ECLECTIC EDUCATIONAL SERIES

RAY'S™ NEW TEST EXAMPLES IN ARITHMETIC

BY

B. O. M. De BECK, A.M.

Originally published by
Van Antwerp, Bragg & Co.

This edition published by

MOTT MEDIA

1130 Fenway Circle, Fenton, Michigan 48430

ISBN 10: 0-88062-065-X
ISBN 13: 978-0-88062-065-9
Printed in the United States of America

PRESENT PUBLISHER'S PREFACE

We are honored and happy to bring to you the classic Arithmetics by Joseph Ray. In the 1800s these popular books sold more than any other arithmetics in America, in fact over 120,000,000 copies. Now with this reprinting, they are once again available for America's students.

Ray's Arithmetics are organized in an orderly manner around the discipline of arithmetic itself. They present principles and follow up each one with examples which include difficult problems to challenge the best students. Students who do not master a concept the first time can return to it later, work the more difficult problems, and master the concept. Thus in these compact volumes is a complete arithmetic course to study in school, to help in preparing for ACT and SAT tests, and to use for reference throughout a lifetime.

In order to capture the spirit of the original Ray's, we have refrained from revising the problems and prices. Only a few words have been changed, as we felt it wise. Thus students will have to rely on their arithmetic ability to solve the problems. Also the charm of a former era lives on in this reprinting. Flour and salt are sold by the barrel, kegs may contain tar, and postage stamps cost 3¢ each. Through this content, students learn social history of the 1800s in a unique, hands-on manner at the same time they are mastering arithmetic.

The series consists of four books ranging from Primary Arithmetic to Higher Arithmetic, as well as answer keys to accompany them. We have added a teacher's guide to help today's busy teachers and parents.

We wish to express our appreciation to the staff of the Special Collections Library at Miami University, Oxford, Ohio, for its cooperation in allowing us to use copies of their original Ray's Arithmetics.

George M. Mott
Founder, Mott Media LLC

PREFACE

This revised and enlarged edition of Test Examples is now respectfully presented to the teachers of our country.

It is confidently believed that it will furnish them the necessary number and variety of exercises essential to successful instruction in arithmetic.

While the difficulties likely to be encountered in school and ordinary business will be found here presented, all mere puzzles have been carefully excluded.

No example has been introduced which the average pupil can not solve without assistance, and no solid progress can be expected unless this is required.

The examples in each article have been carefully graded, the first few being suited to very young pupils, while the last half would furnish work for advanced pupils, whose time is limited.

Attention is called to examples occurring in pairs, where a slight variation in statement changes the nature of the problem.

In each article the number of examples presented is made to depend upon the difficulty and importance of the particular subject presented.

B. O. M. De BECK.

Cincinnati,
December, 1883.

CONTENTS

TEST EXAMPLES.

NOTATION.

Article 11.

Numbers to be Written:

1. Nineteen. Ninety. Ninety-nine.
2. Five hundred and two.
3. Three hundred and sixty-seven.
4. Nine hundred. Nine hundred and twenty.
5. Four thousand and seven.
6. Four thousand and seventy.
7. Four thousand and seventy-seven.
8. Nine thousand six hundred and five.
9. Eight thousand four hundred and twenty.
10. Seven thousand six hundred and fifty-four.
11. Ten thousand. Ten thousand and ten.
12. Forty thousand and seventeen.
13. Fourteen thousand and seventy.
14. Eighty-seven thousand.
15. Twelve thousand and forty-one.
16. Ninety-one thousand two hundred.
17. Sixty thousand three hundred and forty.
18. Sixteen thousand three hundred and fourteen.
19. Fifty-five thousand and fifty-five.

20. Ninety thousand nine hundred and one.

21. Forty-eight thousand and six.

22. Eleven thousand seven hundred.

23. Thirty thousand and thirty.

24. Twenty-one thousand one hundred and seven.

25. Eighty thousand and eight.

26. Sixty-nine thousand four hundred and seventy.

27. Seventy thousand two hundred and eighty.

28. Fifty thousand six hundred.

29. Nineteen thousand nine hundred and twenty-three.

30. Two hundred and twenty-five thousand seven hundred and ninety-one.

31. Two hundred and five thousand seven hundred and one.

32. Six hundred and eighty thousand.

33. Three hundred thousand and eighty.

34. Eight hundred and four thousand nine hundred.

35. One hundred and nine thousand.

36. Four hundred thousand nine hundred.

37. Five hundred thousand and thirty-one.

38. Seven hundred and five thousand five hundred and seven.

39. Four hundred thousand and ninety.

40. Two hundred thousand two hundred and two.

41. Nine hundred and eleven thousand and twenty.

42. One hundred and eighty-seven thousand and thirty.

43. One hundred and eighty-seven thousand and three.

44. Six hundred thousand three hundred and twenty.

45. One hundred and two thousand and three.

46. Nine hundred and eighty-seven thousand.

47. Eight hundred thousand and one.

48. Seven hundred and seventy thousand seven hundred.

49. Six hundred and sixty thousand and sixty.

50. Four hundred thousand one hundred and fifty-seven.

51. Seven million seven hundred thousand seven hundred.

52. Nine million four hundred thousand.

53. Eight million five hundred.

54. Twenty million two hundred and twenty thousand five hundred.

55. Sixty million nine hundred and five thousand.

56. Sixty million nine hundred thousand and five.

57. Four hundred million and ninety.

58. Forty million and two hundred.

59. Thirty-eight million five thousand and sixty.

60. Twenty million two thousand two hundred.

61. Ninety-nine million and nine.

62. Fifteen million fifty thousand and fifteen.

63. Fifty million fifteen thousand and fifty.

64. Seventy million and four.

65. Thirty-four million and fifty-six thousand.

66. Fifty-six million and thirty-four.

67. One hundred and forty million two thousand eight hundred.

68. One hundred and forty million and eight hundred.

69. Two hundred million five thousand and sixty.

70. Five hundred million and eight.

71. Six billion six hundred million seven thousand and thirty.

72. Forty billion seven hundred thousand two hundred and three.

73. One hundred billion nine hundred and thirty three.

74. Thirty trillion forty billion fifty million and sixty.

75. Sixty nine billion and four thousand.
76. Eighty billion and ninety.
77. Sixteen trillion six hundred million.
78. Forty trillion two million and three hundred.
79. Thirteen trillion two hundred billion.
80. Forty trillion fourteen thousand.

In the following examples, TH. *stands for thousand,* M *for million,* B *for billion,* TR. *for trillion.*

81. Write 69 B. 43 M. 319.
82. Write 41 TR. 17 TH. and 60.
83. Write 48 B. 90 TH.
84. Write 300 TR. 200 M. and 94.
85. Write 175 B. 13 M. 299.
86. Write 99 TR. 308.
87. Write 167 TR. 44 M. 273 TH.
88. Write 409 TR. 93 M. and 7.
89. Write 900 TR. 9 TH. 900.
90. Write 375 TR. 2 M.

NUMERATION.

ARTICLE 12.

Copy, separate into periods, and read:

23	4000	10000	524358	7564219
223	2309	34000	409126	6000628
500	6008	57900	600888	32400070
809	8054	74210	347000	136629000
890	3456	97526	200014	8029504962
731	5790	20064	870900	90900009

713	2090	43009	166060	4800080008
444	9307	69200	900089	77000009452
440	7114	80005	763005	526300004
506	4017	79046	225200	30300013003
310	8006	30749	840096	9243000000
687	3680	68802	400002	16700054
1600	9502	40200	680400	66055000500
1750	4008	50060	304006	300000936420
1904	6789	10208	560230	840005400
2378	5200	29847	708020	67760800008
3095	7440	91006	940094	10101010101
5120	1005	80770	709000	40005000600
8700	8060	65030	120502	897065403210
7040	6463	60007	402029	19901990199
4001	2008	48016	290000	678900000257
6802	5083	89119	607080	8040050006
2094	1240	53647	550406	900000700001
9530	3402	10203	803590	61100065084

456780993	26375	13700687319
7654019000	123456789	378483852468
69952468308	87654321	2267000007000
2600800430	3000192	6200900004
83004251007	40090283	100010001018
10083682645	29700370	93724561427
967013750	100560460	5720000902
380080545802	406000557	2237000888005
72000974094	73990646	432666000456
80000303080	1462739	58079529000
954270738900	800002824	8076530900700
3000160069	99033910	74040850770
76544599823	123774105	199055805630
500000922356	60005298	9365704004060

ADDITION.

Article 19.

(1)	(2)	(3)	(4)	(5)	(6)
444	476	743	622	208	748
233	340	385	387	759	677
342	546	614	494	437	386
531	784	286	365	666	974
124	937	367	938	384	953
345	542	894	673	759	379

(7)	(8)	(9)	(10)	(11)
5834	3948	4567	1357	6429
2345	5678	8912	9246	7531
768	1234	3456	8135	8642
4367	9999	7891	7924	9753
9843	7654	2345	6813	6767
6438	3467	6789	5897	8345

(12)	(13)	(14)	(15)	(16)
94073	47356	75319	86427	43214
9846	29356	86426	98574	67785
78468	31663	54687	89758	89376
93785	73548	34387	67896	97644
49679	46659	67496	9523	35975
3492	54762	78588	84376	68796
78685	8658	92738	63527	82768

(17)	(18)	(19)	(20)
473826	483736	765432	754218
584937	736475	198765	765432
695346	859648	432198	109876
746578	365439	765432	543210
677365	449563	987654	987654
485956	658757	321987	321098
345567	512934	654321	765432

(21)	(22)	(23)	(24)
864268	798386	946738	234567
975319	837654	784293	376674
876543	425262	367564	456953
234567	667788	852381	716364
426453	445599	177539	168478
777777	374859	796142	579797
638904	465768	265498	923564
135246	556677	437651	437675

(25)	(26)	(27)	(28)
4538762	4321763	5847354	6756453
7465477	3419844	7356819	1237634
5632850	4553735	9868943	7468515
6783219	9676756	8675478	3189743
7546578	6789427	9756986	4581524
2613695	8252178	3868314	6453635
8843617	7843439	7444267	7684813
4684653	5586865	9565479	9792354
6795876	8638274	8947548	2316615
4777656	4871847	4798716	9875243

(29)	(30)	(31)	(32)
8968548	7945	54	7694746
5637225	6723987	7483	887
6096	1496959	4565572	9769938
2375867	58964	4860	985398
9144636	7	438333	47879
6813405	8877898	9873865	4473767
82277	5693887	5687	6838438
1146	836836	798476	689989
3450014	8869	9929	8971524
8129982	9779853	6549590	7318

33. 7467 + 8938 + 5489 + 6756 + 4887 = what?

34. 57364 + 76528 + 79525 + 55772 + 98769 = what?

35. 49586 + 48659 + 39745 + 87685 + 92367 = what?

36. 58737 + 62914 + 13579 + 24682 + 98765 = what?

37. 4359 + 78768 + 90000 + 85076 + 19467 = what?

38. 37648 + 58459 + 39393 + 78978 + 89789 = what?

39. 76543 + 87654 + 98765 + 34567 + 45678 = what?

40. 12398 + 77665 + 99887 + 88776 + 66554 = what?

41. 73842 + 15693 + 17369 + 82456 + 48597 = what?

42. 49386 + 59487 + 69489 + 76563 + 86465 = what?

43. 76834 + 893584 + 4678 + 59356 + 5968 + 4938 = what?

44. 3456 + 34567 + 345678 + 3456789 = what?

45. 7654 + 987 + 9876 + 98765 + 987654 + 876543 + 8765 + 87654 = what?

46. Add 37590, 4856, 938, 4675, 12834, 2753, and 492.

47. Add 3962, 9623, 2639, 6293, 3269, 9326, 2963, and 6392.

48. Add 6783, 75, 4938, 6, 3974, 7788, 48395, and 568.

49. Add 29, 2967, 96, 9672, 67, 6729, 72, 7296, 79, and 796

50. Add 67, 8945, 5873, 88, 6377, 24, 5891, 53, and 492.

51. Add fifty thousand and twenty-six; sixteen thousand two hundred; nine thousand and ninety-four; 47396; twenty-seven thousand six hundred and seven; 84759; ninety-three thousand and nineteen, and 6733.

52. Add 289564; ninety-four thousand six hundred and eight; 763268; 56921; nine hundred thousand and forty; sixteen thousand eight hundred and seven, and 5698.

53. A man owned seven houses, costing as follows: $5860, $4575, $9560, $12750, $6788, $3500, and $7388. What was the cost of all?

54. The following passengers were carried on a railway: Monday, 2567; Tuesday, 894; Wednesday, 1388; Thursday, 3146; Friday, 1098; Saturday, 3834; and Sunday, 675. How many were carried during the week?

55. Eight men weigh as follows: 168 pounds, 195 pounds, 108 pounds, 187 pounds, 136 pounds, 205 pounds, 154 pounds, and 172 pounds. What is the weight of all?

56. In a city the inhabitants numbered as follows: Americans 57465, Germans 32903, Irish 7588, English 4995, Italians 2893, Colored 2566. How many in all?

57. The membership in four churches was as follows: in the first, 295 men and 330 women; in the second, 107 men and 95 women; in the third, 240 men and 277 women; and in the fourth, 150 men and 148 women. How many members in all?

58. A well was sunk through loam 3 feet, gravel 19 feet, clay 24 feet, sand 5 feet, and limestone 29 feet. How deep is the well?

59. What is the sum of all the numbers under 100, whose ten's figure is 7?

60. Find the total weight of 12 bales of hay, weighing as follows: 467, 388, 491, 417, 373, 402, 333, 412, 309, 383, 417, and 398 pounds.

61. A farmer raises 850 bushels of corn, 720 of oats, 560 of wheat, 236 of rye, 13 of millet, 390 of barley, and 78 of buckwheat. How much grain has he in all?

62. Five clerks receive $1275 apiece, and four others $960 apiece. What are their total wages?

63. The pupils in a school are classed as follows: A grade, 77 boys and 69 girls; B grade, 105 boys and 99 girls; C grade, 148 boys and 153 girls; D grade, 195 boys and 196 girls; and E grade, 219 boys and 231 girls. How many pupils in the school?

64. A planing mill sells the following quantities of lumber: pine, 19680 feet; oak, 7845 feet; poplar, 12098 feet; cherry, 2780 feet; ash, 9860 feet; walnut, 5947 feet; maple, 1439 feet; beech, 610 feet; and sycamore, 439 feet. How many feet in all?

65. In a school 340 children are 6 years old, 297 are 7 years, 258 are 8 years, 227 are 9 nine years, 196 are 10 years, 145 are 11 years, 128 are 12 years, 91 are 13 years, 67 are 14 years, and 48 are older. How many pupils in the school?

66. A lady spent as follows: for muslin, 87 cents; calico, 95 cents; flannel, 175 cents; tape, 7 cents; buttons, 15 cents; thread, 25 cents; needles, 5 cents; silk, 280 cents; table cloth, 375 cents; and napkins, 250 cents. Find the amount of her bill.

67. Spent in a market as follows: for beef, 89 cents; chicken, 65 cents; turnips, 13 cents; carrots, 7 cents; oranges, 15 cents; apples, 35 cents; radishes, 10 cents; potatoes, 34 cents; butter, 45 cents; eggs, 56 cents; and beans, 30 cents. How much did I pay for all?

68. A commenced business with $9278, and gained $346; B with $7866, and gained $963; C with $12390, and gained $2240; and D with $1862, and gained $16. How much were the four then worth?

69. A factory makes in a week 960 chairs, 40 sofas, 68 lounges, 93 settees, 38 sideboards, 29 bureaus, 165 wash-stands, 82 wardrobes, 326 tables, 120 desks, and 5 black-boards. How many articles in all?

70. A steamer on a trip carried the following: iron, 475 tons; flour, 76 tons; cotton, 84 tons; coffee, 45 tons; sugar, 119 tons; barley, 84 tons; paper, 9 tons; lumber, 173 tons; rice, 17 tons; corn, 45 tons; cheese, 22 tons; and other articles, 36 tons. What was the weight of the cargo?

71. Write 58487 ten times and add.

72. A vessel sailed per day as follows: 204 miles, 78 miles, 137 miles, 99 miles, 136 miles, 196 miles, 312 miles, 273 miles, 301 miles, and 264 miles. Find the length of the trip.

73. Find the sum of all the numbers between 48 and 60.

74. Eight barrels of salt weighed respectively 372, 401, 294, 277, 336, 348, 299, and 363 pounds. Find the weight of all.

75. A has $450; B $7 more than A. How many have both?

76. A owns 320 acres of land; B, 120 more than A; and C, 100 more than B. How many acres have the three?

77. I lost $68, $23, and $254, and then had $77. How much had I at first?

78. A merchant paid during the year for rent, $1500; repairs, $205; book-keeper, $1500; clerks, $3200; fuel, $205; freight, $688; gas, $1018; advertising, $274; dray-age, $290; taxes, $360; and little expenses, $164. Find his total expenses.

79. The rooms of a school-house contained 63, 61, 59, 57, 55, 53, 51, 49, 47, and 45 pupils respectively. How many pupils in all?

SUBTRACTION.

ARTICLE 26.

1.	From	4368	take	2634.
2.	From	56789	take	9876.
3.	From	33333	take	4040.
4.	From	303030	take	222222.
5.	From	5263743	take	2281429.
6.	From	34567890	take	12345678.
7.	From	34567890	take	1234567.
8.	From	43216723	take	9013861.
9.	From	29345678	take	2934587.
10.	From	2009988	take	1838899.
11.	From	60000254	take	5000169
12.	From	222333444	take	22334455
13.	From	367890000	take	724.
14.	From	8245673432	take	7345582604.
15.	From	99009900	take	88088088
16.	From	90008000	take	2765094
17.	From	21222324	take	12223242
18.	From	3067543581	take	9364.
19.	From	189640054	take	99999999.
20.	From	880088007	take	80059920.
21.	Take	47563	from	128290.
22.	Take	1357924	from	4297531.
23.	Take	98700563	from	100987285.
24.	Take	7654083	from	23582467.
25.	Take	7654083	from	235824674.
26.	Take	30047582	from	40100000.
27.	Take	235643218	from	524870042.
28.	Take	3242526272	from	4252621222.
29.	Take	123456789	from	987654321.

30. From four million and sixty take 239734.

31. From 59 billion and 30 thousand take 9 million 527 thousand 235.

32. 34000527 — 8370263 = what?

33. 200003000 — 5604037 = what?

34. 37360000 less 29504574 = what?

35. How much greater is 234568001 than 42734056?

36. How much less is 2980752 than 3009527?

37. From 1 unit of the eighth order take 5432187.

38. What number must be taken from five million and five to leave five thousand five hundred?

39. What number must be added to 3723489 to make ten million?

40. What is the difference between 3802764 and 3890609?

41. 39 million less 7800973 = what?

42. What is the difference between 8200969 and 7040080?

43. From 17 million 14 thousand take 9 million 99 thousand 900.

44. From 1 trillion take 560000900384.

45. From forty billion sixty million take 7 billion 328 million 9 thousand and 87.

46. A house cost $4000, and was sold at a loss of $968. How much was received for it?

47. A house was sold for $3425, at a gain of $956. Find the cost.

48. I had $843, and gave away all except $96. How much did I give away?

49. A man had 320 acres, of which 47 acres were woodland. How much was cleared?

50. Washington was born in 1732, and died in 1799. How old was he when he died?

51. In what year was a man born, who died in 1875 at the age of 86?

52. Commenced business with $18420, and quit with $16975. How much did I lose?

53. Commenced with $29080, and lost $2364. How much had I left?

54. After gaining $2972, I had forty thousand dollars. With what sum did I commence?

55. A man agrees to build 4270 feet of fence; after completing 1909 feet, how much remains to be built?

56. A published 40000 copies of a book, and sold 37036. How many remain unsold?

57. I had $1807 in bank, and gave a check for $250. How much was in bank after the check was paid?

58. Sold goods at an advance of $12500, and my expenses were $3750. What was my real gain?

59. At an election Brown received 1013 votes and Jones 834 votes. What is Brown's majority over Jones?

60. Floods occurred in the Ohio River in the years 1832 and 1883. How many years between the two?

61. A treasurer received $507320, of which he paid out $498078. How much has he still?

62. From 2004 take 668 twice.

63. Subtract 3728 three times from 12000.

64. Find the excess of 40789 over 30978.

65. From 100000308 take 15700890 four times.

Addition and Subtraction.

66. $453 + 268 + 2000 - 983 = ?$

67. $2500 + 2145 - 485 - 3485 = ?$

68. $489 + 625 - 873 + 341 = ?$

69. $3250 - 2409 + 1783 - 999 = ?$

70. $10000 - 2733 - 2789 - 2648 = ?$

71. $11111 - 2844 - 2557 + 129 = ?$

72. From 2701 take the difference between 2701 and 897.

73. From 2700 take the sum of 598 and 697.

74. I had $2365; I received $2138 for a house, and paid away $3980. How much have I left?

75. A farmer had 300 acres of tilled land, 725 acres of pasture, and 409 acres of woodland; he sells 987 acres. How much has he now?

76. From the sum of 3456 and 6546 take the difference between 10000 and 1001.

77. From the sum of 4783 and 5984 take their difference.

78. A city contained 47850 inhabitants; 1372 moved in, and 679 moved away; 948 were born, and 473 died. How many did it then contain?

79. Had in bank $2125; deposited $267, and afterwards drew out $415 and $290. How much is left in bank?

80. Bought 4 hogsheads of sugar containing 1183, 1211, 1170, and 1293 pounds, and then filled and sold 3 barrels, each containing 219 pounds. How much is left?

81. Sold, the first year, $8760 worth of goods; the next year $2698 more than the first. How much was that for two years?

82. Williams & Co. gained $4200 the first year, $3850 the second year, and then had $30000. What was their capital at first?

83. Had $20880; gained $1706 the first year, and enough the second year to make my capital $25000. What did I gain the second year?

84. A firm owed me $3800; I bought from them $12000 of goods, paying them $5000 cash, and giving them a note for balance due them. What was the amount of the note?

85. A is worth \$4750; B \$988 more than A; C \$47 less than B; and D \$50 less than A. How much have all together?

86. A man died leaving property worth \$60000 to be divided among his widow, two sons, and three daughters; each son received \$9870, and each daughter \$7890. How much remains for the widow?

MULTIPLICATION.

ARTICLE 31.

1. 326 × 5 = ?
2. 734 × 6 = ?
3. 459 × 7 = ?
4. 386 × 8 = ?
5. 597 × 6 = ?
6. 678 × 4 = ?
7. 5678 × 8 = ?
8. 9768 × 7 = ?
9. 7678 × 5 = ?
10. 8986 × 9 = ?
11. 5846 × 7 = ?
12. 6967 × 8 = ?
13. 783419 × 3 = ?
14. 605628 × 7 = ?
15. 577237 × 8 = ?
16. 409846 × 7 = ?
17. 391055 × 6 = ?
18. 732364 × 5 = ?
19. 694573 × 9 = ?
20. 806782 × 7 = ?
21. 798990 × 8 = ?
22. 680401 × 6 = ?
23. 474692 × 5 = ?
24. 696283 × 8 = ?
25. 467670984 × 8 = ?
26. 288076589 × 7 = ?
27. 668948078 × 9 = ?
28. 701539548 × 11 = ?
29. 933697658 × 10 = ?
30. 845786793 × 8 = ?
31. 457868839 × 9 = ?
32. 766854729 × 7 = ?
33. 870896697 × 9 = ?

34. 287 × 23 = ?
35. 493 × 22 = ?
36. 391 × 24 = ?
37. 465 × 34 = ?
38. 386 × 25 = ?
39. 472 × 26 = ?
40. 951 × 35 = ?
41. 587 × 36 = ?
42. 958 × 37 = ?
43. 6254 × 42 = ?
44. 3873 × 47 = ?
45. 6485 × 43 = ?
46. 3129 × 58 = ?
47. 7654 × 69 = ?
48. 8397 × 42 = ?
49. 6549 × 83 = ?

50. 2386 × 94 = ?
51. 786 × 97 = ?
52. 458 × 69 = ?
53. 6083 × 48 = ?
54. 769 × 316 = ?
55. 846 × 527 = ?
56. 846 × 906 = ?
57. 938 × 238 = ?
58. 938 × 709 = ?
59. 776 × 483 = ?
60. 987 × 904 = ?
61. 3456 × 895 = ?
62. 4567 × 786 = ?
63. 5678 × 607 = ?
64. 6789 × 568 = ?
65. 7894 × 409 = ?

66. Multiply 8945 by 645.
67. Multiply 48075 by 376.
68. Multiply 6908 by 489.
69. Multiply 629075 by 3089.
70. Multiply 738306 by 4605.
71. Multiply 923874 by 3837.
72. Multiply 8877655 by 4657.
73. Multiply 1357986 by 5783.
74. Multiply 4378078 by 6329.
75. Multiply 2468642 by 3759.

76. What cost 93 horses at $75 apiece?

77. What cost 75 horses at $93 apiece?

78. How many yards of thread on 84 spools, holding 196 yards each?

79. What will 9568 bushels of wheat cost, at 127 cents a bushel?

80. A butcher sells 2657 pounds of beef, daily, for 93 days. Find the total amount sold.

81. A book contains 288 pages; and each page, 840 ems. How many ems in the book?

82. What is the total capacity of 46 freight cars, each holding 14260 pounds?

83. What will it cost to grade 257 miles of road at $385 a mile?

84. How many links in 289 chains, each chain having 743 links?

85. A horse can draw a load of 1423 pounds. How much could 85 horses draw?

86. A company of soldiers contains 85 men. How many men in 67 companies?

87. A lot is 287 feet front, and worth $162 for each front foot. What is the lot worth?

88. If 2347568 gallons of water pass a certain point in a river in one hour, how many gallons will pass in 48 hours?

89. How far will a star go in 75 days, if it goes 1267893 miles per day?

90. A barrel of flour contains 196 pounds. Find the weight of 472 barrels.

91. What must be paid for grading a railroad 327 miles long, at $1237 a mile?

92. How many peach trees can be planted on 179 acres, each acre having 256?

93. If a seine contains 4365 yards of twine, how many yards will be required for 483 seines?

94. What will be the weight of 96 horses, estimating them at 1387 pounds apiece?

95. If the circulation of a library is 24306 volumes daily, how many would that be in 297 days?

96. If 829 men could dig a canal bed in 248 days, how many men would be required to complete the work in one day?

ARTICLE 32.—*Case I.*

1. 47384 × 63 = ?
2. 60872 × 132 = ?
3. 346891 × 77 = ?
4. 7205674 × 27 = ?
5. 889793 × 72 = ?
6. 426312 × 44 = ?
7. 3784931 × 45 = ?
8. 6292558 × 96 = ?
9. 3490175 × 66 = ?
10. 768793 × 35 = ?
11. 453312 × 42 = ?
12. 673944 × 108 = ?
13. 483576 × 64 = ?
14. 363108 × 144 = ?
15. 273733 × 88 = ?
16. 903465 × 81 = ?
17. 693197 × 48 = ?
18. 843839 × 84 = ?
19. 783571 × 55 = ?
20. 932186 × 56 = ?

ARTICLE 33.—*Case II.*

1. 28734 × 1000 = ?
2. 49865 × 100 = ?
3. 6200945 × 1000 = ?
4. 384503 × 10000 = ?
5. 468357 × 100 = ?
6. 40050008 × 1000 = ?
7. 40070893 × 100000 = ?
8. 37088900 × 1000 = ?
9. 26893845 × 10000 = ?
10. 34779267 × 100 = ?
11. 48596023 × 100000 = ?
12. 76540063 × 1000 = ?

ARTICLE 34.—*Case III.*

Multiply:

1. 590 by 45.
2. 4732 by 730.
3. 66450 by 6600.
4. 38700 by 40800.
5. 96050 by 39000.
6. 483200 by 79610.
7. 738512 by 4850000.
8. 400400 by 640800.
9. 5008 by 50790.
10. 60904 by 384000.
11. 706004 by 80400000.
12. 209800 by 606600.
13. 345678 by 78050000.
14. 46003 by 90020.
15. 97623 by 5648000.
16. 87410 by 809300.
17. 53820 by 256700000.
18. 6767600 by 4760000.
19. 948372 by 138200.
20. 21101 by 6095000.

SHORT DIVISION.

ARTICLE 41.

Divide:

1. 45678936 by 3.
2. 43218765 by 5.
3. 9999992660 by 7.
4. 807006935 by 5.
5. 392919096 by 8.
6. 987652308 by 4.
7. 987652308 by 6.
8. 111111111 by 9.
9. 222222222 by 6.
10. 21026838 by 3.
11. 74060259 by 7.
12. 76587692 by 4.
13. 723645000 by 8.
14. 876543210 by 9.
15. 9876543215 by 7.
16. 346800270 by 5.
17. 6001674864 by 3.
18. 3031674804 by 6.
19. 345680528 by 4.
20. 759274400 by 8.
21. 39291993 by 9.
22. 876543210 by 6.
23. 392919096 by 4.
24. 123456128 by 8.
25. 350364075 by 5.
26. 5555558400 by 7.
27. 618170472 by 9.
28. 617180742 by 6.
29. 1001002002 by 3.
30. 406052983 by 7.

31. Find one fourth of 3738392.
32. Find one eighth of 7360576.
33. Find one third of 26688111.
34. Find one ninth of 28880109.
35. Find one sixth of 45500196.
36. What is one fifth of 56009800?
37. What is one seventh of 54985448?
38. What is one ninth of 23401881?
39. What is one fourth of 23601880?

40. Four men earn $2968: how much is that for each of them?

41. How many 6-pound balls will be required to weigh 7644 pounds?

42. How many hats can be bought for $2075, at $5 apiece?

43. In one week there are 7 days: how many weeks in 8429435 days?

44. A man earns $972 in 6 months: how much is that per month?

45. A car can go 8 miles in an hour: how long will it take it to go 4560 miles?

46. How many 5-gallon jugs can be filled from 2520 gallons of molasses?

47. $3450 was raised among some merchants, each paying $6: how many were there?

48. Five passenger cars can carry 360 persons: how many is that for each car?

49. Eight stoves weigh 2792 pounds: what is the weight of each?

50. A railroad train can go 3003 miles in 7 days: how far is that each day?

51. How long will it take a man to earn $896, if his wages are $7 a week?

52. How many blank books can be made from 5552 sheets of paper, if each book contains 8 sheets?

53. A man dying left $16814 to be equally divided among 7 children: what was the share of each?

54. A bar of soap weighs 4 pounds: how many bars will be required to weigh 9996 pounds?

55. At $6 a day, how many days will be required to earn $1638?

56. How many sashes, of six panes each, can be filled from 7776 panes of glass?

57. If the Government pays $9256320 of debt in 9 months, how much would that be per month?

58. If 125616 soldiers were divided equally into 8 divisions, how many soldiers would that be for each division?

59. How many sixes would it take to make 16008?

LONG DIVISION.

ARTICLE 42.

Divide:

1. 84878 by 31.
2. 223686 by 51.
3. 328233 by 71.
4. 220867 by 41.
5. 898716 by 91.
6. 356500 by 92.
7. 380398 by 82.
8. 675000 by 72.
9. 241552 by 62.
10. 309557 by 43.
11. 1674123 by 33.
12. 6582564 by 83.
13. 3766110 by 94.
14. 2997592 by 74.
15. 4832460 by 54.
16. 1362768 by 44.
17. 3323232 by 36.
18. 3323232 by 48.
19. 1009827 by 27.
20. 1501305 by 39.
21. 4141387 by 59.
22. 38739176 by 19.
23. 45806266 by 902.
24. 18757711 by 611.
25. 48512520 by 713.
26. 16379005 by 421.
27. 45000000 by 338.
28. 15349839 by 771.
29. 36517449 by 893.
30. 11998679 by 197.

31. Divide 240158529 by 6201.
32. Divide 292246250 by 4138.
33. Divide 37021447680 by 9085.
34. Divide 100200300400 by 8251.
35. $234567891000 \div 3456 = ?$
36. $345678912000 \div 4567 = ?$
37. $456789123000 \div 5678 = ?$

38. At 47 cents apiece, how many hammers can be bought for 18565 cents?

39. How many cars, each 24 feet long, can be placed upon a track 3744 feet long?

40. If 986 pounds is a load for one horse, how many horses will be required to carry 493986 pounds?

41. What will one horse cost, if the bill for 293 horses is $89365?

42. How many sewing machines, at $65 each, can be bought for $4225?

43. If a foundry consume 428 bushels of coal in a day, how long will 121980 bushels last?

44. A man traveled 5341 miles in 109 days: how far was that each day?

45. How many years would be required to pay a debt of $2004002154, if $13013001 are paid yearly?

46. A turnpike was constructed at a cost of $2765 per mile, and the total cost was $215670: how long was the road?

47. Divide 57 million 114 thousand and 57 by 19019.

48. If 56 pounds of rye make a bushel, how many bushels would be required to weigh 93744 pounds?

49. 83 iron columns weigh 764264 pounds: find the weight of each.

50. By what number must 706126 be divided to give 89 for a quotient?

51. By what number must 4328 be multiplied, so that the product may be 8331400?

52. If a short-hand writer can write 125 words in a minute, how long will he require to write 13375 words?

53. What was the length of one piece of cloth, if 193 pieces measured 36477 yards?

CONTRACTIONS IN DIVISION.

Article 43.—*Case I.*

Divide:

1. 4524 by 24.
2. 455364 by 36.
3. 372518 by 32.
4. 2736595 by 45.
5. 4728392 by 48.
6. 1168384 by 56.
7. 13413501 by 27.
8. 3742015 by 28.
9. 27253746 by 18.
10. 47351850 by 25.
11. 11111111 by 42.
12. 3579135 by 63.

Article 44.—*Case II.*

1. Divide 47389256 by 1000.
2. Divide 367854001 by 100.
3. Divide 27000008746 by 10000.
4. Divide 1234567892 by 100.
5. Divide 3704605504 by 1000.
6. Divide 9897969594 by 100000.
7. Divide 130027005 by 100.
8. Divide 123843658 by one thousand.
9. Divide 44872362592 by one million.
10. Divide 5000700040 by ten thousand.
11. Divide 37264839527 by ten.
12. Divide 43 million by one hundred.
13. Divide 12345654321 by one thousand.
14. Divide 754000000000400 by one billion.
15. Divide 47638592143 by ten thousand.

Article 45.—*Case III.*

1. Divide 472956 by 40.
2. Divide 124578013 by 140.
3. Divide 56789324 by 8000.
4. Divide 3438725382 by 1900.
5. Divide 263341058 by 470.
6. Divide 738495262 by 4050.
7. Divide 3213213313 by 8800.
8. Divide 345456567 by 3400.
9. Divide 765472384 by 107000.
10. Divide 9236453400000 by 7200.
11. Divide one billion by 706700.
12. Divide 397 billion by 97 thousand.
13. Divide 56784935867 by 3050600.
14. Divide 999999999 by 90990.

ARTICLE 49.—*Promiscuous Examples.*

1. Bought 60 cows at $33 apiece, and 47 at $28 apiece: what was the total cost?

2. What cost 47 hogsheads, each containing 48 gallons of molasses, at 65 cents a gallon?

3. Had 96 horses; 3 died, and the others were sold at $150 apiece. What sum was received for them?

4. A man having $10000, kept $307, and with the rest bought land at $27 an acre. How many acres did he buy?

5. Multiply the sum of 209 and 390 by their difference.

6. Two men had $8550 apiece; one bought cows at $38 each, the other cows at $45 each. How many more did the first buy than the second?

7. Eighty-seven horses were sold at $155 apiece, and the money invested in mules at $93 apiece. How many mules were bought?

8. Four times 1728 are how many less than 10000?

9. Raised 65 bushels of potatoes on each of 85 acres of land; used 180 bushels, and sold the remainder at 63 cents a bushel. How much was received for them?

10. Four men were in partnership, having in all $8560; the first had $2140, the second $3076, and the third and fourth had equal sums. How much had each of the latter?

11. 66 horses were bought at $127 apiece; sold one third at $125 apiece, and the remainder at $135 apiece. What was my gain on all?

12. I have a lot 65 feet front, worth $175 per front foot; if I trade for a farm of 126 acres, worth $90 an acre, how much cash should I receive?

13. Divide 312×273 by $312 - 273$.

14. Forty-eight men can build a bridge in 187 days; how many must be employed to build it in 176 days?

15. Seventy-three horses eat 101835 pounds of hay in 93 days; how much was that daily for each horse?

16. A man borrows $6000, and pays $400 a year for the use of it; how much should he pay back at the end of 4 years?

17. What sum will be received for 137 acres of land, which cost $75 per acre, and were sold at a gain of $49 per acre?

18. What sum will be received for 354 acres of land, which cost $29 per acre, and were sold at a gain of $94?

19. A man received a legacy of $8273; he paid $131 expenses, and with the remainder bought bonds at $118 apiece; how many did he buy?

20. If a sewing machine is worth $45, how many sewing machines must be traded for 117 watches at $65 apiece?

21. How much must be paid for 45 turkeys, so that 95 cents may be gained by selling them at 87 cents apiece?

22. The dividend was 39 times 552, and the divisor 299: find the quotient.

23. Bought 882 acres of woodland; after clearing one ninth of it, I sold the cleared land at $18 an acre, and the woodland at $11 an acre. How much did I receive in all?

24. If a number will contain 322 ninety-six times, how many times will it contain 69?

25. Bought 48 cows at $32 apiece, and 20 horses at $100 apiece; sold them so as to gain $200. What did I receive for them all?

26. A banker buys 52 shares of stock for $5824; for how much must he seil them to gain $8 a share?

27. Bought 293 hogsheads of sugar at $58 apiece; for how much must I sell it to gain $7?

28. A pile of lumber weighing 39039 pounds lost one seventh of its weight in drying: what did it then weigh?

29. How many 20-gallon casks can be filled from 395 barrels of molasses of 48 gallons each?

30. Sold 47 wagons at $50 apiece, and after buying a farm had $495 left. What was the cost of the farm?

31. What number must be multiplied by 47 to make the product equal to the difference between 987 and 11797?

32. What number must be divided by 73 to make the quotient equal to the sum of 456 and 2893?

33. Spent $8880 for horses at $74 apiece; 23 died: how many remain?

34. If 93 horses cost $19158, how many can be bought for $79310?

35. Bought hogs for $893, and sold them at $11 apiece, gaining $9; how many did I buy?

36. Of what number is 526 both divisor and quotient?

37. If 36 men earn $6912 in 12 weeks, how much does each earn per week?

38. How often is one fourth of one thousand contained in one fifth of one million?

39. After selling 68 cows, at $42 apiece, how much must I borrow if I wish to buy 209 hogs at $14 apiece?

40. Sold 923 yards of my cloth at $4 a yard, and the remainder at $5 a yard, and received in all $5222. How many yards had I at first?

41. If 47 men, in 58 weeks, can dig 215354 yards of ditch, how many yards can 29 men dig in 47 weeks?

42. If an army of 23479 men consume 2653127 pounds of food in a month, how many pounds would be required per month after 4839 men have been killed?

43. Bought 356 acres for $2848, and sold at $11 per acre: how much did I gain?

44. 59375 yards of bunting were bought to make a certain number of flags, 19 yards being intended for each; if 5 yards more are needed for each flag, how much more bunting must be bought?

45. Received $5850 for 18 months' rent; the rent was then raised $20 per month. What was the rent for the next 12 months?

46. A car will carry 11700 pounds; what is the weight of a boat-load of wheat which lacks 250 pounds of filling 23 cars?

47. If an acre of ground will produce 52 bushels of turnips or 70 bushels of potatoes, how many bushels of potatoes can be raised on a farm that will produce 9100 bushels of turnips?

48. What number exceeds one ninth of 3096 as much as one eighth of 3096 exceeds one tenth of 3690?

49. Bought land for $8370, and sold it at $31 an acre, losing $248. How many acres were there?

50. A man having $25725, kept one third, and invested the remainder in land at $49 per acre: how many acres did he purchase?

51. Bought 135 mules at $115 apiece; sold one fifth of them at a gain of $18 apiece, and the others at a gain of $16 apiece. What was my total gain?

52. A man has a farm of 260 acres; on each acre he can raise 35 bushels of oats, worth 93 cents a bushel, or 130 bushels of potatoes, worth 24 cents a bushel. How much more would he realize from oats than from potatoes?

53. From 8 times 7317 take 9 times 5328, and divide the result by the difference between one eighth of 504 and one ninth of 1008.

UNITED STATES MONEY.

Article 53.

Write the following sums:

1. Thirteen dollars ninety-three cents.
2. Eighty-seven dollars forty-nine cents and three mills.
3. Twenty-nine dollars and eight cents.
4. One hundred and fifty-seven dollars and fifty cents.
5. Nine dollars nine cents and nine mills.
6. Twelve dollars and two mills.
7. Five hundred dollars and ten cents.
8. Two hundred dollars and three mills.
9. Ninety-nine dollars and ninety cents.
10. Ninety dollars and ninety-nine cents.

Read the following:

$ 73.38	$ 34.20	$ 96.011	$ 309.806
$ 73.028	$457.02	$ 49.102	$4561.25
$ 70.328	$ 2.909	$600.888	$ 3.092
$ 45.006	$ 6.099	$100.16	$ .59
$ 74.05	$ 5.005	$116.03	$ 739.11
$300.10	$ 88.10	$ 11.603	$ 46.03
$ 59.00	$393.25	$821.018	$1000.97

Article 55.—*Reduction of United States Money.*

1. Reduce $93 to cents.
2. Reduce 800 cents to dollars.
3. Reduce 46 cents to mills.
4. Reduce 187 mills to cents.
5. Reduce 76 dimes to cents.
6. Reduce $45 to mills.
7. Reduce 3009 mills to dollars.
8. Reduce $89.17 to cents.
9. Reduce $700 to cents.

10. Reduce $10000 to mills.
11. Reduce 4 dollars 4 cents 4 mills to mills.
12. Reduce $467.02 to cents.
13. Reduce $467 to cents.
14. Reduce $83 and 9 mills to mills.
15. Reduce 123000 mills to dollars.

ARTICLE 56.—*Addition of United States Money.*

1. What is the sum of 19 dollars 85 cents; 43 dollars and 79 cents; 76 dollars and 21 cents; 58 dollars and 15 cents; and 29 dollars and 75 cents?

2. Add $74.19, $15.01, $46.28, $9.60, $17.81, $25.72, $9.93, and $7.46.

3. $7.007 + $70.70 + $7.07 + $77.77 + $777.77 + $99.00 + $4.683 + $500 = ?

4. A man owes A $750, B $99.65, C $427.80, D $3.47, E $697.29, F 50 dollars, and G 45 cents. What is his total indebtedness?

5. A man bought 2 coats, costing $7.50 and $18; 2 vests, costing $3.20 and $7.80; 2 pairs of pants, costing $4.60 and $9; 2 hats costing $1.85 and $5.50; and 3 shirts costing $1.75, $1.75 and $3. What did he pay for all?

6. I paid for digging cellar, $59.75; for limestone masonry, $195.40; for freestone, $168.90; for brick-work, $897.60; for carpenter work, $528.65; for tin roof, $179; for iron work, $40.60; for plastering, $237.85; for painting, $153.70; for plumbing, $67.60; for gas-fitting, $39; and for lightning-rods, $78.90. How much did these items cost?

7. Bought a farm for $2750, a horse for $127.50, a cow for $53.60, mules for $286, sheep for $69, hogs for $268.90, a wagon for $60.85, harness $55.60, and plows, harrows, etc., $186.40. How much did I pay for all?

ARTICLE 57.—*Subtraction of United States Money.*

1. From $120.63 take $87.29.

2. Take $39.82 from $90.15.

3. Take $76.09 from $100.

4. $1025 — $800.80 = ?

5. $90 less 90 cents = ?

6. $78.15 less $15.78 = ?

7. How much must be taken from $1000 to leave $690.09?

8. A man commenced business with $16208, and lost $1069.40; how much had he then?

9. How much must a man invest, so that after gaining $1690.18 he may have $8008?

10. From $2000 take $739.84 twice.

11. A man owes $529.60, and has $900; how much will he have after paying his debts?

12. A man has $429.13, and owes $600; after paying his money, how much will he still owe?

ARTICLE 58.—*Multiplication of United States Money.*

1. Multiply $8.293 by 24.

2. Multiply $9.835 by 36.

3. Multiply $43.75 by 84.

4. Multiply $8.008 by 65.

5. Multiply $9.12 by 60.

6. Multiply $27.008 by 400.

7. Multiply $29.632 by 750.

8. Find 39 times $.636.

9. What is 891 times 13 cents 6 mills?

10. $87, 3 cents × 3000 = ?

11. $68, 5 mills × 560 = ?

12. What cost 49 barrels of flour at $6.75 a barrel?

13. What cost 67 acres of land at $159.60 an acre?

14. What must be given for 34 horses at $88.40 each?

15. What cost 54 yards of grading at $7.282 per yard?

16. What must be given for 89 hogs at $8.34 apiece?

17. What cost 956 gallons of vinegar at 12 cents a gallon?

18. What will be paid for 526 quarts of berries at 22 cents a quart?

19. Sold 351 sheep at $2.50 apiece; how much did I receive for them?

20. What cost 5000 tickets at 18 cents apiece?

21. What cost 42357 yards of calico at 8 cents a yard?

22. What cost 4500 bolts at 6 mills each?

23. How much will a man earn in 57 days at $2.25 a day?

24. What cost 40 boxes of starch, containing 33 pounds each, at $.075 per pound?

25. If a soldier receives a pension of $1.75 per month, how much will 38 receive in 19 months?

26. What cost 40 boxes of candy, 40 pounds each, at 40 cents a pound?

27. What cost 808 bales of cotton, containing 465 pounds each, at 3 cents 6 mills per pound?

28. What cost 87 boxes of eggs, each containing 72 dozen, at $.125 per dozen?

29. What cost 9388 papers of pins, each containing 30 dozen pins, at 2 mills per dozen?

30. What will the glass cost for 8 houses, each containing 8 rooms, each room having 4 windows, and each window 4 panes, at 37 cents 5 mills per pane?

31. A man has 10 casks of stove polish, containing 425 pounds each; each pound will fill 6 papers, sold at 5 cents a paper. How much will be received for the entire amount?

32. What cost 40 bundles of paper, containing 2 reams each, each ream weighing 60 pounds, at 8 cents 3 mills per pound?

33. What cost 708 boxes of tomatoes, each containing 24 cans of 2 pounds each, at 11 cents a pound?

34. Find the cost of 82 boxes of calico, each box containing 40 bolts, and each bolt 30 yards, at $.066 per yard.

35. Find the amount received for 5 blocks of building lots, each block containing 12 lots, each lot being 25 feet front, the whole being sold at $8.75 per front foot.

36. What will be the wages of 240 men, employed 17 days, of 10 hours each, at 17 cents 5 mills per hour?

ARTICLE 59.—*Division of United States Money.*

1. Divide $49.50 cents by 33 cents.

2. Divide $393.75 by 75 cents.

3. Divide $200 by 32 cents.

4. Divide $333 by 45 cents.

5. Divide $1186.98 by $2.71.

6. Divide $3677.94 by $5 and 4 mills.

7. Divide $1608.88 by 33 cents 8 mills.

8. Divide $2162.45 by 30 cents 5 mills.

9. How much muslin, at 13 cents a yard, can be bought for $23.66?

10. How many sheep, at $3.75 apiece, can be bought for $600?

11. How many needles, at 3 mills apiece, can you buy for $19.38?

12. At $1.25 an acre, how much land can you buy for $995?

13. How many apples, at 1 cent 5 mills each, must be sold to realize $3?

14. How many planes, costing 85 cents each, can be bought for $129.20?

15. How many 20-cent tickets must be sold to make the receipts $500?

16. Divide $99.48 by 4.

17. Divide $95.004 by 7.

18. Divide $326.36 by 8.

19. Divide $436.032 by 9.

20. Divide $389 by 25.

21. Divide $440.44 by 77.

22. Divide $1500.496 by 491.

23. Divide $4226.427 by 603.

24. Nine horses cost me $1025.01; find the cost of each.

25. Sold 43 bushels of peaches for $120.40; how much was that per bushel?

26. $528.44 was divided equally among 11 heirs; find the share of each.

27. What must I charge per bushel for apples, so as to realize $526.50 for 2340 bushels?

28. 144 penknives cost $90; how much was that apiece?

29. 900 pounds of cheese cost $49.50; how much did one pound cost?

30. 600000 pounds of cotton cost $45000; how much is that per pound?

31. If 40 horses cost $5318, what would 76 horses cost?

32. If 38 men earn $1136.20 in 26 days, what is each man's daily wages?

33. If grape settings sell at $3.50 per hundred, how much is that apiece?

34. What cost 750 pickles at $1.20 per hundred?

35. If 16 chests of tea sell for $460.80, at 60 cents a pound, how many pounds in each chest?

ARTICLE 60.—*Promiscuous Examples.*

1. Paid for land, $970.50; for buildings, $1963.60; for horses, $180.75; for cattle, $217.50; for seeds, $29.50; for tools, $36.40; for harness, $82.50; for provisions, $200; and for hogs, $319.25. Find the total expenditure.

2. What cost 5 sofas, at $13.75 each, and 7 lounges, at $4.60 each?

3. Gave $108 for 45 yards of cloth, which I sold for $116.10; find my gain per yard.

4. A dealer bought peaches at $2.50 a bushel; how many bushels must he sell, at a profit of 70 cents a bushel, to receive $144?

5. What cost 1750 picture cards at $1.40 a hundred?

6. I saved $104.52 in 6 months; if my salary was $80 a month, what were my expenditures each month?

7. I saved $130.56 in 8 months; if my expenses were $80 a month, what was my monthly salary?

8. What cost 3700 papers at $2.20 a hundred?

9. A company owes $120000, and its assets amount to $30780; the deficit is collected from 15000 shares of stock. How much is that on each share?

10. How much will be left from a hundred dollar bill after spending the following amounts: $3.60, $11.17, 50 cents, $1.96, $6.40, $8.33, $29.08, and 98 cents.

11. A contractor agrees to grade a road for $14000; he pays a foreman $5 a day, for 80 days; 25 cart drivers $2.25 a day, for 75 days; and 83 laborers $1.30 a day for 77 days. Find his profit.

12. Sold 29 horses for $1914, losing $159.50; what did each cost?

13. Sold a farm of 46 acres for $3000, gaining $7.10 per acre; what did the farm cost?

14. What will I save in 14 months, if I earn $75 each month, and spend $39.25 per month?

15. I worked 13 weeks at $13.75 per week, and saved $58.50 during that time; what were my weekly expenses?

16. How many dimes in $40?

17. How many half-eagles in $1080?

18. How many 3-cent pieces should be given for 240 eagles?

19. How many 5-cent pieces should be given for 720 quarter-eagles?

20. If a man had one of each of the gold coins, how many quarter-dollars could he get for them?

21. Invested $4329 in cattle at $18.50 a head, and sold them at $23.08 a head; what was my gain?

22. Bought a house for $3300; made some repairs, and sold it for $4250, gaining $487.75. What was the cost of the repairs?

23. How many days, of 11 hours each, must a man work to earn $499.07, at 13 cents an hour?

24. Bought 40600 pounds of sugar for $2639, and sold it at a gain of 5 mills per pound; what was my gain?

25. Bought 15600 pounds of coffee for $5850, and sold it for $6162; how much was my gain per pound?

26. Bought rice for $3573; sold it for 5 cents per pound, gaining 5 mills per pound; how many pounds did I buy?

27. What cost 2468 pounds of butter, on which $86.38 was gained by selling it at 30 cents a pound?

28. Forty barrels of coal oil were bought for $241; how much was gained by selling at 15 cents a gallon, there being 50 gallons in each barrel?

29. Fifty barrels of molasses cost $1152, at 48 cents a gallon; how many gallons in each barrel?

30. A team pays $1.75 for toll, at the rate of 25 cents for 10 miles; how far does it go?

31. The expenses of a church festival were $237.52, and the gain was $701.98; how many 25-cent tickets had been sold?

32. A worked 47 days, at $2.55 per day; B worked 4 days longer than A, but received only the same amount. How much did B earn per day?

33. Find the cost of 40 boxes, each containing 24 cans, and each can holding 6 pounds of canned peaches, boxes costing 25 cents each, cans 5 cents each, and peaches 4 cents per pound.

Find the amount of the following bills:

34.	35	yards	Muslin,	at	$0.12	per yard.
	47	do	Calico,	"	.08	do.
	23	do	Delaine,	"	.16	do.
	13	do	Alpaca,	"	.35	do.
	21	do	Silk,	"	1.05	do.
	10	do	Satin,	"	1.25	do.
	7	do	Velvet,	"	2.40	do.
35.	4	pounds	Tea,	at	$1.15	per pound.
	7	do	Coffee,	"	.32	do.
	15	do	Sugar,	"	.13	do.
	20	do	Beef,	"	.09	do.
	17	do	Ham,	"	.12	do.
	12	do	Cheese,	"	.15	do.
	19	do	Starch,	"	.09	do.
36.	400	feet	Pine,	at	$0.025	per foot.
	720	do	Poplar,	"	.03	do.
	560	do	Walnut,	"	.07	do.
	875	do	Oak,	"	.02	do.
	94	do	Beech,	"	.045	do.
	120	do	Cedar,	"	.06	do.

REDUCTION.

ARTICLE 63.—*Dry Measure.*

1. Reduce 4 bu. 3 pk. 2 qt. 1 pt. to pints.
2. Reduce 9 bu. 2 qt. 1 pt. to pints.
3. Reduce 18 bu. 3 pk. 1 pt. to pints.
4. Reduce 36 bu. 3 qt. to pints.
5. Reduce 89 bu. 2 pk. to quarts.
6. Reduce 4789 pt. to bushels.
7. Reduce 5766 qt. to bushels.
8. Reduce 99 bu. 3 pk. 7 qt. 1 pt. to pints.
9. Reduce 583 bu. 1 pt. to pints.
10. Reduce 123456 pt. to bushels.
11. Reduce 4933 pk. to pints.
12. Reduce 25616 bu. to pints.
13. Reduce 25616 pt. to bushels.
14. Reduce 12345 qt. to pecks.
15. Reduce 7 million bushels to quarts.

ARTICLE 64.—*Liquid Measure.*

1. Reduce 38 gal. 3 qt. to pints.
2. Reduce 1025 gi. to gallons.
3. Reduce 87634 gal. to pints.
4. Reduce 93 gal. 2 qt. 1 pt. to gills.
5. Reduce 23867 pt. to gallons.
6. Reduce 8642 gal. to gills.
7. Reduce 99 gal. 3 qt. 2 gi. to gills.
8. Reduce 3732 gills to quarts.
9. Reduce 73 gal. 3 qt. 1 pt. 1 gi. to gills.
10. How many gallons in 33033 cubic inches?
11. How many cubic inches in 500 gallons?
12. A vessel measures 52206 cubic inches; how many gallons would it hold?

ARTICLE 65.—*Avoirdupois Weight.*

1. Reduce 3 T. to pounds.
2. Reduce 5 T. 13 cwt. to pounds.
3. Reduce 9 T. 1 cwt. 50 lb. to pounds.
4. Reduce 7 T. 19 cwt. 99 lb. to pounds.
5. Reduce 13 T. 13 lb. to pounds.
6. Reduce 4 T. 17 cwt. to ounces.
7. Reduce 3 T. 20 lb. 5 oz. to ounces.
8. Reduce 12945 lb. to tons.
9. Reduce 98400 lb. to tons.
10. Reduce 876543 lb. to tons.
11. Reduce 38742 T. to ounces.
12. Reduce 160080 oz. to tons.
13. Reduce 71 T. 17 cwt. 71 lb. to pounds.
14. Reduce 711771 lb. to tons.
15. Reduce 40000000 oz. to tons.
16. Find the weight of 375 balls weighing 32 pounds each.
17. Find the weight of 3000000 candles weighing 3 ounces each.
18. Find the weight of 3456 20-pound cannon balls.
19. Reduce 15999999 oz. to tons.
20. What is the weight of 357 boxes of alum, weighing 56 pounds each?

ARTICLE 66.—*Long Measure.*

1. Reduce 49 yd. 2 ft. 9 in. to inches.
2. Reduce 53 yd. 7 in. to inches.
3. Reduce 41 mi. 200 rd. to rods.
4. Reduce 77 yd. 2 ft. to inches.
5. Reduce 4953 mi. to rods.
6. Reduce 5678 in. to yards.

7. Reduce 38257 rd. to miles.
8. Reduce 498 yd. 11 in. to inches.
9. Reduce 373845 rd. to miles.
10. Reduce 39601 in. to yards.
11. Reduce 39601 mi. to rods.
12. Reduce 39601 rd. to miles.

ARTICLE 67.—*Square Measure.*

1. Reduce 7 A. 100 sq. rd. to square rods.
2. Reduce 3 sq. mi. 300 A. to square rods.
3. Reduce 19 sq. mi. 19 A. 19 sq. rd. to square rods.
4. Reduce 18 sq. yd. 8 sq. ft. 118 sq. in. to square inches.
5. Reduce 39 sq. mi. 90 sq. rd. to square rods.
6. Reduce 99 sq. yd. 99 sq. in. to square inches.
7. Reduce 50000000 sq. mi. to square rods.
8. Reduce 1 billion square inches to square yards.

ARTICLES 68 AND 69.—*Rectangles.*

Find the area of the following:

1. A floor 18 ft. long and 15 ft. wide.
2. A carpet 27 ft. long and 22 ft. wide.
3. A platform 80 ft. long and 16 ft. wide.
4. A pavement 40 ft. long and 9 feet wide.
5. A ceiling 36 ft. long and 20 ft. wide.
6. A lot 72 rd. long and 60 rd. wide.
7. A farm 80 rd. long and 76 rd. wide.
8. A field 100 rods square.

Find the cost of the following:

9. The carpet in example 2 at $1.30 a sq. yd.
10. The pavement in example 4 at 30 cents a sq. yd.
11. The farm in example 7 at $17.75 per A.
12. The platform in example 3 at 3 cents per sq. ft.

13. A farm extends along the road 60 rods; how wide must it be to contain 45 A.?

14. A road is 3 rods wide; how long must it be to contain 120 A.?

15. A farm is 100 rods long and 96 rods wide; how much wheat will it produce at the rate of 13 bushels to the acre?

16. A roof 100 feet long requires 300 square yards of roofing; how wide is it?

17. A floor is 40 feet long and requires 120 square yards of carpet; how wide is it?

ARTICLE 70.—*Solid or Cubic Measure.*

1. Reduce 3483648 cu. in. to cubic yards.

2. Reduce 3 cu. yd. 300 cu. in. to cubic inches.

3. Reduce 746496 cu. in. to cubic yards.

4. Reduce 9856 cu. ft. to cords.

5. Reduce 11 C. 111 cu. ft. 1111 cu. in. to cubic inches.

6. How many cubic yards in a cellar 40 feet long, 18 feet wide, and 9 feet deep?

7. How many cords in a wood-pile 120 feet long, 8 feet high, and 4 feet wide?

8. How many cubic yards of masonry in a stone pier 320 feet long, 36 feet wide, and 12 feet thick?

9. What will be the cost of a breakwater 900 feet long, 6 feet thick, and 12 feet high, at $2.75 per cubic yard?

10. Find the cost of a pile of wood 40 feet long, 40 feet wide, and 8 feet high, at $3.75 a cord.

11. How many inch cubes of lead can be cast from a mass 3 feet long, 1 foot high, and 2 feet wide?

12. Find the cost of digging a ditch 12 feet wide, 6 feet deep, and 285 feet long, at $.75 a cubic yard.

ARTICLE 71.—*Time Measure.*

1. Reduce 3 da. 2 hr. 30 min. to seconds.
2. Reduce 11 weeks to minutes.
3. Reduce 3 wk. 3 da. 3 hr. 3 min. 3 sec. to seconds.
4. Reduce 9 wk. 9 hr. to seconds.
5. Reduce 43 da. 43 sec. to seconds.
6. Reduce 777600 sec. to weeks.
7. Reduce 45678 min. to days.
8. Reduce 87500 days to seconds.
9. Reduce 72000 min. to weeks.
10. How many minutes in the year 1890?
11. How many minutes in the last three months of the year?
12. How many seconds in February, 1889?
13. How many seconds in 5 leap years?
14. Reduce 3 common years to hours.
15. A clock ticks 120 times in a minute; how many ticks will it make in the year 1892?
16. Reduce 19 wk. 5 da. 21 hr. 20 min. to minutes.

ARTICLE 73.—*Miscellaneous Tables.*

1. Reduce 17 lb. 10 oz. 16 pwt. to grains.
2. Reduce 18 lb. 18 gr. to grains.
3. Reduce 24 lb. 11 oz. 19 pwt. 23 gr. to grains.
4. Reduce 87340 gr. to pounds.
5. Reduce 50660 pwt. to pounds.
6. Reduce 31275 lb. to pennyweights.
7. Reduce 15 thousand gr. to pounds.
8. Reduce 4 lb. 4 oz. 4 gr. to grains.
9. Reduce 10 lb. 10 pwt. to grains.
10. Reduce 3 ℔ 9 ℥ 3 ʒ 1 ℈ 14 gr. to grains.
11. Reduce 9 ℔ 3 ʒ 2 ℈ to scruples.

12. Reduce 14 ℔ 7 ℥ 7 gr. to grains.

13. Reduce 45677 gr. to pounds.

14. Reduce 3478 ʒ to pounds.

15. Reduce 12345 ℈ to pounds.

16. Reduce 7 Cong. to f. ℥.

17. Reduce 3 O. 2 f. ℥ to minims.

18. Reduce 71 Cong. 3 f. ʒ to f. ʒ.

19. Reduce 4 ft. 6 in. to lines.

20. Reduce 5 feet to hands.

21. Reduce 17 leagues to miles.

22. Reduce 16 spans to yards.

23. In 17 hands how many feet?

24. In 20 yards how many spans?

25. Reduce 52 spans to hands.

26. Reduce 80 paces to fathoms.

27. Reduce 75 hands to fathoms.

28. Reduce 25 chains to rods.

29. Reduce 37°, 37′, 37″ to seconds.

30. Reduce 19°, 19″ to seconds.

31. Reduce 37864″ to degrees.

32. Reduce 450° to seconds.

33. How many things in 30 dozen?

34. How many things in 15 gross?

35. How many things in 5 great gross?

36. Reduce 15 score to dozens.

37. Reduce 360 score to gross.

38. What cost 12 kegs of nails at 6 cents a pound?

39. What cost 12 barrels of flour at 3 cents a pound?

40. What cost 12 barrels of pork at 8 cents a pound?

41. What cost 12 casks of lime, at 6 mills per pound?

42. What cost 1872 rings at 80 cents a gross?

43. What cost 7 great gross of needles, at 3 cents a dozen?

44. What cost 7 great gross of pins at 3 cents a gross?

45. What cost 9 gross of braces, at 7 cents apiece?

46. What cost 18 quires of drawing paper at 4 cents a sheet?

47. How many sheets of paper in 6 bundles?

48. A ream of paper will make how many 8vo. leaves?

49. Three reams of paper will make how many 12mo. pages?

50. How many reams of paper will be required for 3000 octavo books of 320 pages each?

ARTICLE 74.—*Promiscuous Examples.*

1. Reduce 49 yd. 2 ft. to inches.
2. Reduce 7 lb. 3 pwt. to grains.
3. Reduce 174528 sq. in. to square yards.
4. Reduce 12500″ to degrees.
5. Reduce 504000 cu. in. to cubic yards.
6. Reduce 3 ℔ 7 ℥ 2 ℈ to grains.
7. Reduce 863990 sec. to weeks.
8. Reduce 3329 pt. to bushels.
9. Reduce 14 great gross to dozens.
10. Reduce 7 T. 13 cwt. to pounds.
11. Reduce 3734 in. to yards.
12. Reduce 15 cords to cubic inches.
13. Reduce 5678 pt. to gallons.
14. Reduce 1016064 lb. flour to barrels.
15. Reduce 5400 scores to gross.
16. Reduce 3456 bu. to quarts.
17. Reduce 39750 pwt. to pounds.
18. Reduce 14 T. 14 lb. to ounces.
19. Reduce 23 gallons to f. ℥.
20. Reduce 333360 min. to weeks.
21. Reduce 7599 pt. to gallons.
22. Reduce 435670 sq. rd. to square miles.

23. Reduce 240 mi. to rods.
24. Reduce 78 gal. 3 qt. 1 pt. to pints.
25. Reduce 19 wk. 20 sec. to seconds.
26. Reduce 310 mi. 310 rd. to rods.
27. Reduce 49600 oz. to T.
28. Reduce one million sec. to weeks.
29. Reduce 384 cu. yd. to cords.
30. Reduce 5350 lb. to grains.
31. Reduce 12345 qt. to bushels.
32. Reduce 13 common years to minutes.
33. Reduce 12 cu. yd. 23 cu. ft. to cubic inches.
34. Reduce 39 T. 39 lb. to pounds.
35. Reduce 8 ℔ 8 ℥ 8 gr. to grains.
36. Reduce 46 sq. yd. 2 sq. ft. 36 sq. in. to sq. in.
37. Reduce 9876 pt. to gallons.
38. Reduce 10000 in. to yards.
39. Reduce 1284 pt. to bushels.
40. Reduce 11 ℥ 7 ʒ 2 ℈ to grains.
41. Reduce 5 sq. mi. 5 sq. rd. to square rods.
42. Reduce 162 C. to cubic yards.
43. Reduce 26 reams to 16mo. leaves.
44. Reduce 47580'' to degrees.
45. Reduce one million pt. to gallons.
46. Reduce 3500 gr. to ℥.
47. Reduce 6399 pt. to bushels.
48. Reduce 24 reams to sheets.
49. Reduce 793863 sq. in. to square yards.
50. Reduce one million oz. to tons.
51. Reduce 79 yd. 11 in. to inches.
52. Reduce 19 C. 1600 cu. in. to cubic inches.
53. Reduce 704000 sq. rd. to square miles.
54. Reduce 137 bu. 3 pk. to pints.
55. Reduce 5 wk. 5 da. 15 hr. 55 sec. to seconds.
56. Reduce 13 mi. 130 rd. to rods.

57. Reduce 1600 barrels of pork to pounds.

58. Reduce 30 T. 1 cwt. to ounces.

59. Reduce 217728 cu. in. to cubic yards.

60. Reduce 6920 pt. to gallons.

61. Reduce 10 great gross to scores.

62. Reduce 456789 oz. to tons.

63. Reduce ten thousand pt. to bushels.

64. Reduce 14° 23″ to seconds.

65. Reduce 4720 qt. to gallons.

66. Reduce one million sq. in. to square yards.

67. Reduce 6732 in. to yards.

68. Reduce 5280 minims to f. ℥.

69. Reduce 565 bu. 1 pt. to pints.

70. Reduce 3456000 sec. to weeks.

71. Reduce 3456000 12mo. pages to reams.

72. Reduce 288000 oz. to tons.

73. Reduce 387 A. 100 sq. rd. to square rods.

74. Reduce 17 leagues to rods.

75. Reduce 87 cu. yd. 25 cu. ft. to cords.

76. What cost 35 bushels of apples at 18 cents a peck?

77. What cost 13 bushels of salt at 3 cents a pint?

78. How much iron will be required to make 1000 4-oz. spikes?

79. How much milk will be needed to fill 80 dozen pint bottles?

80. A man's expenses are $1.17 a day; how much is that for July?

81. How many rings, weighing 6 pwt. each, can be made from 3 lb. of gold?

82. 414 gallons of cider were put in bottles containing 3 gills each; how many dozen bottles were required?

83. Find the cost of a pile of wood 40 feet long, 8 feet wide, and 8 feet high, at $3.75 per cord.

84 What cost 20 bushels of apples at 20 cents a peck?

85. A lawn 120 feet long, and 54 feet wide, was sodded at a cost of 19 cents per square yard; what was the total cost?

86. 561 pounds of iron were made into horse-shoes weighing 6 ounces each; how many were made?

87. How many 3-grain pills can be made from 5ʒ of quinine?

88. If sound moves 1124 feet per second, how long will it be in passing over 39340 yards?

89. How many bottles, holding 1 pt. 3 gi. each, can be filled from 168 gallons?

90. A comet moves 40″ per day; how far will it move in 120 days?

91. What cost a carpet 21 feet long and 15 feet wide, at $1.75 per square yard?

92. How many pounds in 480 dozen boxes of baking powder holding 15 ounces each?

93. How much silver will be required to make 10 dozen spoons, each weighing 15 pwt.?

94. How many cords of wood can be cut on 25 acres, at the rate of 72 cubic feet to a square rod?

95. If bottles hold 1 pt. 2 gi. each, how many dozen bottles can be filled from 126 gallons?

96. How many sashes, each 3 yd. 1 ft. long, can be cut from 200 yards of silk?

97. 500 bushels of peaches were packed in baskets, each holding 3 pk. 1 qt.; how many baskets were required?

98. A paper containing 2 ʒ 1 ℈ of medicine was divided into pills weighing 5 grains each, which were sold at 2 cents apiece; how much was received for it?

99. If 25 sq. rd. produce 1 bushel of wheat, how many bushels can be raised on a square mile?

100. If a weaver can weave 10 sq. ft. of carpet in an hour, how many sq. yd. can he weave in 15 days, working 12 hours per day?

101. How many plates, each weighing 2 lb. 8 oz., would be required to weigh 7 tons?

102. What cost 3 lb. 4 oz. of gold plate, at $.95 per pwt.?

103. Three cwt. of indigo was put up in ounce papers; how many dozen papers would that give?

104. A cistern containing 3003 gallons is emptied by a pipe carrying 1 gal. 1 gi. per minute; how long will it take to empty it?

105. A boy walks a rod in 3 seconds; how long will he be in walking 15 miles?

106. At 5 cents a pint, how many bushels of strawberries can be bought for $20?

107. A publisher issued an edition of 5000 12mo. books of 288 pages each; how many reams of paper were required?

108. If a pint of water weigh one pound, how many gallons will be required to make a weight of 8 tons?

109. What cost 13 yards of antique lace, at $20 per inch?

110. What sum will be received for 57 bushels of apples, at 24 cents per peck?

111. What will be the cost of fencing a field 180 rods long and 56 rods wide, at 75 cents per rod?

112. Three ounces and two drams of medicine was divided into powders weighing 13 grains each; how much would be received for the powders, at 15 cents apiece?

113. Fifteen bushels of cherries cost $33.60; how much is that per pint?

114. How much will a man earn in 9 weeks, at $2.25 per day?

115. A ship sails 10′ 30″ per hour; how many days will it take to sail 28°?

116. What will milk cost, to fill 40 dozen bottles, holding 3 gills each, at $2.50 a gallon?

117. A block of stone is 8 ft. long, 8 ft. wide, and 8 ft. thick; how much will it weigh if a cu. ft. weighs 625 lbs?

118. Find the cost of 300 bushels of oysters, at 12 cents per peck.

119. If a railway train can go 22 miles 160 rods in 1 hour, how long will it require to go 1710 miles?

120. What cost 9 tons of hay, at 9 mills per pound?

121. A tank will hold 1000 gallons of water; how many cubic feet in it?

122. A steel plate is 2 feet long and 16 inches wide, and weighs 2 ounces to each square inch; what is it worth, at $0.075 per pound?

123. A man's income being $1.33 every hour, what will it be in the year 1895?

124. What cost 375 fathom of rope, weighing 2 pounds per foot, at 5 cents 5 mills per pound?

125. How many score in 30 great gross?

126. Sold berries at 6 cents a pint, and realized $15.12; how many bushels were sold?

127. What cost 400 gallons of molasses, at 7 ct. a pint?

128. How many rings, weighing 6 ounces each, can be made from 141 pounds of iron?

129. How many plates, weighing 6 ounces each, can be made from 141 pounds of silver?

130. Wheat weighs 60 pounds per bushel; find the cost of 30720 pounds, at 90 cents a bushel.

131. What will be the cost of paving a street 2700 feet long, and 40 feet wide, at $0.72 per square yard?

132. If a machine will peg a shoe in 4 minutes, how many dozen will it peg in 6 days of 10 hours each?

133. A cistern containing 480 gallons of water has two leaks: from one, 3 gills run out per minute; from the other, 13 gallons per hour. How much will be left in the cistern at the end of 8 hours?

134. 550 bushels of corn were bought at 44 cents a bushel, and retailed at 14 cents a peck; how much was gained?

135. How long would it take a tortoise to crawl a league, moving 4 rods an hour and 15 hours a day?

136. A man eats 2 lb. 3 oz. daily; how many weeks would 2 T. 9 cwt. last him?

137. A had 150 barrels of flour; B had the same weight of beef; how many barrels would it fill?

138. How many bags, of 2 bu. 2 qt. each, will be required to contain 2145 bushels of wheat?

139. How long would it take to build a road 86 mi. 20 rd. long, if 1 mi. 20 rd. can be made in a day?

140. What cost 256 cubic yards of wood, at $3.17 a cord?

141. If 3 bu. 2 pk. of berries cost $8.40, how much is that per quart?

142. A man poured 48 gallons of milk into bottles containing 1 qt. 1 pt. each, and sold them at 60 cents per bottle; how much did he receive?

143. How many gallons of essence will be required to fill 40 gross of bottles, each to contain 1 fluid ounce?

144. How many labels, 2 in. long and 1 in. wide, can be cut from 6 sheets of paper, each 4 ft. wide and 8 ft. long?

145. If 1 bu. 1 pk. of peaches cost $3, what will 1 bushel cost?

146. Twenty-four sheets were folded in 12mo.; how many sheets would be required to make as many quarto leaves?

COMPOUND NUMBERS.

ARTICLE 75.—*Addition of Compound Numbers.*

1. Add together 4 bu. 2 pk. 5 qt.; 17 bu. 3 pk. 1 qt.; 9 bu. 2 pk. 6 qt.; 16 bu. 3 pk. 5 qt.; 5 bu. 1 pk. 3 qt.; 2 bu. 7 qt.; 1 pk. 2 qt.; and 3 bu. 3 qt.

2. Add together 199 bu. 2 pk.; 83 bu. 3 pk.; 65 bu. 1 pk.; 88 bu. 2 pk.; 100 bu. 2 pk.; 116 bu. 1 pk.; 134 bu. 3 pk.; and 111 bu. 2 pk.

3. 27 gal. 3 qt. 1 pt. + 27 gal. 2 qt. 1 pt. + 27 gal. 1 qt. 1 pt. + 27 gal. 1 pt. + 27 gal. 3 qt. + 27 gal. 2 qt. + 27 gal. 1 qt. = ?

4. 3 T. 17 cwt. 60 lb. + 5 T. 15 cwt. 70 lb. + 4 T. 90 lb. + 9 T. 19 cwt. 99 lb. + 7 T. 16 cwt. + 5 cwt. 92 lb. = ?

5. 15 gal. 1 pt. + 16 gal. 1 qt. + 17 gal. 1 qt. 1 pt. + 18 gal. 2 qt. + 19 gal. 1 pt. + 20 gal. 3 qt. + 21 gal. 1 pt. + 22 gal. 3 qt. 1 pt. = ?

6. Find the sum of 7 cwt. 29 lb.; 9 cwt. 40 lb.; 16 cwt. 67 lb.; 13 cwt. 28 lb.; 12 cwt. 71 lb.; 10 cwt. 60 lb.; 3 cwt. 33 lb.; and 16 cwt. 72 lb.

7. 29 gal. 2 qt. 1 pt. + 29 gal. 2 qt. 1 pt. + 29 gal. 2 qt. 1 pt. + 29 gal. 2 qt. 1 pt. + 29 gal. 2 qt. 1 pt. + 29 gal. 2 qt. 1 pt. = ?

8. Find the sum of 7 yd. 2 ft. 11 in.; 4 yd. 1 ft. 7 in.; 12 yd. 2 ft. 5 in.; 9 yd. 1 ft. 1 in.; 12 yd. 1 in.; 15 yd. 1 ft. 5 in.; 6 yd. 7 in.; and 10 yd. 1 ft. 11 in.

9. Add together 7 yd. 2 ft.; 7 yd. 2 in.; 6 yd. 1 ft. 7 in.; 4 yd. 11 in.; 9 yd. 2 ft. 6 in.; 3 yd. 3 in.; 12 yd. 2 ft.; and 6 yd. 10 in.

10. 75 A. + 75 sq. rd. + 76 A. 76 sq. rd. + 77 A. 77 sq. rd. + 78 A. 78 sq. rd. + 72 A. 72 sq. rd. + 119 A. 140 sq. rd. = ?

11. 7 sq. yd. 7 sq. ft. 77 sq. in. + 8 sq. yd. 8 sq. ft. 88 sq. in. + 22 sq. yd. 22 sq. in. + 49 sq. yd. 4 sq. ft. 48 sq. in + 39 sq. yd. 96 sq. in. = ?

12. Find the sum of 3 sq. mi. 300 A.; 7 sq. mi. 500 A.; 4 sq. mi. 444 A.; 2 sq. mi. 222 A.; 10 sq. mi. 229 A.; and 5 sq. mi. 555 A.

13. 27 cu. yd. 26 cu. ft. + 26 cu. yd. 25 cu. ft. + 25 cu. yd. 24 cu. ft. + 24 cu. yd. 23 cu. ft. + 23 cu. yd. 22 cu. ft. + 22 cu. yd. 21 cu. ft. = ?

14. 25 C. 17 cu. ft. + 25 C. 1700 cu. in. + 25 C. 117 cu. ft. 1170 cu. in. + 252 C. 1717 cu. in. + 28 C. 127 cu. ft. + 19 C. 127 cu. ft. 1727 cu. in. = ?

15. 3 da. 13 hr. 20 min. + 7 da. 17 hr. 27 min. + 3 da. 13 hr. 33 min. + 6 da. 23 hr. + 4 da. 6 hr. 56 min. + 11 da. 11 hr. 11 min. + 19 da. 19 hr. 59 min. = ?

16. 5 da. 59 min. + 5 da. 58 min. + 5 da. 57 min. + 5 da. 56 min. + 5 da. 55 min. + 5 da. 54 min. + 5 da. 53 min. = ?

17. 4 lb. 9 oz. 12 pwt. + 6 lb. 7 oz. 18 pwt. + 3 lb. 10 oz. 10 pwt. + 5 lb. 11 oz. + 2 lb. 11 pwt. + 6 lb. 6 oz. 16 pwt. + 13 lb. 13 pwt. = ?

18. 2 ℨ 2 ℈ 10 gr. + 7 ℨ 19 gr. + 5 ℨ 1 ℈ 16 gr. + 5 ℨ 10 gr. + 2 ℨ 2 ℈ 1 gr. + 5 ℨ 1 ℈ 4 gr. = ?

19. 5 ℥ 3 ℨ 2 ℈ + 4 ℥ 2 ℨ 1 ℈ + 7 ℥ 2 ℈ + 7 ℨ 2 ℈ + 2 ℥ 4 ℨ 1 ℈ + 3 ℥ 5 ℨ 2 ℈ + 7 ℨ 1 ℈ + 7 ℥ 1 ℈ = ?

20. 4 score and 6 + 3 score and ten + 4 score and 8 + 4 score and 9 + 2 score and 18 + 3 score and 12 = ?

21. 14° 35′ 23″ + 17° 49′ 49″ + 26° 30′ 10″ + 30° 59′ 1″ + 7° 24′ 48″ + 13° 29′ 50″ + 9° 59″ = ?

22. 8° 15′ 28″ + 6° 28′ 29″ + 7° 30′ 30″ + 11° 44′ 32″ + 13° 31′ 31″ + 13° 30′ 31″ = ?

23. 3 cong. 7 O. 11 f. ℥ + 5 cong. 4 O. 9 f. ℥ + 7 cong. 7 O. 7 f. ℥ + 9 cong. 5 f. ℥ + 7 cong. 7 O. + 5 O. 15 f. ℥ = ?

24. 2 f. ℥ 4 f. ʒ 20 ♏ + 3 f. ℥ 5 ʒ 40 ♏ + 7 f. ℥ 3 f. ʒ 40 ♏ + 6 f. ℥ 2 f. ʒ 20 ♏ = ?

25. Seven barrels of coal oil were gauged as follows: 49 gal. 3 qt.; 51 gal. 2 qt.; 48 gal. 3 qt.; 55 gal. 2 qt.; 52 gal. 2 qt.; 53 gal. 1 qt.; and 50 gal. 2 qt. How much in all?

26. How much wood in 5 piles, containing respectively 25 C. 87 cu. ft.; 56 C. 112 cu. ft.; 39 C. 41 cu. ft.; 43 C. 16 cu. ft.; and 88 C. 88 cu. ft.?

27. Eggs were packed in 6 boxes: 29 doz. and 7; 40 doz. and 10; 35 doz. and 5; 60 doz. and 10; 38 doz. and 9; and 52 doz. and 7. How many dozen in all?

28. Find the weight of 8 hogsheads of sugar, weighing as follows: 11 cwt. 83 lb.; 12 cwt. 46 lb.; 11 cwt. 55 lb.; 12 cwt. 19 lb.; 13 cwt. 1 lb.; 12 cwt. 52 lb.; 11 cwt. 93 lb.; and 12 cwt. 51 lb.

29. A farmer planted 17 A. 100 sq. rd. in wheat, 21 A. 120 sq. rd. in oats, 30 A. 50 sq. rd. in corn, 13 A. 60 sq. rd. in potatoes, 7 A. 40 sq. rd. in sorghum, and 11 A. 110 sq. rd. in broom-corn. How much land had he in cultivation?

30. A vessel sailed 13 da. 7 hr. to the first port, and stopped there 2 da. 20 hr; then 25 da. 20 hr. to the second port, and stopped there 3 da. 23 hr.; then 40 da. 5 hr. to the third port, and stopped there 2 da. 19 hr.; then 60 da. 16 hr. to the starting point. How long was the voyage?

31. A railroad train traveled as follows: 14 mi. 125 rd. to first station; 9 mi. 77 rd. to second; 16 mi. 62 rd. to third; 31 mi. 35 rd. to fourth; 11 mi. 83 rd. to fifth; and then 18 mi. 98 rd. to its destination. What was the length of the trip?

32. Set down 3 da. 13 hr. 39 min. 26 sec. seven times, and then add them.

ARTICLE 76.—*Subtraction of Compound Numbers.*

1. From 40 bu. take 20 bu. 3 qt.

2. 39 bu. 1 pk. 1 qt. — 19 bu. 3 pk. 3 qt. = ?

3. From 100 gal. take 49 gal. 3 qt. 2 gi.

4. From 353 gal. 1 pt. take 203 gal. 3 qt.

5. From 3 T. 13 cwt. 23 lb. take 1 T. 18 cwt. 5 lb.

6. From 1 T. 1 cwt. 1 lb. 1 oz. take 11 cwt. 11 lb. 11 oz.

7. From 47 mi. 180 rd. take 23 mi. 250 rd.

8. From 16 yd. 2 ft. 1 in. take 9 yd. 1 ft. 2 in.

9. 81 yd. 6 in. — 18 yd. 8 in. = ?

10. From 9 sq. mi. 100 A. take 4 sq. mi. 370 A.

11. 39 sq. yd. 4 sq. ft. 44 sq. in. — 21 sq. yd. 7 sq. ft. 89 sq. in. = ?

12. From 300 sq. mi. 300 A. 100 sq. rd. take 100 sq. mi. 300 A. 150 sq. rd.

13. From 36 cu. yd. 10 cu. ft. 800 cu. in. take 8 cu. yd. 19 cu. ft. 900 cu. in.

14. Take 18 C. 1500 cu. in. from 81 C. 1478 cu. in.

15. 5 hr. 6 min. 22 sec. — 2 hr. 20 min. 20 sec. = ?

16. From 7 wk. 6 da. 5 hr. 4 min. 3 sec. take 3 wk. 4 da. 5 hr. 6 min. 7 sec,

17. Take 9 lb. 7 oz. 16 pwt. from 15 lb. 3 oz. 3 pwt.

18. 5 ℔ 4 ℥ 3 ʒ 1 ℈ — 2 ℔ 6 ℥ 6 ʒ 2 ℈ = ?

19. From 14° 7′ 10″ take 9° 18′ 30″.

20. From 19 reams take 12 reams 4 quires.

21. From 3 gross 4 dozen take 1 gross 8 dozen.

22. From 1 O. 3 f. ℥ 2 f. ʒ take 13 f. ℥.

23. If 25 bu. 3 pk. 2 qt. have been sold from 40 bu. of peanuts, what quantity is left?

24. A farmer has 450 bu. of potatoes; if he sells 273 bu. 2 pk. what quantity will he have left?

25. The time between two cities by steamer is 2 wk. 2 hr.; by railroad, 5 da. 19 hr.; how much time is gained by the railroad route?

26. From a tank containing 327 gal. 2 qt. 1 pt., 10 gal. 3 qt. 1 pt. leaked out; how much remains?

27. If a tract of 36 A. 120 sq. rd. be cut from a farm of 120 A., how much will be left?

28. A quantity of pig iron, weighing 17 T. 5 cwt. 48 lb., was melted to make stove castings, which, when cast, weighed 17 T. 1 cwt. 90 lb.; how much metal was lost in the work?

29. From a pile of wood containing 106 C. 105 cu. ft., there was taken away a boat load of 87 C. 120 cu. ft.; how much remained?

30. A cart weighed 13 cwt. 80 lb., and, after being filled with coal, weighed 3 T. 11 cwt. 90 lb.; what was the weight of the coal?

31. A ship was 13° 7′ 20″ from a port, and sailed 4° 43′ 40″ toward it; how far from the port was it then?

32. How much will be left of a mass of medicine weighing 1 ℔ 1 ʒ., after 7 ℥ 5 ʒ 2 ℈ 10 gr. have been made into pills?

33. A boat laden with 750 T. 60 lb. was sunk, and 473 T. 90 lb. of the freight was saved; how much was lost?

34. The regular time between two cities was 100 hr. 10 min., and the train arrived 3 hr. 52 min. ahead of time; how long had it taken to make the run?

35. A man contracted to deliver 100 C. of wood, and has only 78 C. 96 cu. ft.; how much does he lack?

36. A man having 89 bu. 1 pk. of clover seed, sold 37 bu. 3 pk. to each of his two brothers; how much has he remaining?

37. From 30 days subtract 5 da. 12 hr. 19 minutes three times.

ARTICLE 77.—*Time between two dates.*

1. Money was borrowed May 18, 1882, and returned Jan. 6, 1884; how long had it been kept?

2. The battle of Monmouth was fought June 28, 1778, and the battle of Antietam September 17, 1862; what time elapsed between the two events?

3. Washington was born February 22, 1732, and died December 14, 1799; at what age did he die?

4. The pilgrims landed December 21, 1620; how long was that before the Declaration of Independence, July 4, 1776?

5. What time elapsed between the surrender at Yorktown, October 19, 1781, and the signing of the treaty of peace, September 3, 1783?

6. A child born December 3, 1876, commenced school August 27, 1883; at what age was that?

7. How old was Washington at the battle of Monmouth? (See examples 2 and 3.)

8. What time elapsed from the battle of Lexington, April 19, 1775, to the firing on Fort Sumter, April 12, 1861?

ARTICLE 78.—*Time in days between two dates.*

1. Find the number of days from Aug. 5 to the second day of the next December.

2. How many days from Nov. 15, 1871, to Jan. 18, 1872?

3. How many days from Oct. 20, 1877, to Mar. 15, 1878?

4. How many days from Jan. 12, 1880, to Oct. 15, 1880?

5. How many days from June 5 to Dec. 25?

6. A servant was hired May 18, and discharged November 29; for how many days should she be paid?

7. How many days from Apr. 6, 1875, to Apr. 1, 1876?

8. Corn was planted April 18, and was ripe September 27; how many days was that?

Article 79.—*Multiplication of Compound Numbers.*

1. 3 bu. 2 pk. 5 qt. 1 pt. × 8 = ?

2. 7 gal. 3 qt. 1 pt. 3 gi. × 8 = ?

3. 3 cwt. 27 lb. 8 oz. × 10 = ?

4. 5 yd. 2 ft. 7 in. × 11 = ?

5. 3 sq. yd. 7 sq. ft. 72 sq. in. × 6 = ?

6. 7 cu. ft. 700 cu. in. × 10 = ?

7. 3 oz. 7 pwt. 10 gr. × 24 = ?

8. 3 ℥ 2 ℈ 12 gr. × 60 = ?

9. 3 gal. 1 pt. 1 gi. × 72 = ?

10. 2° 10′ 20″ × 36 = ?

11. 3 quires 10 sheets × 120 = ?

12. 3 mi. 190 rd. × 77 = ?

13. 13 hr. 24 min. 36 sec. × 99 = ?

14. What will be the weight of 27 castings, 1 T. 12 cwt. 42 lb. each?

15. If an acre will produce 6 bu. 3 pk. 5 qt. of wheat, how much can be raised on 20 acres?

16. If a stream flows 17 yd. 2 ft. 8 in. in a minute, how far would that be in an hour?

17. If a square rod produces 7 qt. 1 pt. of strawberries, what quantity could be raised on 1 A.?

18. A steamer makes a trip in 1 da. 5 hr. 19 min.; what time would be required for 20 trips?

19. If a quart of berries can be picked in 14 min. 20 sec., how long would it take to pick 1 pk.?

20. If a herd of cattle consumes 9 T. 3 cwt. 18 lb. daily, how much fodder would be required for the month of November?

21. If 34 sq. yd. 8 sq. ft. 60 sq. in. of flooring are required for one floor, how much will be needed for 14 floors?

22. If 1 qt. of seed will produce 1 bu. 1 pk. 1 qt. of grain, how much grain will 1 bu. of seed produce?

Article 80.—*Division of Compound Numbers.*

1. Divide 32 bu. 1 pk. 3 qt. by 9.
2. Divide 1 T. 9 cwt. 80 lb. 8 oz. by 8.
3. Divide 22 yd. 2 ft. by 6.
4. Divide 8 sq. yd. 4 sq. ft. 16 sq. in. by 10.
5. Divide 2 da. 15 hr. 12 min. by 18.
6. Divide 3 oz. 11 pwt. 16 gr. by 20.
7. Divide 2 ℥ 6 ʒ by 12.
8. Divide 225 gal. 3 qt. 1 pt. 2 gi. by 30.
9. Divide 238 yd. 1 ft. by 33.
10. Divide 67 sq. yd. by 54.
11. Divide 230 da. 13 hr. 20 min. by 100.
12. Divide 19 cu. yd. 9 cu. ft. 864 cu. in. by 19.

13. A man raised 237 bu. 3 pk. 2 qt. of raspberries on 10 A.; how much was that per acre?

14. If 19 jars would contain 103 gal. 3 qt. 1 pt. 1 gi., what would one contain?

15. If 11 cwt. 79 lb. 12 oz. of sugar be packed in 12 kegs, how much will each contain?

16. One hundred cu. yd. of earth are to be hauled away in 18 carts; how much will that be for each?

17. A glacier moved 43 yd. in 701 da. 13 hr. 22 min.; how long did it take to move 1 yd.?

18. A planet moved 13° 30′ 50″ in 25 days; what would be the average motion per day?

19. Fifteen equal bins contain 3740 bu. 2 pk. 4 qt. of wheat; how much is in each?

20. A steamer goes 183 mi. 144 rd. per day; how far is that per hour?

21. In 7 days, of 10 hours each, a furnace will turn out 242 T. 18 cwt. of blooms; how much is that per hour?

22. A gardener raised 275 bu. of beets on an acre of ground; what was the yield per square rod?

LONGITUDE AND TIME.

ARTICLES 81 AND 82.

Find the differences in time, corresponding to the following differences in longitude:

1. 40°.	**5.** 100° 10′.	**9.** 99° 9′.
2. 33° 20′.	**6.** 49° 13′ 30″.	**10.** 111° 51′ 30″.
3. 36° 17′.	**7.** 66° 45″	**11.** 58° 58′ 15″.
4. 69° 51′.	**8.** 70° 17′ 15″.	**12.** 97° 53′.

Find the differences in longitude, corresponding to the following differences of time:

13. 11 hr. 17 min. 13 sec.	**17.** 15 hr. 14 min. 29 sec.
14. 6 hr. 59 min. 17 sec.	**18.** 4 hr. 45 min. 10 sec.
15. 10 hr. 10 min. 10 sec.	**19.** 5 hr. 29 min. 25 sec.
16. 7 hr. 17 min. 27 sec.	**20.** 47 min. 47 sec.

21. A man travels east 29°; will his watch be fast or slow then, and how much?

22. A boat sails 47° west; how much will her chronometer gain or lose on the time at the point reached?

23. A team travels eastward 45′ a day; will its day be lengthened or shortened, and how much?

24. What is the difference of time between two places whose longitudes are 29° east, and 54° west?

25. When it is 7 o'clock A. M. at a place in 93° west longitude, what is the time at another place in 39° west longitude?

26. When it is 7 o'clock A. M. at a place in 107° east longitude, what is the time at another place in 40° east longitude?

27. When it is 11 o'clock A. M. at a place in 40° west longitude, what is the time at another place in 70° east longitude?

28. When it is 3 o'clock P. M. at a place in 3° east longitude, what is the time at another place in 68° west longitude?

29. When it is 6 o'clock A. M. in 90° east longitude, what is the time in 90° west longitude?

30. What is the difference of time between two places, one in 37° 35′ east longitude, the other in 47° 10′ west longitude?

FACTORING.

Article 87.

Find the Prime Factors:

1. Of 51.	**8.** Of 120.	**15.** Of 252.
2. Of 52.	**9.** Of 132.	**16.** Of 561.
3. Of 62.	**10.** Of 168.	**17.** Of 882.
4. Of 63.	**11.** Of 196.	**18.** Of 828.
5. Of 72.	**12.** Of 198.	**19.** Of 2662.
6. Of 75.	**13.** Of 204.	**20.** Of 3087.
7. Of 76.	**14.** Of 207.	**21.** Of 4356.

Article 88.

What Prime Factors are common to:

1. 60 and 80?
2. 90 and 120?
3. 80 and 120?
4. 135 and 180?
5. 126 and 210?
6. 324 and 432?
7. 324 and 594?
8. 264 and 638?
9. 462 and 819?
10. 385 and 595?
11. 363 and 1419?
12. 48, 72, and 84?
13. 78, 104, and 143?
14. 192, 252, and 348?
15. 64, 104, 144, and 376?
16. 135, 180, 210, and 375?
17. 144, 168, 192, and 240?
18. 117, 143, 286, and 390?
19. 126, 196, 238, and 266?
20. 187, 231, 275, and 308?
21. 147, 210, 315, and 364?
22. 384, 486, 324, and 510?

Article 89.—*Greatest Common Divisor.*

Find the Greatest Common Divisor:

1. Of 48 and 84.
2. Of 40, 60, and 90.
3. Of 117 and 171.
4. Of 889 and 560.
5. Of 124 and 600.
6. Of 390 and 702.
7. Of 392 and 637.
8. Of 770 and 891.
9. Of 873 and 378.
10. Of 656 and 1066.
11. Of 980 and 2401.
12. Of 3003 and 21000.
13. Of 1008 and 1584.
14. Of 1296 and 2304.
15. Of 16983 and 18574.
16. Of 243, 324, and 432.
17. Of 56, 84, and 126.
18. Of 80, 120, and 180.
19. Of 468, 648, and 864.
20. Of 675, 945, and 1053.
21. Of 980, 2002, and 15001.
22. Of 289, 391, and 493.
23. Of 288, 387, and 486.
24. Of 3375, 8205, and 15000.
25. Of 81, 135, 450, and 780.
26. Of 63, 144, 216, and 297.
27. Of 1120, 960, 888, and 666.

Article 90.—*Least Common Multiple.*

Find the Least Common Multiple:

1. Of 8, 12, 16, and 20.
2. Of 9, 12, 16, and 20.
3. Of 12, 16, 20, and 24.
4. Of 16, 20, 25, and 40.
5. Of 36, 42, 48, and 54.
6. Of 24, 30, 42, and 28.
7. Of 60, 66, 30, and 36.
8. Of 21, 35, 55, and 84.
9. Of 16, 18, 20, and 22.
10. Of 16, 18, 20, and 30.
11. Of 16, 18, 20, and 24.
12. Of 18, 20, 24, and 36.
13. Of 24, 54, 84, and 144.
14. Of 121 and 122.
15. Of 221 and 323.
16. Of 169 and 325.
17. Of 343 and 735.
18. Of 150, 225, and 375.
19. Of 100, 200, and 300.
20. Of 14, 24, 44, and 42.
21. Of 143 and 175.
22. Of 143 and 176.
23. Of 12, 16, 24, 36, and 72.
24. Of 30, 36, 48, 64, and 80.
25. Of 18, 26, 54, and 78.
26. Of 576, 384, 288, 768, and 256.
27. Of 8, 9, 10, 11, and 12.
28. Of 45, 75, 81, 72, and 54.
29. Of 245, 343, 441, and 98.
30. Of 123, 205, 287, and 246.

Article 91.—*Cancellation.*

1. How often is 12 contained in 4 times 27?
2. Divide 18×21 by 14×9.
3. In 16 times 18 how many times 12?
4. How often is 6×8 contained in 16×18?
5. How many score in 12×25?
6. How many flower-beds 4 feet long and 3 feet wide, can be made from a plat 36 feet long and 18 feet wide?
7. Divide $8 \times 9 \times 10 \times 12$ by $3 \times 4 \times 5 \times 6$.

8. Sold six dozen tumblers at 8 cents apiece, and spent the money for yarn at 18 cents a pound; how many pounds did I receive?

9. How many barrels of sugar, at $15 a barrel, will pay for 18 hogs, at $20 apiece?

10. Divide $18 \times 20 \times 24 \times 32$ by $27 \times 16 \times 40$.

11. How many lots 5 feet square can be cut from a lot 30 feet square?

12. Divide $18 \times 17 \times 16 \times 15$ by $2 \times 3 \times 4 \times 5 \times 6$.

13. A quantity of iron will make three hundred 30-lb. castings; how many 25-lb castings will it make?

14. Twenty reams of paper, of 20 quires each, and each quire 24 sheets, and each sheet making 24 pages, were made into books containing 160 pages each; how many dozen books would there be?

15. How many hundred blocks 3 in. long, 2 in. wide, and 1 in. thick, can be made from a block 5 ft. long, 3 ft. wide, and 5 in. thick?

FRACTIONS.

ARTICLE 103.—*Reduction of Integers to Fractions of given Denominators.*

Reduce:

1. 14 to sevenths.
2. 23 to elevenths.
3. 7 to twenty-thirds.
4. 63 to eighteenths.
5. 90 to ninths.
6. 31 to thirty-seconds.
7. 3 to fifty-sixths.
8. 26 to eighths.
9. 315 to ninths.
10. 200 to twelfths.
11. 37 to eighteenths.
12. 34 to fortieths.
13. 14 to twentieths.
14. 27 to thirteenths.
15. 31 to sixteenths.
16. 67 to twenty-seconds.
17. 19 to ninetieths.
18. 81 to twenty-ninths.

Article 104.—*Case II.*

Reduce the following to Improper Fractions:

1. $15\frac{7}{8}$.
2. $19\frac{5}{7}$.
3. $99\frac{1}{9}$.
4. $73\frac{1}{10}$.
5. $36\frac{8}{15}$.
6. $42\frac{11}{18}$.
7. $176\frac{2}{7}$.
8. $19\frac{1}{19}$.
9. $28\frac{17}{18}$.
10. $45\frac{5}{22}$.
11. $73\frac{8}{73}$.
12. $29\frac{3}{100}$.
13. $272\frac{8}{11}$.
14. $396\frac{4}{27}$.
15. $562\frac{3}{14}$.
16. $100\frac{1}{100}$.
17. $682\frac{11}{16}$.
18. $129\frac{14}{41}$.
19. $29\frac{4}{111}$.
20. $21\frac{1}{19}$.
21. $73\frac{73}{99}$.

Article 105.—*Case III.*

Reduce the following to Integers or Mixed Numbers:

1. $\frac{457}{6}$.
2. $\frac{368}{8}$.
3. $\frac{1239}{7}$.
4. $\frac{1289}{10}$.
5. $\frac{4710}{13}$.
6. $\frac{2617}{15}$.
7. $\frac{4618}{19}$.
8. $\frac{2468}{17}$.
9. $\frac{3753}{23}$.
10. $\frac{739}{22}$.
11. $\frac{5647}{14}$.
12. $\frac{3973}{26}$.
13. $\frac{4140}{18}$.
14. $\frac{4678}{33}$.
15. $\frac{3003}{77}$.
16. $\frac{9876}{100}$.
17. $\frac{3402}{42}$.
18. $\frac{1234}{15}$.
19. $\frac{7630}{35}$.
20. $\frac{12345}{23}$.
21. $\frac{4678}{97}$.

Article 106.—*Case IV.*

1. Reduce $\frac{4}{11}$ to thirty-thirds.
2. Reduce $\frac{5}{12}$ to sixtieths.
3. Reduce $\frac{3}{8}$ to fortieths.
4. Reduce $\frac{4}{5}$ to thirty-fifths.
5. Reduce $\frac{17}{20}$ to hundredths.

Reduce the following fractions:

6. $\frac{8}{9}$ to a fraction whose denominator is 126.
7. $\frac{16}{21}$ " " " " " 105.
8. $\frac{12}{13}$ " " " " " 156.
9. $\frac{17}{19}$ " " " " " 171.

Reduce the following fractions:

10. $\frac{17}{20}$ to a fraction whose denominator is 280.
11. $\frac{14}{23}$ " " " " " 345.
12. $\frac{17}{28}$ " " " " " 336.
13. $\frac{15}{29}$ " " " " " 464.
14. $\frac{17}{32}$ " " " " " 416.
15. $\frac{27}{38}$ " " " " " 1368.
16. $\frac{81}{88}$ " " " " " 7744.
17. $\frac{73}{80}$ " " " " " 4560.
18. $\frac{13}{212}$ " " " " " 3604.
19. $\frac{29}{273}$ " " " " " 1911.
20. $\frac{179}{197}$ " " " " " 6698.

ARTICLE 107.—*Case V.*

Reduce the following to their Lowest Terms:

1. $\frac{144}{169}$.
2. $\frac{84}{126}$.
3. $\frac{405}{705}$.
4. $\frac{567}{1001}$.
5. $\frac{407}{999}$.
6. $\frac{407}{990}$.
7. $\frac{803}{876}$.
8. $\frac{9200}{12075}$.
9. $\frac{1625}{3055}$.
10. $\frac{1234}{4319}$.
11. $\frac{1681}{1763}$.
12. $\frac{999}{1350}$.
13. $\frac{3456}{4356}$.
14. $\frac{3465}{4356}$.
15. $\frac{945}{1785}$.
16. $\frac{1296}{1620}$.
17. $\frac{2345}{3685}$.
18. $\frac{3468}{5202}$.
19. $\frac{1950}{4050}$.
20. $\frac{3025}{7744}$.
21. $\frac{4001}{5001}$.

ARTICLE 108.—*Case VI.*

Reduce the following to Least Common Denominators:

1. $\frac{2}{3}$, $\frac{1}{4}$, $\frac{3}{5}$.
2. $\frac{4}{5}$, $\frac{5}{6}$, $\frac{8}{9}$.
3. $\frac{3}{8}$, $\frac{3}{4}$, $\frac{3}{7}$.
4. $\frac{4}{9}$, $\frac{7}{10}$, $\frac{8}{15}$.
5. $\frac{2}{5}$, $\frac{3}{10}$, $\frac{4}{15}$, $\frac{9}{20}$.
6. $\frac{7}{8}$, $\frac{7}{12}$, $\frac{7}{16}$, $\frac{7}{24}$.
7. $\frac{9}{10}$, $\frac{7}{12}$, $\frac{9}{20}$, $\frac{7}{24}$.
8. $\frac{4}{15}$, $\frac{5}{24}$, $\frac{7}{30}$, $\frac{9}{40}$.
9. $\frac{13}{20}$, $\frac{13}{40}$, $\frac{13}{60}$, $\frac{13}{80}$.
10. $\frac{9}{14}$, $\frac{9}{22}$, $\frac{9}{26}$.
11. $\frac{7}{9}$, $\frac{5}{6}$, $\frac{3}{4}$, $\frac{3}{8}$, $\frac{5}{12}$.
12. $\frac{3}{25}$, $\frac{7}{20}$, $\frac{9}{10}$, $\frac{11}{50}$.
13. $\frac{3}{4}$, $\frac{1}{6}$, $\frac{7}{9}$, $\frac{11}{12}$, $\frac{1}{3}$.
14. $\frac{1}{2}$, $\frac{1}{12}$, $\frac{1}{22}$, $\frac{1}{32}$.

15. $\frac{3}{10}$, $\frac{11}{20}$, $\frac{5}{12}$, $\frac{7}{8}$.
16. $\frac{1}{12}$, $\frac{4}{9}$, $\frac{5}{16}$, $\frac{13}{18}$.
17. $\frac{4}{15}$, $\frac{5}{18}$, $\frac{7}{10}$, $\frac{1}{6}$.
18. $\frac{4}{15}$, $\frac{5}{18}$, $\frac{7}{10}$, $\frac{1}{16}$.
19. $\frac{3}{8}$, $\frac{5}{18}$, $\frac{9}{28}$, $\frac{7}{48}$.
20. $\frac{11}{15}$, $\frac{7}{10}$, $\frac{2}{3}$, $\frac{5}{6}$.
21. $\frac{2}{9}$, $\frac{3}{10}$, $\frac{2}{7}$, $\frac{3}{11}$.
22. $\frac{5}{8}$, $\frac{7}{9}$, $\frac{7}{16}$, $\frac{7}{18}$.
23. $\frac{2}{11}$, $\frac{2}{33}$, $\frac{3}{22}$, $\frac{3}{44}$.
24. $1\frac{2}{3}$, $1\frac{3}{4}$, $1\frac{5}{6}$, $1\frac{7}{12}$.
25. $2\frac{4}{5}$, $\frac{7}{15}$, $3\frac{3}{10}$, $\frac{11}{20}$.
26. $\frac{11}{12}$, $\frac{15}{16}$, $\frac{17}{18}$, $\frac{23}{24}$.
27. $\frac{4}{7}$, $\frac{4}{8}$, $\frac{4}{9}$, $\frac{4}{10}$.
28. $\frac{13}{16}$, 2, $\frac{13}{24}$, $\frac{13}{36}$, $\frac{13}{48}$.
29. $\frac{17}{20}$, $\frac{18}{21}$, $\frac{9}{14}$, $\frac{17}{18}$, $\frac{11}{12}$.
30. $\frac{4}{9}$, $\frac{3}{8}$, $5\frac{5}{6}$, $\frac{7}{4}$, $8\frac{11}{12}$.

Article 110.—*Addition of Fractions. Case I.*

Add the following fractions:

1. $\frac{7}{18}$, $\frac{12}{18}$, $\frac{15}{18}$, $\frac{14}{18}$.
2. $\frac{5}{12}$, $\frac{7}{12}$, $\frac{11}{12}$, $\frac{9}{12}$.
3. $\frac{13}{24}$, $\frac{14}{24}$, $\frac{15}{24}$, $\frac{16}{24}$.
4. $\frac{18}{36}$, $\frac{21}{36}$, $\frac{24}{36}$, $\frac{27}{36}$.
5. $\frac{11}{48}$, $\frac{12}{48}$, $\frac{13}{48}$, $\frac{14}{48}$.
6. $\frac{4}{77}$, $\frac{13}{77}$, $\frac{18}{77}$, $\frac{9}{77}$.
7. $\frac{53}{80}$, $\frac{63}{80}$, $\frac{73}{80}$, $\frac{23}{80}$.
8. $\frac{24}{72}$, $\frac{27}{72}$, $\frac{18}{72}$, $\frac{32}{72}$.
9. $\frac{12}{84}$, $\frac{16}{84}$, $\frac{21}{84}$, $\frac{28}{84}$.
10. $\frac{56}{112}$, $\frac{63}{112}$, $\frac{64}{112}$, $\frac{34}{112}$.
11. $\frac{72}{120}$, $\frac{80}{120}$, $\frac{96}{120}$, $\frac{27}{120}$.
12. $\frac{75}{144}$, $\frac{85}{144}$, $\frac{95}{144}$, $\frac{105}{144}$.
13. $\frac{47}{160}$, $\frac{48}{160}$, $\frac{49}{160}$, $\frac{50}{160}$.
14. $\frac{77}{180}$, $\frac{87}{180}$, $\frac{97}{180}$, $\frac{107}{180}$.

Article 111.—*Case II.*

Add the following quantities:

1. $\frac{5}{16}$, $\frac{5}{6}$, $\frac{5}{12}$.
2. $\frac{16}{21}$, $\frac{17}{28}$, $\frac{19}{42}$, $\frac{15}{56}$.
3. $\frac{7}{12}$, $\frac{7}{8}$, $\frac{7}{9}$, $\frac{7}{18}$.
4. $\frac{14}{15}$, $\frac{17}{18}$, $\frac{13}{45}$, $\frac{11}{30}$
5. $\frac{6}{7}$, $\frac{5}{8}$, 4, $\frac{3}{4}$.
6. $\frac{5}{11}$, $\frac{7}{12}$, $\frac{8}{13}$.
7. $\frac{4}{27}$, $\frac{11}{18}$, $\frac{19}{72}$, $\frac{17}{36}$.
8. $\frac{2}{3}$, $\frac{3}{4}$, $\frac{4}{5}$, $\frac{5}{7}$.
9. $\frac{2}{3}$, $\frac{3}{4}$, $\frac{4}{5}$, $\frac{5}{8}$.
10. $4\frac{7}{8}$, $3\frac{2}{3}$, $8\frac{1}{2}$, $6\frac{3}{4}$.
11. $5\frac{1}{5}$, $6\frac{1}{6}$, $8\frac{1}{8}$, $10\frac{1}{10}$.
12. $12\frac{1}{2}$, $16\frac{2}{3}$, $29\frac{1}{6}$, $40\frac{1}{4}$.
13. $38\frac{7}{8}$, $38\frac{7}{12}$, $38\frac{7}{9}$, $38\frac{7}{18}$.
14. $123\frac{1}{4}$, $135\frac{1}{6}$, $147\frac{1}{8}$, $156\frac{1}{3}$.
15. $725\frac{1}{3}$, $87\frac{3}{4}$, $93\frac{7}{8}$, $591\frac{5}{6}$.
16. $\frac{4}{5}$, $\frac{3}{8}$, $\frac{5}{6}$, $\frac{5}{8}$, $\frac{1}{6}$.
17. $\frac{4}{9}$, $\frac{5}{8}$, $\frac{2}{5}$, $\frac{5}{9}$.
18. $1\frac{1}{3}$, $1\frac{1}{4}$, $1\frac{1}{6}$, $1\frac{1}{8}$, $1\frac{1}{12}$.
19. $2\frac{2}{3}$, $2\frac{3}{4}$, $2\frac{5}{6}$, $2\frac{7}{8}$, $2\frac{11}{12}$.
20. $1\frac{3}{8}$, $1\frac{5}{9}$, $2\frac{2}{3}$, $7\frac{3}{8}$.
21. $3\frac{1}{2}$, $2\frac{1}{3}$, $3\frac{1}{4}$, $4\frac{1}{3}$.
22. $\frac{3}{16}$, $\frac{3}{20}$, $\frac{5}{16}$, $\frac{5}{24}$, $\frac{7}{12}$, $\frac{7}{8}$.

23. $1\frac{2}{3}$, $1\frac{3}{4}$, $1\frac{5}{6}$, $1\frac{1}{8}$, $1\frac{5}{12}$.
24. $6\frac{1}{2}$, $6\frac{2}{3}$, $7\frac{1}{4}$, $7\frac{1}{3}$, $8\frac{3}{8}$.
25. $16\frac{1}{3}$, $17\frac{3}{4}$, $8\frac{11}{12}$, $7\frac{5}{12}$, $4\frac{7}{12}$.
26. $1\frac{1}{3}$, $1\frac{2}{5}$, $1\frac{4}{15}$, $1\frac{5}{18}$, $1\frac{7}{9}$.
27. $\frac{6}{7}$, $\frac{5}{8}$, $\frac{3}{4}$, $\frac{3}{14}$.
28. $234\frac{2}{7}$, $236\frac{3}{8}$, $238\frac{1}{4}$, $239\frac{1}{9}$.
29. $12\frac{4}{5}$, $124\frac{5}{6}$, $1\frac{3}{8}$, $17\frac{1}{4}$, $18\frac{1}{3}$.
30. $1\frac{2}{5}$, $1\frac{5}{6}$, $1\frac{7}{8}$, $11\frac{1}{3}$, $19\frac{11}{40}$.

ARTICLE 113.—*Subtraction of Fractions. Case I.*

1. From $18\frac{15}{16}$ take $5\frac{5}{16}$.
2. $47\frac{17}{20} - 23\frac{11}{20} = ?$
3. $29\frac{15}{18} - 21\frac{7}{18} = ?$
4. $24\frac{17}{20} - 15\frac{9}{20} = ?$
5. $91\frac{5}{6} - 19\frac{2}{6} = ?$
6. $42\frac{19}{20} - 31\frac{7}{20} = ?$
7. $23\frac{7}{16} - 14\frac{11}{16} = ?$
8. $193\frac{17}{18} - 34\frac{11}{18} = ?$
9. $39\frac{17}{24} - 29\frac{19}{24} = ?$
10. $100\frac{14}{25} - 80\frac{21}{25} = ?$
11. $38\frac{17}{27} - 26\frac{26}{27} = ?$
12. $237\frac{1}{80} - 37\frac{21}{80} = ?$
13. $327\frac{11}{24} - 184\frac{16}{24} = ?$
14. $168\frac{15}{36} - 93\frac{19}{36} = ?$
15. $299\frac{1}{8} - 11\frac{5}{8} = ?$
16. $73\frac{18}{35} - 47\frac{11}{35} = ?$
17. $400 - 47\frac{3}{5} = ?$
18. $736 - 367\frac{18}{49} = ?$
19. $19\frac{7}{100} - 7\frac{19}{100} = ?$
20. $365 - 37\frac{11}{100} = ?$
21. $423\frac{18}{23} - 237 = ?$
22. $146\frac{17}{32} - 92\frac{19}{32} = ?$
23. $1473\frac{7}{8} - 597\frac{3}{8} = ?$
24. $573\frac{109}{120} - 294\frac{47}{120} = ?$

ARTICLE 114.—*Case II.*

1. From $\frac{2}{3}$ take $\frac{5}{8}$.
2. From $\frac{5}{7}$ take $\frac{6}{11}$.
3. From $\frac{11}{12}$ take $\frac{9}{10}$.
4. From $\frac{7}{18}$ take $\frac{3}{16}$.
5. From $\frac{4}{5}$ take $\frac{5}{12}$.
6. From $\frac{19}{20}$ take $\frac{7}{15}$.
7. From $\frac{17}{18}$ take $\frac{7}{12}$.
8. From $\frac{8}{7}$ take $\frac{7}{8}$.
9. From $\frac{13}{16}$ take $\frac{13}{20}$.
10. From $\frac{7}{11}$ take $\frac{7}{12}$.
11. From 6 take $2\frac{7}{12}$
12. From $6\frac{5}{8}$ take $2\frac{11}{12}$.
13. From $1\frac{7}{9}$ take $\frac{17}{28}$.
14. From $15\frac{3}{16}$ take 8.
15. From $8\frac{1}{3}$ take $7\frac{1}{7}$.
16. From $13\frac{18}{19}$ take $5\frac{7}{18}$.
17. From $6\frac{7}{11}$ take $\frac{17}{20}$.
18. From 800 take $147\frac{13}{21}$.
19. From $728\frac{1}{2}$ take $149\frac{15}{28}$.
20. From $24\frac{17}{48}$ take $19\frac{19}{40}$.
21. From $48\frac{17}{24}$ take $26\frac{19}{25}$.
22. From $432\frac{7}{8}$ take $329\frac{9}{10}$.
23. From $16980\frac{5}{6}$ take $7991\frac{8}{11}$.

ARTICLE 115.—*Multiplication of Fractions.*

Multiply together:

1. $\frac{7}{8}$, $\frac{9}{10}$.
2. $\frac{5}{12}$, $\frac{8}{15}$.
3. $\frac{15}{28}$, $\frac{14}{25}$.
4. $\frac{49}{80}$, $\frac{40}{63}$.
5. $\frac{33}{50}$, $\frac{17}{55}$.
6. $\frac{15}{14}$, $\frac{21}{10}$.
7. $\frac{7}{8}$, $\frac{4}{9}$, $\frac{6}{21}$.
8. $\frac{3}{5}$, $\frac{11}{12}$, $\frac{25}{22}$.
9. $\frac{2}{3}$, $\frac{8}{9}$, $\frac{15}{56}$.
10. $\frac{6}{11}$, $\frac{26}{21}$, $\frac{33}{13}$.
11. $\frac{18}{7}$, $\frac{20}{9}$, $\frac{28}{11}$.
12. $3\frac{4}{7}$, $2\frac{2}{5}$.
13. $5\frac{1}{3}$, $5\frac{1}{4}$, $5\frac{1}{5}$.
14. $2\frac{2}{7}$, $3\frac{3}{8}$, $4\frac{4}{9}$.
15. $5\frac{1}{2}$, $5\frac{1}{3}$, $5\frac{1}{4}$.
16. $4\frac{2}{5}$, 6, $3\frac{2}{11}$.
17. $35\frac{3}{5}$, 9.
18. $\frac{5}{7}$, 150, $6\frac{3}{10}$.
19. $325\frac{5}{8}$, $10\frac{2}{3}$.
20. $13\frac{3}{4}$, $13\frac{3}{4}$.
21. $1562\frac{1}{2}$, $1562\frac{1}{2}$.
22. $3\frac{1}{4}$, $3\frac{1}{5}$, $3\frac{1}{6}$.
23. 8, $7\frac{2}{3}$, 5.
24. $4\frac{4}{7}$, $5\frac{5}{8}$, $5\frac{5}{9}$, $3\frac{1}{2}$.
25. $5\frac{1}{3}$, $6\frac{1}{4}$, $7\frac{1}{5}$, $8\frac{1}{6}$.
26. $\frac{6}{35}$, 6, $4\frac{2}{3}$, $5\frac{5}{9}$.
27. $\frac{11}{12}$, $3\frac{1}{2}$, $1\frac{1}{5}$, $2\frac{2}{5}$.
28. $8\frac{8}{9}$, $3\frac{3}{4}$, 7, $3\frac{3}{5}$.
29. $2\frac{2}{3}$, $2\frac{2}{5}$, $2\frac{2}{9}$, $2\frac{2}{11}$.
30. 7, $7\frac{1}{2}$, 8, $8\frac{1}{2}$, 9.
31. 8, $8\frac{1}{3}$, $8\frac{2}{3}$, 9.
32. $\frac{4}{15}$, $3\frac{1}{7}$, $3\frac{1}{8}$, $3\frac{1}{9}$, 6.

ARTICLE 116.—*Fractional Parts of Integers.*

1. What is $\frac{7}{11}$ of 100?
2. What is $\frac{9}{5}$ of 87?
3. What is $\frac{31}{32}$ of 80?
4. What is $\frac{14}{45}$ of 70?
5. What is $\frac{8}{91}$ of 9?
6. What is $\frac{13}{30}$ of 43?
7. What is $\frac{18}{19}$ of 18?
8. What is $\frac{14}{27}$ of 72?
9. What is $\frac{11}{120}$ of 17?
10. What is $\frac{53}{16}$ of 200?
11. What is $\frac{21}{25}$ of 120?
12. What is $\frac{16}{19}$ of 67?

ARTICLE 117.—*Compound Fractions.*

Reduce the following to Simple Fractions:

1. $\frac{3}{4}$ of $\frac{18}{19}$.
2. $\frac{5}{7}$ of $\frac{17}{20}$.
3. $\frac{4}{9}$ of $2\frac{1}{2}$.
4. $\frac{5}{8}$ of $13\frac{1}{3}$.
5. $\frac{17}{18}$ of $\frac{15}{28}$.
6. $\frac{11}{13}$ of $\frac{19}{15}$.
7. $\frac{4}{81}$ of $\frac{9}{20}$.
8. $\frac{14}{15}$ of $11\frac{1}{3}$.

9. $\frac{11}{3}$ of $\frac{14}{5}$.
10. $\frac{3}{100}$ of $\frac{4}{81}$.
11. $\frac{15}{26}$ of $11\frac{1}{7}$.
12. $\frac{3}{4}$ of $\frac{7}{8}$ of $10\frac{2}{3}$.
13. $\frac{5}{8}$ of $\frac{5}{9}$ of $13\frac{1}{5}$.
14. $\frac{3}{10}$ of $\frac{7}{5}$ of $24\frac{2}{7}$.
15. $\frac{16}{17}$ of $\frac{14}{15}$ of $\frac{3}{8}$ of $4\frac{2}{7}$.
16. $\frac{9}{16}$ of $\frac{25}{36}$ of $\frac{7}{4}$ of $3\frac{3}{5}$.
17. $\frac{5}{12}$ of $\frac{5}{6}$ of $\frac{4}{15}$ of $\frac{9}{13}$.
18. $\frac{27}{32}$ of $\frac{14}{21}$ of $\frac{20}{3}$ of $6\frac{2}{7}$.
19. $\frac{19}{30}$ of $\frac{7}{11}$ of $\frac{6}{28}$ of $\frac{33}{38}$.
20. $\frac{13}{16}$ of $\frac{8}{9}$ of $\frac{5}{3}$ of $4\frac{4}{5}$.
21. $\frac{19}{50}$ of $\frac{15}{90}$ of $\frac{7}{5}$ of $4\frac{2}{3}$.
22. $\frac{3}{4}$ of $\frac{5}{6}$ of $\frac{16}{21}$ of $5\frac{1}{4}$.
23. $\frac{3}{11}$ of $\frac{4}{7}$ of $\frac{5}{9}$ of $\frac{11}{13}$ of $18\frac{1}{5}$.
24. $\frac{11}{9}$ of $\frac{14}{6}$ of $\frac{5}{22}$ of $130\frac{1}{2}$.
25. $\frac{15}{28}$ of $\frac{15}{32}$ of $\frac{16}{25}$ of $4\frac{4}{5}$.
26. $\frac{11}{20}$ of $\frac{18}{13}$ of $\frac{17}{9}$ of $17\frac{1}{3}$.
27. $\frac{16}{33}$ of $\frac{14}{27}$ of $\frac{11}{21}$ of $\frac{9}{19}$ of 90.
28. $\frac{5}{14}$ of $\frac{18}{29}$ of $\frac{21}{25}$ of $\frac{7}{9}$ of $6\frac{1}{4}$.

ARTICLE 118.—*Miscellaneous Examples.*

Find the cost :

1. Of $3\frac{3}{4}$ lb. of sugar, at $8\frac{1}{3}$ ct. a lb.
2. Of 5 yd. muslin, at $11\frac{1}{4}$ ct. a yd.
3. Of $7\frac{3}{4}$ lb. cheese, at $8\frac{1}{3}$ ct. a lb.
4. Of $312\frac{1}{2}$ lb. of brass, at $27\frac{1}{5}$ ct. a lb.
5. Of $4\frac{2}{3}$ yd. of fence, at \$$2\frac{2}{5}$ a yd.
6. Of $17\frac{1}{2}$ lb. of coffee, at \$$\frac{3}{8}$ a lb.
7. Of $2\frac{2}{5}$ mi. of road, at \$17200 a mi.
8. Of 18 bu. of potatoes, at \$$\frac{3}{5}$ a bu.
9. Of $38\frac{3}{4}$ lb. of steel, at $12\frac{1}{2}$ ct. a lb.
10. Of $6\frac{3}{4}$ lb. of rice, at $6\frac{2}{3}$ ct. a lb.
11. Of $13\frac{1}{3}$ oz. of copper wire, at $7\frac{1}{2}$ ct. an oz.
12. Of 4728 lb. of pork, at $3\frac{3}{4}$ ct. a lb.
13. From $\frac{1}{2}$ of $17\frac{1}{3}$ take $\frac{1}{3}$ of $17\frac{1}{2}$.
14. To $\frac{3}{4}$ of $5\frac{2}{3}$ add $\frac{4}{7}$ of $5\frac{3}{4}$.
15. Multiply $\frac{4}{5}$ of $7\frac{1}{3}$ by $\frac{3}{4}$ of $7\frac{1}{5}$.
16. How far can a boat move in $6\frac{3}{5}$ hours, at the rate of $13\frac{1}{2}$ miles per hour?

17. What cost $8\frac{1}{5}$ T. of hay, at \$$16\frac{2}{3}$ a T.?

18. A man owning $47\frac{1}{2}$ A. of land, sold $\frac{3}{5}$ of it; how many acres has he remaining?

19. A man had $25\frac{5}{6}$ cords of wood, and burned $\frac{5}{8}$ of it; how much remains?

20. What cost 8000 torches at $\frac{1}{5}$ ct. each?

21. What would be the value of $\frac{2}{7}$ of a farm of $58\frac{1}{3}$ acres, at \$$7\frac{1}{2}$ an acre?

22. A man earned \$$7\frac{1}{2}$ a week, for $6\frac{5}{6}$ weeks, and saved $\frac{1}{4}$ of his wages; how much did he save?

23. An iron bar was $8\frac{1}{4}$ feet long; $\frac{1}{5}$ of it being broken off, the remainder was sold for $2\frac{1}{2}$ ct. a lb. How much was received for it, the weight being $8\frac{1}{3}$ lb. per foot?

24. A had $57\frac{1}{3}$ acres; B, $49\frac{1}{5}$ acres; each gave the other $\frac{1}{8}$ of his own land; how much more had A then than B?

ARTICLE 119.—*Division of Fractions.*

1. Divide $\frac{7}{8}$ by $\frac{3}{4}$.
2. Divide $\frac{3}{4}$ by $\frac{7}{8}$.
3. Divide $9\frac{1}{4}$ by $6\frac{1}{6}$.
4. Divide $18\frac{1}{3}$ by $2\frac{3}{4}$.
5. Divide $17\frac{7}{9}$ by $\frac{5}{6}$.
6. Divide $\frac{3}{8}$ by 20.
7. Divide $4\frac{1}{4}$ by $4\frac{1}{5}$.
8. Divide $19\frac{3}{10}$ by $3\frac{3}{5}$.
9. Divide $2\frac{1}{5}$ by $5\frac{1}{2}$.
10. Divide $13\frac{1}{13}$ by $4\frac{1}{4}$.
11. Divide $27\frac{1}{2}$ by $1\frac{4}{7}$.
12. Divide $2\frac{2}{9}$ by $8\frac{1}{3}$.
13. Divide $19\frac{1}{5}$ by $4\frac{4}{11}$.
14. Divide $18\frac{3}{7}$ by $4\frac{3}{10}$.
15. Divide 180 by $3\frac{5}{7}$.
16. Divide $\frac{2}{5}$ by 25.
17. Divide 800 by $\frac{8}{17}$.
18. Divide $15\frac{9}{11}$ by $4\frac{1}{7}$.
19. Divide $18\frac{5}{9}$ by $13\frac{1}{3}$.
20. Divide $7\frac{1}{7}$ by $1\frac{1}{4}$.
21. Divide $3\frac{1}{3}$ by $4\frac{1}{5}$.
22. Divide 675 by $1\frac{4}{5}$.
23. Divide $39\frac{1}{10}$ by $4\frac{1}{4}$.
24. Divide $396\frac{1}{3}$ by $4\frac{1}{6}$.
25. Divide $13\frac{1}{5}$ by $47\frac{2}{3}$.
26. Divide $8\frac{4}{5}$ by 400.
27. Divide $67\frac{3}{8}$ by $3\frac{1}{7}$.
28. Divide $6\frac{2}{3}$ by $11\frac{1}{9}$.
29. Divide 44589 by $39\frac{5}{9}$.
30. Divide $347\frac{1}{3}$ by $123\frac{5}{8}$.

31. What cost 1 egg, at $17\frac{1}{2}$ ct. a dozen?

32. If 7 men earn $\$243\frac{1}{2}$, what will each man's share be?

33. A farm of $287\frac{3}{4}$ acres was divided among 5 children; what would be the share of each?

34. How much silk could be bought for $\$\frac{1}{4}$, at \$3 a yard?

35. If $4\frac{1}{2}$ lb. cheese cost 80 ct., find the cost of 1 lb.

36. At $4\frac{3}{10}$ ct. a lb., how many pounds of rice can be bought for 75 ct.?

37. How much coffee, at $37\frac{1}{2}$ ct. a pound, can be bought for 10 ct.?

38. How many apples, at $\frac{1}{3}$ ct. each, can be bought for 15 cents?

39. How much saffron, at \$16 an ounce, can be bought for $\$\frac{2}{3}$?

40. If $1\frac{1}{3}$ oz. of quinine cost $\$4\frac{1}{4}$, how much is that per ounce?

41. At $\$2\frac{2}{5}$ per day, how many days must a man work to earn $\$22\frac{1}{2}$?

42. How much must a man charge per hour to receive $\$1\frac{3}{5}$ for $9\frac{1}{2}$ hours?

43. How many yards of muslin, at $6\frac{2}{9}$ ct. a yd., can be bought for 80 ct.?

44. If $2\frac{2}{5}$ lb. of butter cost $\$1\frac{1}{4}$, how many pounds can be bought for $\$4\frac{1}{2}$?

45. A man chops $14\frac{1}{2}$ C. in $4\frac{3}{5}$ da.; how long will it take him to chop $23\frac{1}{5}$ C.?

ARTICLE 120.—*To find what part one number is of another.*

1. $7\frac{1}{2}$ is what part of 20?

2. $16\frac{2}{3}$ is what part of $62\frac{1}{2}$?

3. $\frac{4}{7}$ is what part of 28?

4. $4\frac{2}{5}$ is what part of $5\frac{1}{13}$?

5. $7\frac{3}{10}$ is what part of $10\frac{3}{7}$?
6. $8\frac{3}{4}$ is what part of 105?
7. $19\frac{5}{7}$ is what part of $30\frac{2}{3}$?
8. $84\frac{6}{7}$ is what part of $90\frac{3}{4}$?
9. What part of 102 is $4\frac{1}{4}$?
10. What part of $77\frac{7}{9}$ is $3\frac{4}{7}$?
11. What part of $91\frac{2}{3}$ is $13\frac{3}{4}$?
12. What part of $19\frac{4}{5}$ is $3\frac{6}{7}$?
13. $\frac{4}{5}$ of $16\frac{2}{3}$ is what part of $\frac{5}{9}$ of $34\frac{2}{7}$?
14. $\frac{7}{8}$ of $33\frac{1}{2}$ is what part of $\frac{3}{4}$ of $50\frac{1}{4}$?
15. $\frac{19}{20}$ of $\frac{19}{20}$ is what part of $\frac{3}{10}$ of $90\frac{1}{4}$?
16. $\frac{1}{30}$ of $30\frac{1}{3}$ is what part of $\frac{1}{10}$ of $20\frac{4}{5}$?

ARTICLE 121.—*Reduction of Complex Fractions.*

Reduce the following to Simple Fractions:

1. $\dfrac{4\frac{1}{2}}{5\frac{5}{7}}$.

2. $\dfrac{9\frac{1}{3}}{9\frac{4}{5}}$.

3. $\dfrac{17\frac{3}{5}}{24\frac{3}{4}}$.

4. $\dfrac{\frac{3}{8}}{15\frac{5}{7}}$.

5. $\dfrac{4}{19\frac{3}{11}}$.

6. $\dfrac{18\frac{5}{12}}{37\frac{2}{5}}$.

7. $\dfrac{13\frac{3}{5}}{4\frac{1}{4}}$.

8. $\dfrac{\frac{7}{8}}{19\frac{1}{3}}$.

9. $\dfrac{15\frac{3}{8}}{51\frac{2}{3}}$.

10. $\dfrac{8\frac{4}{7}}{84}$.

11. $\dfrac{69\frac{3}{8}}{95\frac{1}{7}}$.

12. $\dfrac{46\frac{1}{2}}{69\frac{3}{4}}$.

13. $\dfrac{23\frac{1}{3}}{75\frac{1}{4}}$.

14. $\dfrac{48\frac{4}{9}}{109}$.

15. $\dfrac{53\frac{4}{9}}{120\frac{1}{4}}$.

ARTICLE 122.

1. By what must $7\frac{1}{5}$ be multiplied, to give the product $20\frac{1}{4}$?

2. By what must $7\frac{1}{5}$ be divided to make the quotient $2\frac{1}{4}$?

3. How many pounds of sugar can be bought for $42\frac{1}{2}$ ct., at $9\frac{1}{3}$ ct. a lb.?

4. Bought $5\frac{3}{5}$ A. of land for \$77; what was the price per A.?

5. Divide $\frac{2}{3}$ of $\frac{5\frac{2}{5}}{7\frac{1}{8}}$ by $\frac{2}{5}$ of $\frac{3\frac{1}{7}}{4\frac{2}{5}}$.

6. I had $23\frac{3}{4}$ A. of land, and sold $\frac{5}{7}$ of it for \$1045; how much was that per A.?

7. If $2\frac{1}{2}$ yd. of cloth cost $\$3\frac{1}{2}$, how much can be bought for $\$4\frac{1}{2}$?

8. If $2\frac{1}{2}$ lb. of honey cost $\$\frac{3}{4}$, how much can be bought for $\$10\frac{1}{10}$?

9. How often will $\frac{5\frac{1}{4}}{2\frac{1}{3}}$ contain $\frac{2\frac{1}{4}}{5\frac{1}{3}}$?

10. A boy had $\$\frac{4}{5}$, and spent $\frac{2}{5}$ of it for cherries; how many straps, at $\$\frac{3}{50}$ each, can he buy with the balance of his money?

11. I am offered $14\frac{1}{3}$ A. for $\$103\frac{1}{5}$; I have only \$100; how many acres should I receive for my money?

12. Divide $\frac{3\frac{3}{7}}{8\frac{4}{5}}$ by $\frac{13\frac{1}{3}}{9\frac{3}{7}}$.

13. I had $\$43\frac{2}{10}$, which I paid for gold at $\$\frac{9}{10}$ a pwt.; I had the gold made into rings weighing $1\frac{1}{5}$ pwt. each; how many rings were made?

14. By what must $\frac{3\frac{8}{9}}{5\frac{3}{5}}$ be divided to make a quotient equal to $\frac{1\frac{1}{3}}{3\frac{3}{4}}$?

15. By what must 10 be multiplied, so that the product may be $\frac{1}{10}$?

16. I had $4\frac{4}{7}$ bl. of glue, and gave $\frac{1}{3}$ of my lot to my brother for $\$25\frac{3}{5}$; how much was that per bl.?

17. If $7\frac{7}{8}$ yd. of cloth cost $\$16\frac{4}{5}$, how many yards can be purchased for $\$28\frac{4}{9}$?

Article 123.—*Fractional Compound Numbers.*

1. How many yards in 24 rd.?

2. How many sq. yd. in 1 A.?

3. How many years in 14690 days?

4. What cost $14\frac{1}{6}$ lb. of coffee at 27 ct. a lb.?

5. Reduce 84 sq. rd. to sq. ft.

6. What cost $112\frac{3}{4}$ yd. of paving, at $\$8\frac{4}{5}$ per rod.?

7. A field is $37\frac{1}{3}$ rd. long, and $25\frac{1}{2}$ rd. wide; how many sq. rd. in it?

8. What cost 1463 yd. of telegraph wire, at 20 ct. a rod?

9. How much will 43560 sq. yd. of land cost at $13.75 an acre?

10. What cost $51\frac{1}{2}$ bu. of wheat at $16\frac{1}{4}$ ct. a peck?

11. Reduce 12 yr. 300 da. to hr.

Find the cost of:

12. $17\frac{1}{2}$ yd. of silk, at $87\frac{1}{2}$ ct. a yd.

13. $37\frac{1}{2}$ bu. of potatoes, at $56\frac{2}{3}$ ct. a bu.

14. $26\frac{4}{5}$ yd. of tape, at $1\frac{1}{3}$ ct. a yd.

15. $6\frac{6}{7}$ oz. of pepper, at $4\frac{1}{4}$ ct. an oz.

16. $18\frac{1}{2}$ lb. of ham, at $10\frac{1}{4}$ ct. a lb.

17. $14\frac{1}{2}$ oz. of copper, at $2\frac{1}{4}$ ct. an oz.

18. Reduce 53000 ft. to mi.

19. Reduce 3 A. 120 sq. rd. to sq. yd.

20. Reduce 127512 in. to mi.

21. How many sq. in. in 3 A.?

22. A field $93\frac{1}{3}$ rd. long contains 7 acres; how wide is it?

23. How many steps 2 ft. 9 in. long must be taken in going 5 mi.?

24. A glacier moves $2\frac{1}{4}$ in. in a day; how long will it take it to move one mile?

ARTICLES 124 AND 125.—*Reduction to Lower Denominations.*

1. Reduce $\frac{3}{128}$ bu. to the fraction of a quart.
2. Reduce $\frac{7}{90}$ gal. to the fraction of a pint.
3. Reduce $\frac{1}{2000}$ cwt. to the fraction of an oz.
4. Reduce $\frac{1}{5000}$ A. to the fraction of a sq. yd.
5. Reduce $\frac{2}{135}$ cu. yd. to the fraction of a cu. ft.
6. Reduce $\frac{3}{1461}$ yr. to the fraction of a day.
7. Reduce $\frac{17}{400}$ lb. to the fraction of an oz (Iron).
8. Reduce $\frac{3}{1000}$ lb. to the fraction of a pwt.
9. Reduce $\frac{11}{480}$ ℥ to the fraction of a scruple.
10. Reduce $\frac{1}{104000}$ sq. mi. to the fraction of a sq. rd.
11. Reduce $\frac{3}{1000000}$ cu. yd. to the fraction of a cu. in.
12. Reduce $\frac{1}{90000}$ da. to the fraction of a sec.
13. Reduce $\frac{1}{8000}$ bu. to the fraction of a pt.
14. Reduce $\frac{11}{147000}$ wk. to the fraction of a min.
15. Reduce $\frac{12}{875}$ gal. to the fraction of a gill.
16. Reduce $\frac{19}{32}$ gal. to integers.
17. Reduce $\frac{7}{11}$ T. to integers.
18. Reduce $\frac{17}{18}$ mi. to integers.
19. Reduce $\frac{23}{24}$ A. to integers.
20. Reduce $\frac{5}{9}$ yr. to integers.
21. Reduce $\frac{7}{9}$ lb. Troy to integers.
22. Reduce $\frac{59}{60}$ gal. to integers.
23. Reduce $\frac{15}{16}$ ℥ to integers.
24. Reduce $\frac{15}{32}$ T. to integers.
25. Reduce $\frac{1}{880}$ mi. to integers.
26. Reduce $\frac{3}{100}$ of a degree to integers.
27. Reduce $\frac{1}{121}$ sq. mi. to integers.
28. Reduce $\frac{4}{5}$ chain to integers.
29. Reduce $\frac{25}{81}$ C. to integers.
30. Reduce $\frac{1}{5}$ O. to integers.
31. Reduce $\frac{37}{81}$ da. to integers.

ARTICLE 126.—*Reduction to Higher Denominations*

1. Reduce $\frac{4}{5}$ min. to the fraction of a day.
2. Reduce $\frac{1}{20}$ cu. ft. to the fraction of a cord.
3. Reduce $\frac{9}{8}$ sq. in. to the fraction of a sq. yd.
4. Reduce $\frac{32}{45}$ oz. to the fraction of a cwt.
5. Reduce $\frac{16}{19}$ pt. to the fraction of a gal.
6. Reduce $\frac{32}{5}$ pt. to the fraction of a bu.
7. Reduce $\frac{3}{10}$ gr. to the fraction of an oz.
8. Reduce $\frac{243}{16}$ cu. in. to the fraction of a cu. yd.
9. Reduce $\frac{36}{11}$ ℈ to the fraction of a pound.
10. Reduce $\frac{22}{3}$ yd. to the fraction of a mile.
11. Reduce $\frac{363}{400}$ sq. yd. to the fraction of a sq. mi.
12. Reduce $\frac{487}{5}$ hr. to the fraction of a year.
13. Reduce $\frac{25}{36}$ lb. to the fraction of a ton.
14. Reduce $\frac{11}{3}$ in. to the fraction of a chain.
15. Reduce $\frac{18}{7}$ gi. to the fraction of a gal.
16. Reduce $\frac{1}{16}$ qt. to the fraction of a bu.

ARTICLE 127.

1. What part of 1 mi. 10 rd. is 88 rd.?
2. What part of 2 bu. 1 qt. is 1 bu. 2 qt.?
3. What part of 9 C. is 16 cu. ft.?
4. What part of 39 lb. is 7 lb. 8 oz.?
5. What part of 1 wk. 5 da. is 1 da. 8 hr.
6. 3 A. 6 sq. yd. is what part of 9 A.?
7. 17 bu. 3 pk. 4 qt. is what part of 65 bu.?
8. 3 ʒ 1 ℈ is what part of 5 ℥ 2 ℈?
9. 8 yd. 1 ft. is what part of 5 rd. 1 yd.?
10. 2° 37′ 30″ is what part of 8° 45′?
11. What part is 5 gal. 1 gi. of 10 gal.?
12. What part is 3 doz. and 6, of a gross?
13. What part is 12 lb. 8 oz. of 2 T. 5 cwt.?

Article 128.

1. $\frac{5}{24}$ sq. yd. — $\frac{3}{8}$ sq. ft. = ?
2. $\frac{4}{5}$ C. + $\frac{4}{5}$ cu. yd. = ?
3. $\frac{3}{4}^{\circ} - \frac{4}{5}' = ?$
4. $\frac{3}{7}$ lb. — $\frac{4}{7}$ oz. + $\frac{4}{7}$ pwt. = ?
5. $\frac{3}{8}$ T. — $\frac{4}{5}$ cwt. = ?
6. $\frac{4}{3}$ Cong. + $\frac{2}{3}$ O. = ?
7. $\frac{3}{5}$ mi. — $\frac{5}{9}$ rd. = ?
8. $\frac{8}{9}$ chain — $\frac{1}{4}$ pace = ?
9. $\frac{3}{4}$ wk. + $\frac{4}{9}$ da. + $\frac{3}{5}$ hr. = ?
10. $\frac{4}{5}$ bu. + $\frac{3}{5}$ pk. + $\frac{2}{5}$ qt. + $\frac{2}{5}$ pt. = ?
11. $\frac{4}{9}$ gal. + $\frac{4}{9}$ qt. + $\frac{4}{9}$ pt. + $\frac{4}{9}$ gi. = ?
12. $\frac{7}{12}$ T. + $\frac{5}{12}$ cwt. + $\frac{11}{12}$ lb. = ?
13. $\frac{3}{11}$ mi. + $\frac{4}{11}$ rd. + $\frac{1}{4}$ yd. + $\frac{1}{4}$ ft. = ?
14. $\frac{2}{9}$ ℥ + $\frac{4}{9}$ ʒ + $\frac{1}{3}$ ℈ = ?
15. $\frac{13}{28}$ C. + $\frac{17}{45}$ cu. yd. + $\frac{13}{35}$ cu. ft. = ?

Article 129.—*Promiscuous Examples.*

1. From $8\frac{1}{3}$ take $7\frac{7}{10}$.
2. Reduce $\frac{5}{22}$ sq. mi. to integers.
3. Add $3\frac{1}{3}$ to the difference between $4\frac{1}{4}$ and $6\frac{1}{6}$.
4. From $7\frac{7}{9} \times 6\frac{6}{7}$ take $6\frac{6}{7} \times 5\frac{5}{6}$.
5. Reduce $\frac{4}{9}$ to a fraction whose denominator is 126.
6. Reduce $\frac{91117}{131769}$ to its lowest terms.
7. Reduce $\frac{810}{900}$ to twentieths.
8. Find a number which multiplied by $8\frac{1}{3}$ gives 60.
9. What number divided by $4\frac{5}{7}$ gives $4\frac{5}{11}$?
10. From $\frac{7}{8} \div \frac{5}{4}$ take $\frac{3}{8} \div \frac{7}{4}$.
11. Reduce $\frac{7}{11}$ to a fraction whose numerator is 77.
12. What part of \$5 is $\frac{4}{5}$ of 5 cents?
13. Reduce $\frac{1}{7750}$ T. to the fraction of a pound.
14. \$$4\frac{1}{2}$ will buy $1\frac{2}{5}$ yd. of cloth; how much will $1\frac{2}{3}$ yd. cost?
15. Bought 3750 lb. of iron, at \$3.50 per cwt.; what is the amount of the bill?

16. A boy works 3 days at the rate of $\$5\frac{3}{4}$ a week; how much does he earn?

17. I have 55 A. of land, worth $\$17\frac{1}{2}$ an acre; B wishes to trade me 7 hogs, worth $\$7\frac{1}{3}$ each; what part of my land should be given for them?

18. Bought $32\frac{1}{2}$ T. of iron for $1218.75; at that rate, what quantity can I buy for $1000?

19. A man lost $\$13\frac{3}{4}$, and borrowed $\$57\frac{3}{5}$; he then had $\$106\frac{1}{2}$; what sum had he at first?

20. What number is as much greater than $15\frac{1}{2}$ as $15\frac{1}{2}$ is greater than $7\frac{5}{11}$?

21. A farmer raised 208 bu. 1 pk. of wheat, and sold 119 bu.; what part of his crop has he remaining?

22. A lady bought $35\frac{1}{4}$ yd. carpet for $47; had she bought 6 yd. more, what would the bill have been?

23. A farm is worth $5500, and A owns $\frac{5}{12}$ of it; what part of his share should A sell for $825?

24. How much would a family consume in August, at the rate of 8 lb. 5 oz. daily?

25. $\frac{5}{7}$ of a certain number is $389\frac{1}{7}$; what is the number?

26. Multiply $4\frac{2}{5} \times 8\frac{1}{3}$ by $2\frac{2}{11} \times 3\frac{3}{8}$.

27. A farmer sold $\frac{4}{11}$ of his flock of geese, and has 14 dozen remaining; how many geese had he at first?

28. Reduce $\frac{7\frac{1}{3}}{8\frac{4}{5}}$, $\frac{11\frac{1}{3}}{12\frac{3}{4}}$, $\frac{7\frac{1}{2}}{12\frac{6}{7}}$, and $\frac{7\frac{1}{4}}{11\frac{3}{5}}$ to a common denominator.

29. Hats cost $\$3\frac{1}{3}$ apiece, but late in the season are sold at $\frac{4}{5}$ of the cost; how many can I then buy for $48?

30. Sold a house for $2373, which was $\frac{7}{9}$ of the cost; how much did I lose?

31. A lawyer collected $18.80, and kept $\frac{3}{8}$ of it; how much did he pay over?

32. What number is that, to which, if you add $\frac{3}{8}$ of itself, the sum will be $82\frac{1}{2}$?

33. Find the value of a lot 88 ft. long and $49\frac{1}{2}$ ft. wide, at $700 per acre.

34. $\frac{5}{6}$ of a farm are worth $$3157\frac{1}{2}$; what are $\frac{8}{9}$ of it worth?

35. $53\frac{1}{3}$ yards of cloth cost me $88; what will I lose by selling $8\frac{1}{2}$ yd. for $10?

36. Three men found a sum of money, of which the first took $\frac{1}{5}$, and the second $\frac{5}{8}$, leaving the third man $69.44; what was the sum found?

37. A expended $347 for land, at $$\frac{2}{5}$ an acre; and B, $4243 for land, at $$5\frac{1}{2}$ an acre; how many acres have both together?

38. What was the cost of 47 head of cattle, if $47 was lost by selling 13 head for $$26\frac{1}{2}$ apiece?

39. From a lot 100 rd. long and $72\frac{1}{2}$ rd. wide, was sold a lot 45 rd. long and 29 rd. wide; what part of the whole lot was sold?

40. A owns 405 A. 39 sq. rd., and B owns 391 A. 109 sq. rd.; how much land must A sell B, so that their farms may be of equal size?

ARTICLE 130.—*Practice.*

Find the cost of:

1. 450 lb. butter, at 25 ct. a pound.
2. 784 yd. muslin, at $6\frac{1}{4}$ ct. a yard.
3. 462 gal. vinegar, at $16\frac{2}{3}$ ct. a gallon.
4. 673 yd. delaine, at $62\frac{1}{2}$ ct. a yard.
5. 96 gal. milk, at $$1.87\frac{1}{2}$ ct. a gallon.
6. 5726 lb. whiting, at $1\frac{1}{2}$ ct. a pound.
7. 538 bu. wheat, at $$1.12\frac{1}{2}$ a bushel.
8. 788 yd. cloth, at $$1.62\frac{1}{2}$ a yard.
9. 375 lb. cheese, at $8\frac{1}{3}$ ct. a pound.
10. 424 A. land, at $$3.18\frac{3}{4}$ an acre.

11. 398 bu. barley, at 75 ct. a bushel.

12. 666 lb. feathers, at $33\frac{1}{3}$ ct. a pound.

13. 78 C. wood, at $4.75 a cord.

14. 3786 lb. twine, at $16\frac{2}{3}$ ct. a pound.

15. 5 gal. 3 qt. of vinegar, at $2.50 a gallon.

16. 17 yd. 2 ft. of paving, at $2.40 a yard.

17. 69 bu. 3 pk. of potatoes, at 68 ct. a bushel.

18. 4 lb. 11 oz. of honey, at 36 ct. a pound.

19. 3 hr. 45 min. work, at 40 ct. an hour.

20. 7 oz. 7 pwt. of silver, at 88 ct. an ounce.

21. 3 bu. 3 pk. of clover seed, at $3.60 a bushel.

22. 49 sq. yd. 6 sq. ft. of plastering, at 27 ct. a square yard.

23. 3 ℥ 2 ʒ 1 ℈ of quinine, at $3.60 an ounce.

24. 4 bu. 2 pk. 5 qt. of berries, at $3.20 a bushel.

25. 15 gal. 3 qt. 1 pt. 1 gi. of milk, at $1.92 a gallon.

26. 5 C. 96 cu. ft. of wood, at $4.40 a cord.

27. How many bushels of oats, at $37\frac{1}{2}$ ct. a bu., can be bought for $\$7.87\frac{1}{2}$?

28. How much cloth, at $\$2.12\frac{1}{2}$ a yard, can be bought for $\$90.31\frac{1}{4}$?

29. What cost 18 lb. 12 oz. of coffee, at $33\frac{1}{3}$ ct. a lb.?

30. Find the cost of 500 screws, at 36 ct. a gross.

31. Find the cost of 18 bu. 2 pk. of apples, at $\$.66\frac{2}{3}$ a bushel.

32. What cost 40 rubbers, at 40 cents a dozen?

33. At $\$3.37\frac{1}{2}$ an acre, how many acres of ground can be bought for $281.25?

34. What cost 5 bu. 2 pk. of strawberries, at $33\frac{1}{3}$ ct. a quart?

35. A week's work is 6 da., of 10 hr. each; how much can a man earn in 4 da. 6 hr., if his weekly wages are $10.50?

36. Find the cost of 11 T. 940 lb. of hay, at $12 a ton.

DECIMAL FRACTIONS.

ARTICLE 135.—*Writing Decimals.*

Write the following Decimal Numbers:

1. 803 *thousandths.*
2. Fifty-one *thousandths.*
3. Nine *thousandths.*
4. Forty-six *ten-thousandths.*
5. Two hundred and one *ten-thousandths.*
6. 7735 *hundred-thousandths.*
7. 86 *hundred-thousandths.*
8. 3 *hundred-thousandths.*
9. Nine hundred and nineteen *thousandths.*
10. Nine thousand and twenty *ten-thousandths.*
11. Ten thousand and one *hundred-thousandths.*
12. Five thousand and sixty-seven *ten-thousandths.*
13. 381257 *millionths.*
14. 40703 *millionths.*
15. 2008 *millionths.*
16. 88 *millionths.*
17. 7 *millionths.*
18. Forty seven thousand and eighteen *millionths.*
19. Five hundred and fifty-five *millionths.*
20. Three hundred thousand and eight *millionths.*
21. Sixty-seven *millionths.*
22. Fifty-seven *tenths.*
23. 2406391 *ten-millionths.*
24. 65400 *ten-millionths.*
25. 49 *ten-millionths.*
26. 880004 *ten-millionths.*
27. 6 *ten-millionths.*
28. 31000722 *ten-millionths.*
29. Four hundred and eighty *hundredths.*

30. 14 *units* and 5 *hundredths.*
31. 3 *units* and 17 *thousandths.*
32. 3000 *units* and 4 *thousandths.*
33. 3004 *thousandths.*
34. 8354 *hundredths.*
35. One *unit* and one *millionth.*
36. One million *units* and one *millionth.*
37. Three hundred *millionths.*
38. Seven hundred *units* and seven *hundredths.*
39. 19 *billionths.*
40. 39704 *ten-billionths.*
41. 800004 *hundred-millionths.*
42. Eight thousand and five *tenths.*
43. Eight thousand *units* and five *ten-thousandths.*
44. 379000 *units* and 379 *thousandths.*
45. Fifty thousand and one *hundred billionths.*
46. $\frac{3}{10}$, $\frac{7}{100}$, $\frac{19}{1000}$, $\frac{483}{100}$, $\frac{39}{10000}$.
47. $\frac{88}{100}$, $\frac{903}{10000}$, $\frac{7}{1000}$, $\frac{21}{100000}$, $\frac{89}{10}$.
48. $5\frac{87}{100}$, $16\frac{8}{1000}$, $200\frac{17}{100}$, $30\frac{30}{100000}$.

ARTICLE 136.—*Reading Decimals.*

Read the following Decimal Numbers:

1. 4.18; 6.008; .0006; 36.036; 3.4075.
2. .702; .078; .02005; 50.09; .0006.
3. .00066; .30066; .00456; .000036.
4. .01; .016; .0162; .01624.
5. 4736.2; 3.8914; .356; 283.67.
6. 2000.20002; 304.0506; 7.24006.
7. .3703; 3.703; 37.03; 370.3.
8. 4.4; 4.04; 4.004; 4.0004.
9. .056; 30.07; .00009; .010203.
10. 45.0009; .005009; 60.016.
11. 37.03; 4638.9; 364.005.

12. .0102 ; .001002 ; .00010002.

13. 5.806 ; 50.4903 ; 6.8938.

14. 3700.0004 ; .3704 ; 3000.0704.

Change the following to Common Fractions:

15. .64 ; .165 ; .0375 ; .9375.

16. .024 ; .00008 ; .0000088.

17. .875; .4375; .15625.

18. .1024; .83875; .873642.

ARTICLE 141.—*Reduction of Decimals. Case III.*

Reduce the following to Common Fractions or Mixed Numbers:

1. .875.
2. .64.
3 .512.
4. .625.
5. .025.
6. .256.
7. .0025.
8. .2224.
9. .975.
10. .0084.
11. .1875.
12. .46875.
13. 4.045.
14. 26.18.
15. .0125.
16. 19.625.
17. 300.25.
18. 46.875.
19. 13.92.
20. 20.02.
21. .6875.
22. 14.01875.
23. 9.008.
24. .34375.

ARTICLE 142.—*Reduction of Decimals. Case IV.*

Reduce the following to Decimals:

1. $\frac{3}{8}$.
2. $\frac{9}{20}$.
3. $\frac{5}{16}$.
4. $\frac{11}{25}$.
5. $\frac{13}{50}$.
6. $\frac{15}{80}$.
7. $\frac{13}{32}$.
8. $\frac{17}{32}$.
9. $\frac{21}{16}$.
10. $\frac{3}{160}$.
11. $\frac{1}{800}$.
12. $\frac{17}{250}$.
13. $\frac{9}{500}$.
14. $\frac{137}{160}$.
15. $\frac{11}{640}$.
16. $\frac{61}{64}$.
17. $\frac{89}{50}$.
18. $\frac{50}{89}$.
19. $\frac{17}{71}$.
20. $\frac{28}{70}$.
21. $\frac{36}{48}$.
22. $\frac{49}{52}$.
23. $\frac{27}{200}$.
24. $\frac{13}{811}$.

ARTICLE 143.—*Addition of Decimals.*

1. Add 3.12; 41.3; 68.94; 39.77.

2. 18 and 54 hundredths + 19 and 5 tenths + 53 and 73 hundredths + 37 and 56 hundredths + 16 and 9 tenths = ?

3. 5 and 17 thousandths + 73 and 29 hundredths + 128 and 3 tenths + 94 and 983 thousandths + 26 and 71 hundredths + 271 and 7 tenths = ?

4. Add 413 thousandths; 413 ten-thousandths; 413 hundred-thousandths, and 413 millionths.

5. 25.7 + 6.009 + .4309 + 509.7 + 38.08 + 8.983 + 73.38 = ?

6. Add 46 and 89 thousandths; 60 and 894 thousandths; 8 and 946 thousandths; 9 and 468 thousandths; 89 and 46 thousandths; 460 and 89 thousandths, and 20.

7. Add 400.009; 40.09; 4.0009; 40.9; 400.09; 4.009; 100; and .002.

8. 738.84 + 388.47 + 884.73 + 847.38 + 473.88 + 59.99 + 59.099 + 99.59 = ?

9. Add 17.38; 18.37; 19.36; 20.35; 21.34; 22.33; 23.32; 24.31 and 25.3.

10. Write 395.4276 seven times and add.

11. Write 234.056 eight times and add.

12. Add 893 thousandths; 753 hundredths; 49 tenths; 3739 thousandths; 5 hundredths; 55 hundredths; 5500, and 127 thousandths.

13. 46.8 + 48.6 + 68.4 + 64.8 + 84.6 + 86.4 + 44.4 + 66.6 + 88.8 = ?

14. Add 74 and 8 ten-thousandths; 36 and 5-thousandths; 637 and 4 ten-millionths; 29 and 8 tenths; 3 and 8914 hundred-thousandths; 55 and 93 hundredths; 84 millionths, and 637 and 27306 ten-millionths.

ARTICLE 144.—*Subtraction of Decimals.*

1. From 47.378 take 19.89.
2. From 60.06 take 50.89.
3. From 48.937 take 13.0609.
4. From 300 take 46.875.
5. From 345.6789 take 88.88.
6. Take 8.76 from 234.372.
7. Take 23.9564 from 32.404.
8. Take 22.222 from 111.11.
9. Take 6.0008 from 22.93004.

Find the difference between the following:

10. 39.81 and 20.985.
11. 100.001 and 50.09.
12. 324.137 and 199.9994.
13. 64 thousandths and 64 hundredths.
14. From 147 and 39602 hundred-thousandths take 58 and 545986 millionths.
15. Take 73421 and 397 ten-thousandths from 124316 and 397 thousandths.

ARTICLE 147.—*Multiplication of Decimals.*

Multiply:

1. .643 by .89.
2. 3.56 by 62.5.
3. 7.875 by 94.
4. .125 by .126.
5. 48.76 by 48.75.
6. .03 by .02.
7. .744 by .125.
8. .0375 by .036.
9. $9.9 \times .098$.
10. $666. \times 5.55$.
11. $.048 \times .04375$.
12. $.9375 \times 2400$.
13. $7.39 \times .0043$.
14. $.2502 \times .0848$.
15. 42.075×100.
16. 3.956×42.75.

17. Multiply 48 units and 75 hundredths by 6 units and 32 thousandths.

18. Multiply 893 thousandths by 893 ten-thousandths

19. Multiply 38400 by 19 units and 28 thousandths.

20. Multiply 27 thousand by 27 thousandths.

21. Multiply 78 and 125 thousandths by 1024.

22. Multiply 67 thousand 2 hundred by 67 and 2 hundredths.

23. Multiply 7936 ten-thousandths by 390 and 625 thousandths.

24. Multiply 6.625 by 14.32.

ARTICLE 150.—*Division of Decimals.*

Divide:

1. 5.845 by 3.5.
2. 9.4125 by 1.25.
3. .7614 by .36.
4. 2.875 by 1.15.
5. 4.752 by 198.
6. .897 by .06.
7. .897 by 260.
8. .7375 by .059.
9. 1287.7651 by 3.217.
10. 160 by .04.
11. 6.5667 by 31.27.
12. 17429.1 by .4251.
13. 3.1 by 3.2.
14. .004 by 160.
15. 8.91 by 1.98.
16. 1 by 16.

17. Divide 37 units and 37 thousandths by 4 units and 4 thousandths.

18. Divide 12 units and 12 hundredths by 16 units and 16 hundredths.

19. Divide 1 hundred by 1 hundredth.

20. Divide 208 millionths by 65 hundred-thousandths.

21. Divide 8.76 by 132.

22. Divide .9 by 2.99.

23. Divide .001 by 150.

24. Divide 27.5 by .28.

Decimal Compound Numbers.

Article 151.—*Reduction to Lower Denomination.*

1. Reduce .0125 bu. to the decimal of a pint.
2. Reduce .0273 gal. to the decimal of a pint.
3. Reduce .00043 T. to the decimal of a pound.
4. Reduce .0275 yd. to the decimal of an inch.
5. Reduce .0000075 sq. mi. to the decimal of a sq. rd.
6. Reduce .0000025 cu. yd. to the decimal of a cu. in.
7. Reduce .00001125 da. to the decimal of a second.
8. Reduce .00375 C. to the decimal of a cu. ft.
9. Reduce .000575 sq. yd. to the decimal of a sq. in.

Article 152.—*Reduction of Decimals to Integers.*

Find the value of the following, in Integers:

1. .4375 bu.
2. .4375 gal.
3. .15625 T.
4. .15625 mi.
5. .390625 sq. mi.
6. .7 C.
7. .38 yr.
8. .047 of a circle.

Article 153.—*Reduction to Higher Denominations.*

1. Reduce .352 pt. to the decimal of a bushel.
2. Reduce .48 gi. to the decimal of a gallon.
3. Reduce .648 sq. in. to the decimal of a sq. yd.
4. Reduce .5832 cu. in. to the decimal of a cu. yd.
5. Reduce .472 qt. to the decimal of a bushel.
6. Reduce .486 min. to the decimal of a day.
7. Reduce .4096 oz. to the decimal of a cwt.
8. Reduce .39 pt. to the decimal of a gallon.
9. Reduce .1296 sec. to the decimal of a day.
10. Reduce .015 pt. to the decimal of a bushel.

11. Reduce .13824 cu. in. to the decimal of a cord.
12. Reduce .17532 hr. to the decimal of a year.
13. Reduce .792 in. to the decimal of a mile.
14. Reduce 7.68 oz. to the decimal of a ton.
15. Reduce .17424 sq. in. to the decimal of an acre.

Article 154.—*Promiscuous Examples.*

1. Find the value of .05 da. in integers.

2. If 3.7 yards cost $10.36, what will 5.8 yards cost?

3. If 3.5 acres of land cost $430.43, how many acres could be bought for $614.90?

4. Find the cost of 4 bu. 3 pk. of oats, at 46 cents a bushel.

5. A man sold 55 gal. 1 pt. of milk, at $1.80 a gallon, and was paid in tea at 84 ct. a pound; how many pounds did he receive?

6. A field 40 rods wide contains 10 A. 80 sq. rd.; how long is it?

7. How much wood, at $2.90 a cord, can be bought for $105.125?

8. .4 mi. + .3 rd. + .7 yd. = ?

9. Find the value of .7475 T. in integers.

10. How much vinegar, at 24 ct. a gallon, can be bought for $7.77?

11. What cost 1000 cu. yd. of embankment, at the rate of $0.37 per cu. ft.?

12. Find the value of .234375 bu. in integers.

13. What cost 7227 feet of wire fence, at 14 ct. a rod?

14. A locomotive runs 17 mi. 32 rd. in an hour; how far will it run in 13 hr. 39 min.?

15. .1 yr. + .2 wk. + .3 da. + .4 hr. = ?

16. Reduce $\frac{4}{9}$ of $\frac{13\frac{1}{2}}{16}$ to a decimal.

17. 1.4 bu. — 3.7 pk. = ?

18. How much land, at $500 an acre, can be bought for $131.25?

19. .03 T. + .73 cwt. + .75 lb. = ?

20. Find the cost of 7 lb. 7 oz. of silverware, at $1.20 an ounce.

21. How much cloth, at $1.44 a yd., must be given for 6 bu. 6 qt. of strawberries, worth $4.80 a bushel?

22. At $12\frac{1}{2}$ ct. a pound, how much cheese can be bought for $$19.81\frac{1}{4}$?

23. What cost 4350 lb. iron, at $2.80 a hundred pounds?

24. What cost 8764 pickles, at 75 ct. a hundred?

25. What cost 108 screws, at $1.08 per gross?

26. Find the value of .77 yr. in integers.

27. A locomotive runs 16 mi. 256 rd. per hour; how long will it be in running 154 mi. 280 rd.?

28. A man can earn $18\frac{3}{4}$ ct. per hour, and a boy $12\frac{1}{2}$ ct.; how much will the man earn while the boy earns $4?

29. Grading a road cost $10312.50, at 62 ct. 5 m. per foot; how long is the road?

30. Find the value of a lot 70 rods square, at $20 an acre.

THE METRIC SYSTEM.

ARTICLE 156.—*Measures of Length.*

Reduce:

1. 394.5 Hm. to dm.

2. 93.64 m. to kilometers.

3. 1234.56 Dm. to Mm.

4. 987.65 Km. to Dm.

5. .34 m. to myriameters.

6. 74.6 Dm. to cm.

7. 83.7 Hm. to Mm.

8. .37 Mm. to meters.

9. 4600 Km. to dm.

10. 58000 cm. to Hm.

11. 374.5 Mm. to cm.

12. 67.25 Dm. to Km.

13. 8936.4 cm. to Dm.

14. .456 Km. to Hm.

ARTICLE 157.—*Metric Square Measure.*

Reduce:

1. 374680 m^2 to hektars.
2. 493.2 A. to centars.
3. 387.43 ca. to ars.
4. 387.43 m^2 to ars.
5. 43.875 A. to m^2.
6. .457 ca. to hektars.
7. 8973.4 m^2 to hektars.
8. 5839 A. to m^2.
9. 3843 ca. to hektars.
10. 3970 A. to centars.

ARTICLE 158.—*Measures of Capacity.*

Reduce:

1. 4800 cl. to liters.
2. 39.5 Dl. to centiliters.
3. 493.7 dl. to Hl.
4. 58.39 Hl. to centiliters.
5. .457 Dl. to liters.
6. 6.789 l. to centiliters.
7. 34.692 Hl. to Dl.
8. 42.789 dl. to liters.
9. 325.84 l. to hektoliters.
10. 4.7 dl. to dekaliters.
11. 3800 Hl. to deciliters.
12. 29.7 l. to dekaliters.
13. 468.3 cl. to hektoliters.
14. 38700 Dl. to deciliters.
15. 49 m^3 to liters.
16. 37282 cl. to m^3.
17. 678 l. to cubic meters.
18. .0303 m^3 to deciliters.

ARTICLE 159.—*Metric Weights.*

Reduce:

1. 6.5 Mg. to M. T.
2. 489.31 Dg. to mg.
3. .04653 Q. to Dg.
4. 654.3 Hg. to quintals.
5. 87 M. T. to kilograms.
6. .937 mg. to grams.
7. 123.456 Hg. to dg.
8. 873.4 dg. to Dg.
9. 88.736 Mg. to cg.
10. .0086 g. to quintals.
11. .0765 Kg. to M. T.
12. 3945 cg. to Hg.
13. 3.894 M. T. to grams.
14. 87300 Kg. to mg.
15. 89900 Dg. to Mg.
16. .00489 Q. to dg.
17. 4000 G. to Mg.
18. 12000000 mg. to Kg.
19. 9876541 dg. to quintals.
20. 34.56 Kg. to grams.
21. 48004800 cg. to Hg.
22. .09083 M. T. to mg.

ARTICLE 160.

Find the value of:

1. 40 meters.
2. 50 hektars.
3. 375 kilograms.
4. .6375 kilometers.
5. 13 tonneaux.
6. 93.75 sters.
7. 875 grams.
8. 500 cubic meters.
9. 625 square meters.
10. 37.5 ars.

Reduce:

11. 45 hektoliters to bu.
12. 100 inches to meters.
13. 100 mi. to kilometers.
14. 100 sq. yd. to m^2.
15. 100 acres to hektars.
16. 100 cu. yd. to m^3.
17. 48 sq. rd. to ars.
18. 18 T. to metric tons.
19. 454 bu. to hektoliters.
20. 66 gal. to liters.
21. 1 lb. 4oz. 1 pwt. 12 gr. to grams.
22. 3000 sq. ft. to m^2.
23. 56 bu. 3 pk. to Hl.
24. 2 ℔ 8 ℥ 1 ʒ 12 gr. to the metric system.

ARTICLE 161.—*Miscellaneous Examples.*

1. What cost 475 kilos of iron, at 4 ct. a pound?

2. What cost 6 hektometers of fence, at 15 ct. a foot?

3. What cost 40 sters of wood, at $6.25 per cord?

4. What cost 327 cubic meters of stone-work, at $5.30 per cubic yard?

5. Find the weight of a stone 4 m. long, 4 dm. wide, and 8 cm. thick, if a cubic meter weighs 3 cwt.

6. What cost a field 300 meters square, at $30 per ar?

7. What cost a pile of wood 8 m. long, 3 m. wide, and 1.5 m. high, at $1.30 per ster?

8. What must be paid for 17 quintals of wheat, at 5 ct. per kilo?

9. A field is 52 yd. wide and 92 yd. long; what is it worth, at $.35 per square meter?

10. A pile of stone is 109 ft. long, 36 ft. wide, and 9 ft. high; what is it worth at $3.80 per cubic meter?

11. Find the cost of 64.3 lb. of gold ore, at 45 ct. per gram.

12. Find the cost of a gold chain weighing 1929 grains, at 60 ct. a gram.

13. What would be the cost of 2 T. 15 cwt. 11 lb. 8 oz. of coal, at $5.60 per metric ton?

14. How long will it take a man to walk 31.0685 mi. if he can walk 6 kilometers in an hour?

PERCENTAGE.

ARTICLE 164.—*Case I.*

Find the following:

1. 28 % of 925.
2. 25 % of 624.
3. 23 % of 900.
4. $13\frac{1}{3}$ % of 744.
5. $16\frac{2}{3}$ % of 390.
6. $37\frac{1}{2}$ % of 8.8.
7. $2\frac{1}{2}$ % of 290.
8. $\frac{3}{10}$ % of 70.
9. $14\frac{2}{7}$ % of 1393.
10. 56 % of 750.
11. 5.6 % of 750.
12. $\frac{1}{9}$ % of 467.
13. 800 % of 800.
14. 900 % of $\frac{1}{900}$.

What is:

15. 22% of 1800 bu. corn?
16. 85% of 7 da.?
17. $\frac{1}{10}$% of $480?
18. 500% of 71 A.?
19. 53% of 3 T.?
20. 20% of 19 gal. 1 qt. 1 pt.?
21. 100% of 3 bu. 2 pk.?
22. $66\frac{2}{3}$% of 87 gal.?
23. $\frac{1}{2}$% of $\frac{1}{2}$?
24. $2\frac{2}{3}$% of $2\frac{1}{2}$?
25. $16\frac{2}{3}$% of $16\frac{2}{3}$?
26. 77% of 187.05?

ARTICLE 165.—*Case II.*

1. What per cent of 275 is 33?
2. What per cent of 48 is 36?
3. What per cent of 60 is 10.2?
4. What per cent of 800 is 600?
5. What per cent of 666 is 499.5?
6. What per cent of 350 is 56?
7. What per cent of 75 bu. is 33 bu.?
8. What per cent of 48 is 96?
9. What per cent of 56 is 560?
10. $172\frac{1}{2}$ is what per cent of 230?
11. 187.5 is what per cent of 150?
12. .5 is what per cent of 250?
13. 4 is what per cent of $17\frac{7}{9}$?
14. 2.3 is what per cent of $18\frac{2}{5}$?
15. .014 is what per cent of 70?
16. $29\frac{1}{5}$ is what per cent of 80?
17. 1 bu. 2 pk. is what per cent of 3 bu. 3 pk.?
18. 6 gal. 3 qt. is what per cent of 4 gal. 2 qt.?
19. What per cent of $\frac{7}{20}$ is $\frac{21}{40}$?
20. What per cent of 1 wk. is 4 da. 4 hr. 48 min.?

ARTICLE 166.—*Case III.*

1. 4.2 is 6% of what number?
2. 153 is 68% of what number?
3. 315 is $\frac{1}{2}$% of what number?
4. 6 is $3\frac{3}{7}$% of what number?
5. $14\frac{2}{5}$ is $4\frac{1}{2}$% of what number?
6. $7\frac{5}{7}$ is 150% of what number?
7. $43\frac{1}{3}$ is $11\frac{1}{9}$% of what number?
8. 35 is $46\frac{2}{3}$% of what number?

9. $1\frac{1}{3}$ is $\frac{1}{20}\%$ of what number?
10. 175 is 1000% of what number?
11. $45\frac{3}{8}$ is $18\frac{3}{4}\%$ of what number?
12. 3 bu. 3 pk. is 24% of what quantity?
13. 5 da. 5 hr. is 150% of what quantity?
14. 18 gal. is 96% of what quantity?
15. 18 T. 9 cwt. is $22\frac{1}{2}\%$ of what quantity?
16. 9 A. 40 sq. rd. is 40% of what quantity?

ARTICLE 167.—*Case IV.*

1. What number, increased by 30% of itself, equals 1690?

2. What number, diminished by 80% of itself, would give 80?

3. 777 is 40% greater than what number?
4. 777 is 40% less than what number?
5. 60 is 60% less than what number?
6. 60 is 60% more than what number?
7. What fraction, less $23\frac{1}{3}\%$ of itself, would equal $\frac{23}{40}$?
8. What number + 26% of itself, would equal $25\frac{1}{5}$?
9. What number, increased by 135% of itself, would give $15\frac{2}{3}$?

10. What number, diminished by $99\frac{1}{6}\%$ of itself, would leave 350?

11. What number, increased by $\frac{4}{5}\%$ of itself, would give 56?

12. Find a number which, added to $18\frac{3}{4}\%$ of itself, will give 36.1.

ARTICLE 169.—*Miscellaneous Examples.*

1. Sold a house for $1805, which was 5% less than the cost; find the cost.

2. In a grade of 560 pupils, 532 passed at examination; what % of the grade passed?

3. A farmer's wife had 20 dozen chickens, and $6\frac{2}{3}\%$ of them died; how many died?

4. A man had 140 hogs, which he sold at $8 apiece, and spent 32% of the money for sheep, at $2.80; how many sheep did he buy?

5. Sold a house for $1840, which was 15% more than the cost; what was the cost?

6. In a school of 950 pupils, 52% were girls; how many boys were there?

7. After 22% of a pole had been broken off by the wind, it was 117 feet high; how high was it at first?

8. A's farm is 30% of B's; if B has 160 A., how many acres has A?

9. A's farm is 30% of B's; if A has 180 A., how many acres has B?

10. A's farm is 30% of B's; if both together have 208 acres, how many has B?

11. A's farm is 30% of B's; if B has 280 acres more than A, how many has B?

12. An engine traversed 15% of a road in 18 hours, at the rate of 14 mi. 128 rd. per hour; what was the length of the entire road?

13. William is 4 ft. 7 in. high; his brother is 20% taller; what is the height of the latter?

14. A trade dollar weighs 420 grains, of which 10% is alloy; how much pure silver in 640 trade dollars?

15. The eagle contains 258 grains, of which 10% is alloy; how much alloy must be mixed with 12.9 oz. of pure gold for the coinage of eagles?

16. What will be the weight of the alloy in $1000 of gold coin?

17. What weight of pure gold must be mixed with 140 oz. Troy of alloy for coinage of gold coin?

18. 26% of a farmer's potatoes spoiled, and he still had 407 bushels of sound ones; how many bushels had he at first?

19. A ship's crew had provision for 18 weeks, but a storm destroyed 25% of it; how long would the remainder last them?

20. What number, less 40% of itself, would be equal to 40% of 930?

21. A man owed $60500; but, being unable to pay in full, settled for $44770; what % of his debt did he pay?

22. A publishing house sold 15% more books this year than last year; if the number this year is 52900 dozen, what was the number last year?

23. What number, increased by 120% of itself, would equal 803?

24. A tenant pays his landlord 3 pk. out of every 5 bu. he raises; what % is that?

25. 34000000 letters were posted, of which 170,000 were sent to the dead letter office; what % was that?

26. A field is 168 rods long, and its length is 40% greater than its breadth; find the area of the field.

27. A field is 168 rods long, and its breadth is 40% less than its length; find the area of the field.

28. A field is 168 rods wide, and its breadth is 40% less than its length; find the area of the field.

29. A farmer raised 450 bu. of oats the first year; the second year his crop was 20% greater than the first; and the third year, 25% less than the second; how many bushels did he raise in the three years?

30. I have 47 A. 40 sq. rd. of beech woods, which is 27% of my woodland; how many acres of timber have I in all?

31. Ore lost 32% in smelting, and 433 T. 10 cwt. of blooms were produced; how much ore was smelted?

Article 172.—*Commission.*

1. An agent sold a house for \$3940, at $2\frac{1}{2}\%$ commission; what sum did he receive?

2. An agent sold a farm for \$2750, at $1\frac{1}{5}\%$ commission; what sum did he send the owner?

3. The commission on \$7500 sales amounted to \$125; what was the % commission?

4. An agent sold a stock of groceries for \$77500, and sent the owner \$75640; what was his % commission?

5. A commission merchant sold goods at $2\frac{1}{2}\%$ commission, and sent the owner \$2281.50; what commission did he retain?

6. An attorney collected a claim at $12\frac{1}{2}\%$ commission, and sent his principal \$934.50; what was the amount of the claim?

7. I sold goods at auction, charging the owner 5%, and sent him \$199.69; what was the amount of the sale?

8. Received \$1300.50 to invest in starch, retaining my commission of 2%; what sum should I invest?

9. An agent received 5% commission for collecting 3 years' rent, and sent the owner \$684; what rent was collected monthly?

10. A farmer allowed a drover 3% commission for selling his hogs, by which the drover realized \$1455; what sum was sent the farmer?

11. A farmer allowed a drover 3% commission for selling his hogs, by which the farmer realized \$1455; what sum did the drover retain?

12. Thompson sold for a refinery 45000 gal. molasses, at 62 ct. a gallon, and 127000 lb. sugar, at $12\frac{1}{2}$ ct. a lb.; what was his commission, at $\frac{1}{2}\%$?

13. A lawyer collected a debt of \$750; he paid \$14.60 expenses, and sent the creditor \$724.15; what % commission did he charge?

14. Sent A \$1025.10, which he invested in sugar, first deducting his commission, at 2%; sent B an equal sum, which he invested in flour, retaining $\frac{1}{2}$% commission; what was the difference in the two purchases?

15. A commission merchant, whose expenses were \$7125, cleared \$2127.25 profit in a year by selling goods at 2% commission; what was the amount of his sales?

Article 173.—*Trade Discount.*

1. Sold 47500 lb. of iron at \$2.75 per cwt., 4% off for cash; what sum was received for it?

2. 500 cases of slates were sold; list price, \$36 per case, with 60 and 60% off; what was realized?

3. Goods were bought at 10 and 10% off, for \$688.50; what was the list price?

4. Goods were bought at 40, 10 and 2% off, for \$1455.30; find the list price.

5. Goods were bought at 10, 2 and 40% off, for \$1455.30; find the list price.

6. Bought goods at 5% off, and the discount was \$16.30; what was the amount of the purchase?

7. Bought goods at 50, 10 and 2% off, and the discounts amounted to \$167.70; what was the amount of the purchase?

Article 174.—*Profit and Loss.*

1. Goods costing \$350 were sold at a gain of 12%; what was the gain?

2. Cost \$750, gain $\frac{1}{2}$%; find the gain.

3. Cost \$400, loss $7\frac{1}{2}$%; find the selling price.

4. Cost \$625, loss $2\frac{2}{5}\%$; find the loss.

5. Selling price \$308.70, gain 5%; find cost.

6. Cost \$75, selling price \$80.10; find the % of gain.

7. Cost \$70, selling price \$65.80; find the % of loss.

8. What % is lost by selling for \$16 that which cost \$20?

9. What % is gained by selling for \$100 that which cost \$80?

10. What % is gained on berries costing \$3 per bu., and sold at 16 ct. per qt.?

11. What % is gained on indigo costing \$45 a cwt., and sold at 5 ct. an oz.?

12. What % is gained on quinine costing \$3 an oz., and sold at 2 ct. a grain?

13. What % is lost by selling for \$84 that which cost \$105?

14. What % is gained by selling for \$105 that which cost \$84?

15. Gained 60% by selling a cow for \$60; what % would have been gained by selling her for \$50?

16. Reducing the selling price 10 ct. reduced the gain 8%; find the original gain.

17. What % does the huckster gain, whose bushel-measure holds only 3 pk. 6 qt.?

18. If I sell 15 acres for as much as 18 acres cost, what % do I gain?

19. If I sell 18 acres for as much as 15 acres cost, what % do I lose?

20. Sugar was bought at $6\frac{7}{8}$ ct. a pound, and sold at $7\frac{1}{8}$ ct. a pound; what % was gained?

21. I gained $\frac{1}{2}\%$ by selling my farm for \$1346.70; find the cost.

22. What was the cost of muslin, on which $11\frac{1}{9}\%$ was gained by selling it at $11\frac{1}{9}$ ct. per yd.?

23. Retaining my commission at 2%, how much can I invest in cotton for a manufacturer who sends me $8000?

24. Retaining my commission at 2%, what amount of cotton goods must I sell for the manufacturer so as to owe him $8000?

25. Bought $8000 worth of cotton; what sum must the manufacturer send me, my commission being 2%?

26. Sold $8000 worth of cotton goods; what sum must I send the manufacturer, my commission being 2%?

27. I gained 150% by selling silk at $1.50 a yard; what % would I gain by selling at $1.60 per yard?

28. A merchant sold molasses to a grocer, gaining 12%; the grocer retailed it for $4120.90, gaining 16%; what was the first cost to the merchant?

29. A bookseller gains 20% by selling a history for $2.10; if the publisher reduces his price 4%, what % will the bookseller then make if he sells at the same price as before?

30. I have a contract to deliver goods, and I gain 15% thereby; if the price to me is lowered 8%, how many % will my income be increased?

ARTICLE 175.—*Miscellaneous Examples.*

1. Jones had wheat costing $8000, which he sold to Smith at 8% profit; Smith afterward sold the wheat back to Jones for $8000; what % did Smith lose?

2. I bought goods at 40 and 40% off, paying for them $294.30; what was the list price?

3. Two farms were sold at $1800 each; one at a gain of 20%, the other at a gain of 25%; what was the difference in their cost?

4. If I sell $\frac{5}{8}$ of a farm for what $\frac{4}{5}$ of it cost, what % do I gain?

5. An architect charged $\frac{1}{2}\%$ for plans and specifications, and $1\frac{1}{4}\%$ for superintending the erection of a house; and he received in all, $151.20; what was the cost of the house, including his fees?

6. Two booksellers expended $3000 each for books, one at 25% off the list, the other at 20% off; if they sold at the list price, how much more did one receive than the other?

7. I buy goods at 20% off the list price; how many % can I take off the list price to gain 10%?

8. By selling at 25% off the list price, I gain 25%; what discount from the list price did I receive when buying?

9. A sells to B at 10% profit; B sells to C at 5% profit; if C paid $5336.10, what did the goods cost A?

10. I buy goods at 20 and 5% off the list price, and sell at 5% off the same list; what % do I gain?

11. What % will a grocer make in selling by using for a pound a weight of only $15\frac{1}{5}$ oz.?

12. What % will he lose, by using the same weight in buying?

13. How much above cost must I mark goods, so that I can take off 20%, and still gain 10%?

14. How much above cost must I mark goods, so that I can take off 10% and still gain 20%?

15. What % off the list must I receive, so that I can gain 12% by selling at 16% off the same list?

Article 177.—*Brokerage.*

1. Seventy-five shares were bought at par by a broker for an operator who paid $7515; what was the % of brokerage?

2. Bought 550 shares of stock, and my brokerage was $165; what was the %?

3. Bought 260 shares at $\frac{1}{4}\%$ brokerage, and afterwards sold them at $\frac{1}{5}\%$; what was my brokerage?

4. The brokerage on 820 shares of Michigan Southern stock was $82; what was the %?

5. Ninety-eight shares of O. and M. stock were sold at $\frac{1}{8}\%$ brokerage; what was received for selling them?

6. How many shares must be bought to make the brokerage $50, at $\frac{1}{5}\%$?

7. What is the brokerage on 8268 shares of Kentucky Central stock at $\frac{1}{6}\%$?

8. What must be paid a broker for buying 78 shares railroad stock, at $\frac{1}{3}\%$; 65 shares steamboat stock, at $\frac{1}{4}\%$; and 48 shares insurance stock, at $\frac{1}{2}\%$?

ARTICLE 178.—*Assessments and Dividends.*

1. What would be the assessment on 60 shares of mining stock, at $32\frac{1}{2}\%$?

2. An insurance company declares a dividend of $3\frac{3}{4}\%$; what will A receive, who owns 46 shares?

3. An assessment of $12\frac{1}{2}\%$ on turnpike stock realized $28000; how many shares were there?

4. What % must be assessed on 2500 shares of steamboat stock, to cover a loss of $75000?

5. What sum will the owner of 58 shares receive from a dividend of $4\frac{1}{2}\%$?

6. What assessment is made when the owner of 35 shares pays $90 more than the owner of 23 shares?

7. A $3\frac{1}{2}\%$ dividend being declared on 8000 shares of stock, $26320 were paid out; how much remained of unclaimed dividends?

8. A stock dividend of 8% was declared, after which the president had 378 shares; how many had he owned before the dividend was declared?

ARTICLE 179.—*Stock Values.*

1. What will be the cost of 40 shares of Reading R. R. stock, at $88\frac{7}{8}$?

2. What will I receive for 280 shares of Lackawanna, at $127\frac{3}{4}$?

3. What must be paid for 300 shares Chesapeake and Ohio, at $20\frac{1}{2}$, brokerage $\frac{1}{5}\%$?

4. How many shares St. Paul, at $104\frac{1}{8}$, brokerage $\frac{1}{8}\%$, can I buy for $5421?

5. My agent sold for me 720 shares Ohio and Mississippi at $$33\frac{1}{2}$, brokerage $\frac{1}{4}\%$; and with the money bought Wabash Pacific preferred, at $44\frac{3}{4}$, brokerage $\frac{1}{4}\%$; how many shares of the latter did I receive?

6. Bought Northern Pacific at $50\frac{3}{8}$, and sold at $50\frac{7}{8}$, and neither lost nor gained; what was the rate of brokerage?

7. Bought 450 shares of North Western at $133\frac{5}{8}$, brokerage, $\frac{1}{4}\%$; and sold at $133\frac{7}{8}$, brokerage $\frac{1}{4}\%$; what was my loss?

8. If gold is worth 102 in currency, what is currency worth in gold?

9. A broker buys Pacific Mail, at a brokerage of $\frac{1}{4}\%$, for which I pay $103750, including his brokerage, $625; what did he pay for that stock?

10. What sum in gold must I pay for $1440 currency, at $\frac{5}{8}\%$ discount?

11. What sum in currency must I pay for $1431 in gold, at $\frac{5}{8}\%$ premium?

12. How many shares, at 5% discount, must be given for 180 shares at 14% premium?

13. Invested $70225 in Canada Southern at 66, and sold at 68; find my gain, each brokerage being $\frac{1}{4}\%$.

ARTICLE 180.—*Stock Investments.*

1. I invest $12168 in 4% bonds, at 4% premium; what annual income will I receive from them?

2. A man bought Covington and Lexington stock at 20, and received 2% dividends annually; what % was that on his investment?

3. A capitalist invested $8214 in 4% bonds at 74; what income will that produce annually?

4. $19600 was invested in 3% bonds, giving an annual income of $840; at what rate were the bonds bought?

5. What income will arise from investing $5488 in 6% bonds at 112?

6. What income will be produced by investing $3000 in 3% bonds, at 30?

7. I had 450 6% bonds, which I sold at 112, and invested the proceeds in a 5% bond at 90; how much did I increase my income?

8. When gold declined from 137 to 120, how much less currency was received per annum for eighteen $500 6% bonds?

9. What must be paid for a 5% bond, to make a $6\frac{1}{4}$% investment?

10. What must be paid for $4\frac{1}{2}$% bonds to realize $7\frac{1}{2}$% income?

11. What must be paid for a 6% bond, to make a 5% investment?

12. What % of income is derived from U. S. 5% bonds costing 112, when gold is 105?

13. Five % mining bonds yield an income of $20\frac{5}{6}$% annually; at what rate were they bought?

14. How much less income will be obtained by investing $2185 in 4% bonds at 95, than in 5% bonds at 115?

INTEREST.

Article 183.—*Case I.*

Find the interest for One Year of:

1. \$500 at 9%.
2. \$750 at 6%.
3. \$72 at 10%.
4. \$3200 at $7\frac{1}{2}$%.
5. \$1950 at 14%.
6. \$5 at 11%.

Find the amount for One Year of:

7. \$585 at 4%.
8. \$75 at $6\frac{2}{3}$%.
9. \$8765 at $4\frac{4}{5}$%.
10. \$470 at 12%.
11. \$940 at $2\frac{1}{2}$%.
12. \$999 at 9%.

Find the interest of:

13. \$392.00 for 3 yr., at 6%.
14. \$137.50 for 6 yr., at $4\frac{4}{5}$%.
15. \$900.10 for 6 yr., at 5%.
16. \$3570.40 for 4 yr., at 10%.
17. \$876.50 for 8 yr., at $6\frac{1}{4}$%.
18. \$3888.20 for 6 yr., at $3\frac{1}{2}$%.

Find the amount of:

19. \$375.00 for 5 yr., at $6\frac{2}{3}$%.
20. \$894.50 for 4 yr., at 5%.
21. \$132.35 for 9 yr., at 4%.
22. \$9.45 for 3 yr., at 9%.
23. \$9000.00 for 10 yr., at 10%.
24. \$9.99 for 9 yr., at 9%.

Find the interest of:

25. \$270.00 for 2 mo., at 8%.
26. \$52.80 for 5 mo., at 5%.
27. \$1346.00 for 8 mo., at 9%.
28. \$876.52 for 11 mo., at $2\frac{1}{2}$%.
29. \$777.77 for 7 mo., at 7%.
30. \$300.06 for 8 mo., at $6\frac{2}{3}$%.

Find the amount of:

31. \$187.50 for 8 mo., at 9%.
32. \$945.00 for 10 mo., at 4%.
33. \$473.20 for 7 mo., at 5%.
34. \$586.20 for 9 mo., at $3\frac{1}{3}$%.
35. \$3948.80 for 8 mo., at $8\frac{3}{4}$%.
36. \$371.20 for 5 mo., at $6\frac{1}{4}$%.

Find the interest of:

37. \$600.00 for 20 da., at 9%.
38. \$825.00 for 12 da., at 6%.
39. \$347.50 for 24 da., at 5%.
40. \$72.00 for 15 da., at $6\frac{2}{3}$%.
41. \$1938.57 for 12 da., at $2\frac{2}{3}$%.
42. \$3847.21 for 11 da., at $3\frac{3}{4}$%.

Find the amount of:

43. \$4740.00 for 10 da., at 6%.
44. \$6.00 for 12 da., at 10%.
45. \$480.00 for 20 da., at 3%.
46. \$16200.00 for 16 da., at $9\frac{1}{9}$%.
47. \$387.50 for 9 da., at 8%.
48. \$474.63 for 11 da., at $7\frac{1}{5}$%.

Find the interest of:

49. \$600.00 for 2 yr. 5 mo., at 6%.
50. \$400.00 for 2 yr. 2 mo. 15 da., at $4\frac{1}{2}$%.
51. \$432.00 for 3 yr. 4 mo. 20 da., at 5%.
52. \$387.00 for 2 yr. 6 mo. 24 da., at 12%.
53. \$486.00 for 3 yr. 5 mo. 7 da., at 5%.
54. \$729.00 for 4 yr. 7 mo. 5 da., at $6\frac{2}{3}$%.
55. \$555.00 for 5 yr. 5 mo. 5 da., at 5%.
56. \$897.31 for 4 yr. 7 mo. 11 da., at 11%.

Find the amount of:

57. \$400.00 for 3 yr. 6 mo., at 8%.
58. \$720.00 for 4 yr. 5 mo., at 5%.
59. \$750.00 for 3 yr. 2 mo. 15 da., at 4%.
60. \$960.00 for 5 yr. 9 mo. 12 da., at 8%.
61. \$471.50 for 3 yr. 7 mo. 12 da., at 5%.
62. \$89.25 for 2 yr. 11 mo. 17 da., at 3%.
63. \$1367.41 for 4 yr. 3 da., at 6%.
64. \$3791.40 for 12 yr. 27 da., at 4%.

Find the interest of:

65. \$360 from May 12, 1872, to July 20, 1877, at 7%.
66. \$450 from July 25, 1880, to Nov. 2, 1884, at 4%.
67. \$540 from Dec. 18, 1880, to May 28, 1881, at 8%.
68. \$960 from May 29, 1883, to June 1, 1885, at 3%.
69. \$1111.50 from Oct. 13, 1879, to May 28, 1888, at 4%.
70. \$999.90 from June 8, 1878, to Dec. 1, 1881, at 8%.
71. \$379.83 from March 3, 1878, to Oct. 16, 1886, at $3\frac{1}{3}$%.

Find the amount of:

72. \$5200 from Sept. 21, 1873, to April 4, 1880, at 9%.
73. \$540 from Oct. 21, 1865, to June 7, 1869, at 8%.
74. \$480 from June 5, 1885, to Nov. 1, 1887, at 6%.
75. \$600 from Nov. 27, 1801, to Aug. 6, 1803, at 3%.
76. \$388.80 from July 7, 1883, to Feb. 15, 1885, at $6\frac{2}{3}$%.
77. \$493.75 from June 7, 1882, to Jan. 1, 1883, at 5%.
78. \$666.66 from July 21, 1881, to Dec. 20, 1883, at $7\frac{1}{2}$%.

ARTICLE 184.—*The Twelve Per Cent Method.*

Find the interest of One Dollar at 12% for:

1. 6 mo. 6 da.
2. 9 mo. 21 da.
3. 2 yr. 5 mo. 13 da.
4. 3 yr. 7 mo. 29 da.
5. 2 yr. 1 mo. 1 da.
6. 5 yr. 28 da.
7. 4 yr. 1 da.
8. 1 yr. 11 mo. 29 da.

Find the interest of One Dollar for:

9. 5 mo. 12 da., at 5%.
10. 8 mo. 12 da., at 10%.
11. 9 mo. 6 da., at 8%.
12. 9 mo. 10 da., at 9%.
13. 2 mo. 4 da., at 9%.
14. 9 mo. 9 da., at 3%.
15. 7 mo. 7 da., at 7%.
16. 4 mo. 1 da., at 6%.
17. 5 mo. 5 da., at 5%.
18. 17 da., at 6%.
19. 3 yr. 6 mo. at 4%.
20. 2 yr. 7 mo. 8 da., at 3%.
21. 1 yr. 4 da., at 8%.
22. 3 yr. 9 mo. 18 da., at 10%.
23. 7 yr. 5 da., at 6%.

Find the interest of:

24. $600.00 for 4 mo. 10 da., at 6%.
25. $720.00 for 2 yr. 5 mo. 15 da., at 5%.
26. $480.00 for 1 yr. 9 mo. 12 da., at 9%.
27. $216.00 for 7 yr. 2 mo. 24 da., at 5%.
28. $500.00 for 3 yr. 3 mo. 6 da., at 15%.
29. $360.00 for 7 yr. 7 mo. 7 da., at 7%.
30. $100.80 for 3 yr. 4 mo. 5 da., at 5%.
31. $297.60 for 3 yr. 1 mo. 15 da., at 6%.
32. $102.40 for 3 yr. 7 mo. 6 da., at 4%.
33. $105.60 for 3 yr. 3 mo. 3 da., at $4\frac{1}{2}$%.
34. $487.50 for 5 yr. 6 mo. 1 da., at 3%.
35. $5000.00 for 12 yr. 1 mo. 10 da., at 8%.
36. $39.75 for 4 yr. 4 da., at 4%.
37. $7.75 for 9 mo., 19 da., at 5%.

Find the amount of:

38. $1296 for 2 yr. 6 mo. 15 da., at 5%.
39. $500.40 for 12 yr. 9 mo. 10 da., at 4%.
40. $840 for 3 yr. 12 da., at 7%.
41. $98.75 for 1 yr. 2 mo. 3 da., at 6%.
42. $5787.28 for 3 yr. 11 mo. 29 da., at 4%.
43. 30 cents for 30 years, at 30%
44. $387.45 for 3 yr. 1 da., at $4\frac{1}{2}$%.

Find the interest of:

45. \$390 from Aug. 15, 1870, to May 21, 1873, at 8%.

46. \$5374 from May 21, 1870, to Aug. 15, 1874, at 6%.

47. \$378.47 from Nov. 12, 1881, to April 6, 1884, at 7%.

Find the amount of:

48. \$538.20 from Aug. 3, 1881, to Jan. 27, 1885, at 5%.

49. \$588.30 from Oct. 19, 1870, to March 4, 1876, at 7%.

50. \$47.38 from Dec. 5, 1790, to May 1, 1820, at $4\frac{1}{2}$%.

Article 185.—*Case II.*

Find the time in the following:

1. Principal \$720, Interest \$108.00, Rate 5%.

2. Principal \$540, Interest \$81.00, Rate 6%.

3. Principal \$600, Interest \$104.00, Rate 8%.

4. Principal \$90, Interest \$90.00, Rate 4%.

5. Principal \$80, Interest \$100.00, Rate 10%.

6. Principal \$80, Amount \$100.00, Rate 10%.

7. Principal \$200, Amount \$400.00, Rate 5%.

8. Principal \$85, Interest \$28.90, Rate 6%.

9. In what time will \$750 amount to \$760, at 6%?

10. In what time will \$450, at 8%, earn \$57.60 interest?

11. In what time will any principal double itself at 9%?

12. In what time will any principal, at 8%, increase one fourth?

13. In what time will any principal, at 6%, increase one fifth?

14. How long will it take \$480 to amount to \$840, at 6%?

15. How long will it take \$75 to amount to \$76, at 5%?

16. How long will it take \$76 to amount to \$95, at 4%?

17. How long will it take \$76 to gain \$95, at 4%?

18. In what time at 8%, will $1500 amount to $1737?

19. In what time will $550, at 8%, gain $81.40?

20. A man paid $3.50 for the use of $70 at 20%; how long had he had it?

ARTICLE 186.—*Case III.*

Find the rate per cent in the following:

1. Principal $400, interest $100, time 4 yr. 2 mo.

2. Principal $750, interest $95, time 1 yr. 7 mo.

3. Amount $315, interest $35, time 2 yr. 1 mo.

4. Amount $390, principal $360, time 1 yr. 8 mo.

5. At what per cent will any principal double itself in 12 years?

6. At what per cent will any principal increase one half in 10 years?

7. Lent $550 for 3 years, and received $682; what per cent was that?

8. At what per cent will any principal treble itself in 40 years?

9. At what per cent will $900 amount to $1000 in 1 yr. 4 mo. 20 da.?

10. A man charged $1 for the use of $40 for 1 month; what per cent was that?

11. A man charged $2 for the use of $50 for 20 days; what per cent was that?

12. Principal $990, interest $338.25, time 5 yr. 1 mo. 15 da.; find the rate.

13. $700, in 6 years, amounted to $847; find the rate per cent.

14. A $5000 U. S. bond has coupons for $50 every 3 months; what is the rate per cent?

15. A railroad mortgage bond for $500 has coupons for $11.25 every six months; what per cent did it pay?

16. A boy paid 1 cent for the use of $1 for 3 days; what rate per cent was that?

17. One loan increased one third in 3 years, another one fourth in four years; what was the difference of the rates?

18. How much must the rate be increased, to increase the interest of $560, in 4 years, $56?

19. The United States exchanged $200000000 of 6% bonds for new bonds, and saved $6000000 a year; what per cent did the new bonds bear?

20. A state owed $2600000 in 7% bonds, for which it gave new bonds, saving $65000 annnally; what rate per cent did the new bonds bear?

ARTICLE 187.—*Case IV.*

1. Interest $65, time 5 yr., rate 5%; find the principal.

2. What principal, in 4 years, at 7%, will produce $203 interest?

3. Interest $50, time 5 yr., rate 5%; find the principal.

4. What sum, in 3% bonds, will give an annual income of $735?

5. What sum, in $4\frac{1}{2}$% bonds, will yield $792 annually?

6. Interest for 5 yr. 5 mo. 13 da., at 8%, was $39.26; what was the principal?

7. Rate $4\frac{1}{2}$%, time 3 yr. 7 mo. 14 da., interest $117.36; find the principal.

8. Rate 8%, time 8 da., interest $8; find the principal.

9. What sum, at $3\frac{3}{4}$%, for 4 yr. 5 mo. 10 da., will gain $327.40?

10. What sum, at 6% interest, would gain $104.43 in 4 yr. 1 mo. 5 da.?

11. What principal will produce $613.70 interest in 10 yr. 10 da., at 10%?

12. The interest for 7 yr. 1 mo. 19 da., at 5%, is $128.45; what is the principal?

ARTICLE 188.—*Case V.*

1. What principal, in 4 yr., at 10%, will amount to $840?

2. What principal will amount to $880 in 2 yr., at 5%?

3. Rate 8%, time 3 yr. 6 mo. 20 da., amount $231.20; find the principal.

4. Amount $147.60, time 2 yr. 10 mo. 15 da., rate 8%; find the principal.

5. Amount $180, rate 5%, time 6 yr. 8 mo.; find the principal.

6. Amount $180, rate 10%, time 3 yr. 4 mo.; find the interest.

7. What sum at interest for 7 yr. 7 mo. 6 da., at $7\frac{1}{2}$%, will amount to $643.70?

8. What sum must I deposit in a savings bank, at 4%, so that at the end of 3 yr. 2 mo. 15 da. I can draw out $169.25?

9. What sum at interest 12 yr., at 12%, will amount to $481.90?

10. What principal will amount to $250.25 in 8 yr. 7 mo. 6 da., at 5%?

11. What principal would amount to $9409, in 540 yr., at 7%?

12. A loaned $990 for 6 yr. 8 mo., at 3%; what sum must B loan for 7 yr., at 5%, to realize the same amount that A does?

ARTICLE 190.—*Compound Interest.*

Find the amount, at compound interest, of:

1. \$400 for 2 yr., at 5%.
2. \$600 for 1 yr. 6 mo., at 10%.
3. \$409.60 for 3 yr., at $6\frac{1}{4}$%.
4. \$500 for 3 yr., at 8%.

Find the compound interest of:

5. \$640 for 5 yr., at 4%.
6. \$640 for 4 yr., at 5%.
7. \$500 for 2 yr. 2 mo., at 6%.
8. \$1562.50 for 4 yr., at 8%.

9. Find the interest of \$2000 for 2 yr. at 8% compound interest, payable semi-annually.

10. Find the compound interest of \$125 for 1 yr. 8 mo., at 8%.

11. Find the compound interest of \$250 for 2 yr., at 6%, payable semi-annually.

12. What is the amount of \$1000 for 1 yr. at 4% compound interest, interest payable quarterly?

13. What is the difference between simple and compound interest on \$1000, for 3 yr., at 4%?

14. What is the difference between simple and compound interest on \$1000, for 4 yr., at 3%?

ARTICLE 191.—*Annual Interest.*

1. No interest having been paid, find the amount due in 3 yr. on a note of \$500, with interest at 6%, payable annually.

2. What would be the amount of the above note, if the interest were payable semi-annually?

3. What would be the interest of $750, for 5 yr., at 6%, annually, no interest having been paid?

4. Interest having been paid for 3 yr., find the amount due on a note for $900, for 7 yr., at 4%, payable annually.

5. A note was given May 15, 1884, for $1500, with 6% interest, payable annually; what was due on this note May 15, 1889?

6. What would have been the interest on the above note Aug. 15, 1887?

7. If the interest on the above note had been paid for 3 yr., what would have been due on the note Oct. 30, 1890?

8. If the interest on the above note had been paid for 2 yr., what would be the interest due on it Dec. 10, 1888?

Article 192.—*Partial Payments.*

1. A note of $500 is dated Oct. 1, 1870. Int., 8%. Indorsed Oct. 1, 1872, $130; Oct. 1, 1874, $100. What was due Oct. 1, 1875?

2. A note of $500 is dated Oct. 1, 1870. Int., 8%. Indorsed Oct. 1, 1872, $30; Oct. 1, 1874, $200. What was due Oct. 1, 1875?

3. A note of $600 is dated Jan. 1, 1865. Int., 6%. Indorsed March 1, 1866, $30; April 1, 1867, $40; May 1, 1868, $100. What was due Jan. 1, 1870?

4. A note of $600 is dated Jan. 1, 1865. Int., 6%. Indorsed April 1, 1866, $30; March 1, 1867, $40; May 1, 1868, $100. What was due Jan. 1, 1870?

5. A note of $800 is dated May 18, 1880. Int., 5%. Indorsed March 24, 1881, $84; July 24, 1881, $42.50; June 4, 1882, $91; Oct. 4, 1883, $34. What was due Jan. 1, 1884?

6. A note of $500 is dated Sept. 19, 1870. Int., 4%. Indorsed June 10, 1871, $10; Oct. 10, 1871, $10; March 19, 1872, $40; Aug. 19, 1872, $38. What was due Feb. 13, 1874?

7. A note of $960 is dated June 23, 1880. Int., 4½%. Indorsed July 8, 1881, $50; July 23, 1882, $50; Aug. 8, 1883, $100; Jan. 1, 1884, $15. What was due June 28, 1884?

8. A note of $875 is dated May 5, 1877. Int., 6%. Indorsed Oct. 12, 1878, $50; July 13, 1879, $100; May 23, 1880, $30; June 16, 1881, $300. What was due Nov. 29, 1881?

ARTICLE 193.—*Mercantile Rule.*

1. A note of $400 is dated Dec. 16, 1882. Indorsements: March 4, 1883, $50; May 28, 1883, $50; Aug. 10, 1883, $50; Oct. 22, 1883, $50. What was due Dec. 4, 1883, interest at 6%?

2. A man owed $325 from Jan. 1, 1879. He paid March 1, 1879, $40; April 1, 1879, $40; May 1, 1879, $80; July 1, 1879, $80; Dec. 1, 1879, $80. What was due Jan. 1, 1880, reckoning 6% interest?

3. A man borrowed $600 July 1, 1881, and paid $100 on the first day of each succeeding month in that year. What was due Jan. 1, 1882, interest at 6%?

4. Borrowed $187.50 May 13, 1884. Paid $30 July 30, 1884; $35 Aug. 12, 1884; $40 Oct. 3, 1884; $50 Dec. 17, 1884; and $40 Feb. 1, 1885. What was due May 1, 1885, interest at 12%?

5. Borrowed $110 Jan. 1, 1882, and paid $10 on the first day of each succeeding month in the year. What was due Jan. 1, 1883, interest at 6%?

DISCOUNT.

ARTICLE 196.—*Bank Discount. Case I.*

Find the date when due, bank discount, and proceeds of:

1. A note of \$400, dated July 8, payable in 60 days, and discounted at 6%.

2. A note of \$450, dated March 18, payable in 90 days, and discounted at 8%.

3. A note of \$400, dated April 18, payable in 90 days, and discounted at 9%.

4. A note of \$520, dated June 16, payable in 90 days, and discounted at $4\frac{1}{2}$%.

5. A note of \$540, dated June 16, payable in 3 months, and discounted at 6%.

6. A note of \$80, dated Feb. 24, 1879, payable in 60 days, and discounted at 9%.

7. A note of \$180, dated Jan. 15, 1881, payable in 90 days, and discounted at 4%.

8. A note of \$480, dated May 19, payable in 5 months, and discounted at 3%.

9. A note of \$320, dated Sept. 13, payable in 4 months, and discounted at $4\frac{1}{2}$%.

10. A note of \$810, dated Jan. 16, 1883, payable in 100 days, and discounted at 8%.

11. A note of \$89.40, dated July 19, payable in 40 days, and discounted at 5%.

12. A note of \$13.93, dated Aug. 18, payable in 6 months, and discounted at 7%.

13. A note of \$399.99, dated Oct. 16, payable in 50 days, and discounted at 10%.

14. A note of \$1122.33, dated Dec. 18, 1879, payable in 90 days, and discounted at 7%.

Find the date when due, time of discount, bank discount, and proceeds of:

15. A note of $400, dated May 18, 1880, payable in 6 months, and discounted Aug. 21, 1880, at 6%.

16. A note of $500, dated July 26, 1870, payable in 90 days, and discounted Aug. 5, 1870, at 12%.

17. A note of $450, dated Jan. 19, 1880, payable in 3 months, and discounted Feb. 16, at 4%.

18. A note of $720, dated Oct. 14, 1875, payable in 90 days, and discounted Nov. 21, 1875, at 5%.

19. A note of $360, dated May 19, 1877, payable in 3 months, and discounted June 26, 1877, at 4%.

20. A note of $360, dated May 19, 1877, payable in 90 days, and discounted June 26, 1877, at 4%.

21. A note of $783.29, dated April 22, 1875, payable in 80 days, and discounted June 3, 1875, at 9%.

22. A note of $400, dated Dec. 16, 1883, payable in 4 months, with interest at 6%, and discounted Feb. 13, 1884, at 9%.

23. A note of $720, dated Jan. 13, 1846, payable in 90 days, with interest at 10%, and discounted March 3, 1846, at 9%.

24. A note of $600, dated March 2, 1884, payable in 8 mo. 7 da., with interest at 9%, and discounted July 14, 1884, at 12%.

25. A note of $450, dated Sept. 19, 1882, payable in 9 mo. 27 da., with interest at 5%, and discounted Jan. 20, 1883, at 8%.

26. A note of $5000, dated June 16, 1888, payable in 90 days, with interest at 6%, and discounted July 16, 1888, at 8%.

27. A note of $475, dated Jan. 1, 1880, payable in 4 months, with interest at 4%, and discounted Jan. 15, 1880, at 10%.

ARTICLE 197.—*Case II.*

1. The proceeds of a note, payable in 60 days, dis counted at a bank at 6%, were $494.75. Find the face of the note.

2. A note payable in 30 days was discounted in bank at 8%; the proceeds were $595.60. What was the face of the note?

3. For what sum must I make a note at 60 days, to obtain $739.50 from a bank discounting at 8%?

4. I wish to obtain $800 on a note payable in 42 days; for what sum must I give my note to a bank discounting at 4%?

5. For what sum must I give a 60-day note, to obtain $1000 from a bank discounting at 9%?

6. Sold 40 acres of land, receiving a note at 6 months, which I at once discounted in bank at 6%, receiving $2326.80; what was the price per acre?

7. I sold 20 horses, receiving a note payable in 3 months, for which I received $2338 from a bank discounting at 10%; what was the price of each horse?

8. A note dated May 3, 1885, payable in 6 months, and drawing 6% interest, was discounted in bank Sept. 27, 1885, at 9%, the proceeds being $2040.39; what was the face of the note?

ARTICLE 199.—*True Discount.*

What is the present worth and discount, at 6%, of:

1. $450.00, due in 3 yr. 4 mo.?
2. $900.00, due in 7 yr. 4 mo.?
3. $685.00, due in 6 yr. 2 mo.?
4. $810.00, due in 2 yr. 1 mo.?
5. $359.00, due in 3 yr. 3 mo. 10 da.?

6. $448.70, due in 1 yr. 1 mo. 20 da.?
7. $622.30, due in 8 yr. 10 da.?
8. $373.10, due in 5 yr. 6 mo. 15 da.?
9. $616.21, due in 7 yr. 9 mo. 13 da.?
10. $888.00, due in 8 yr. 8 mo. 8 da.?

Find the true discount, at 6%, of:

11. $961.00, due in 4 yr.
12. $427.00, due in 3 yr. 8 mo.
13. $262.80, due in 1 yr. 7 mo.
14. $490.10, due in 4 yr. 3 mo. 10 da.
15. $161.21, due in 2 yr. 6 mo. 9 da.
16. $3836.90, due in 2 yr. 1 mo. 21 da.
17. $936.43, due in 6 yr. 11 mo. 23 da.
18. $700.00, due in 9 mo. 13 da.
19. $1000.10, due in 27 da.

20. A bill of merchandise amounted to $364, at 4 months time, or 4% off for cash; if money is worth 12% per annum, how much will the buyer gain by paying cash?

21. What should be paid May 10, 1884, for a debt of $264.20, due Jan. 15, 1886, money being worth 6%?

22. A debt of $1368 is due in 2 years: how much more should be given for it, if money is worth 7%, than if money is worth 10%?

23. A balance of $514.80 is due: one third in 1 yr., one third in 2 yr., and the balance in 3 yr. What sum should pay it now, money being worth 10%?

24. What debt could be settled by paying $561.60 cash, and giving two notes, of $561.60 each, one payable in 6 mo., and the other in 1 yr., money being worth 8%?

25. A lot was bought for $1800, one third cash, one third in 1 yr., and one third in 2 yr., with interest at 6%. If money is worth 10%, what sum in cash should have been paid for the lot?

ARTICLE 201.--*Domestic Exchange.*

1. New York exchange being $\frac{1}{5}\%$ premium, what must be paid for a sight draft on that place for $4700?

2. What must be paid for a sight draft on San Francisco for $730, at $\frac{1}{2}\%$ discount?

3. Find the cost of a sight draft on Philadelphia for $4950, at $\frac{1}{20}\%$ premium.

4. Find the cost of a sight draft on Toronto for $1360, at $\frac{1}{4}\%$ discount.

5. What must be paid for a sight draft on Milwaukee for $373.84, at $\frac{1}{2}\%$ premium?

6. What will be the cost of a sight draft on Santa Fe for $2377.50, at $\frac{3}{4}\%$ discount?

7. What must be paid for a draft on New York for $1000, payable in 30 days, exchange at par, and interest 6%?

8. What must be paid for a draft on Boston for $1000, payable in 30 days, exchange being at $\frac{1}{2}\%$ discount, and interest 6%?

9. Find the cost of a 30-day draft on Savannah for $2400, exchange at $\frac{1}{8}\%$ discount, interest at 8%.

10. What cost a 60-day draft on Cleveland for $1500, exchange at $\frac{1}{5}\%$ premium, interest at 8%?

11. What was the face of a sight draft for which $796 was paid, exchange at $\frac{1}{2}\%$ discount?

12. What was the face of a 60-day draft on New York, for which $792 was paid, exchange being $\frac{1}{20}\%$ premium, and interest 6%?

13. What was the face of a 90-day draft on Mobile costing $1857.83, exchange being at $\frac{1}{4}\%$ premium, interest at 8%?

14. $1000 was paid for a sight draft on Detroit, exchange at $\frac{1}{4}\%$ discount; what was the face of the draft?

ARTICLE 202.—*Foreign Exchange.*

1. What must be paid for a bill of exchange on London for £796 5s., exchange being at $4.84?

2. What will be the cost of a bill of exchange on Edinburgh for £283 15 s., exchange being at $4.88?

3. How large a bill on Manchester can be bought for $5314.41, exchange being at $4.86?

4. How large a bill on Marseilles can be bought for $818.75, exchange being at 5 fr. 16 centimes?

5. What cost a bill on Havre for 5047 francs, exchange being at 5 fr. 15 centimes?

6. What cost a bill on Munich for 4800 reichsmarks, exchange being 96 cents for 4 reichsmarks?

7. What cost a bill on Dresden for 3742 reichsmarks, exchange being at $.98?

8. How large a bill on Stuttgart can be bought for $1000, exchange being at $.965?

INSURANCE.

ARTICLE 204.—*Fire and Marine Insurance.*

1. What must be paid for $4800 insurance on a dwelling at $\frac{7}{10}\%$?

2. A factory is valued at $18000; what must be paid for insuring $\frac{7}{9}$ of its value, at $\frac{3}{5}\%$?

3. What will be the premium for insuring $\frac{2}{3}$ of a steamer valued at $36800, at $\frac{3}{8}\%$?

4. A store is valued at $15000, and the contents at $11000; what will be the premium for insuring $\frac{3}{4}$ of the value of the store, at $\frac{2}{5}\%$, and $\frac{3}{5}$ of the value of the contents, at $\frac{1}{4}\%$?

5. Insured a mill for $\frac{3}{4}$ of its value, at $\frac{5}{8}\%$, the premium being $41.25; what was the value of the mill?

6. A merchant has goods valued at $46000, and pays $184 for insurance at $\frac{1}{2}\%$; what part of the value is insured?

7. I insured $\frac{2}{3}$ of a factory, valued at $35400, and $\frac{3}{4}$ of the stock, valued at $41200, paying $436; what was the rate of insurance?

Article 205.—*Life Insurance.*

1. What must be paid yearly for $6000 life insurance, the premium being $32.18 per $1000?

2. A man paid $382.50 for 5 years insurance on a life policy for $3000; what was the company's annual rate per $1000?

3. A father, at the age of 50, insures his life for $5000, at $47.18 per $1000 annually; his son, aged 21, insures his life for the same sum, at an annual rate of $19.89. If each lives to the age of 71, which will pay the greater sum for insurance, and how much more than the other will he pay?

4. An endowment policy for $2000 costs $107.32 per $1000 annually, for 10 years; what would be the amount of the ten payments, allowing simple interest at 6%?

TAXES.

Article 208.—*To fix the Rate of Taxation.*

1. A tax of $625000 is to be levied upon a valuation of $250000000; what will be the rate of taxation?

2. The valuation in a certain city being $165000000, and the amount of tax to be levied $3795000, what will be the rate of taxation?

3. The expense of building a school-house was estimated at $6600, to be raised by a tax of $2\frac{1}{2}$ mills on $1; what is the valuation?

4. $3471250 is to be levied upon a valuation of $571273600; what will be the rate to the hundredth of a mill?

ARTICLE 209.—*Apportionment of Taxes.*

1. $3400 is to be assessed upon a town; the valuation is $1269531.25, and 100 persons pay $1.50 each for poll tax; find the rate of levy, and construct a table to $9000.

With the above levy, find the tax to be paid by the following persons:

2. William Smith, property $7500, 2 polls.
3. G. W. Wright, property $5610, 1 poll.
4. Ruth Williams, property $6495.
5. Seth Cooper, property $1698, 1 poll.
6. William Simpson, property $1627, 2 polls.
7. Enoch Ayres, property $1240, 3 polls.
8. Matthew Wilson, property $990, 1 poll.

9. The tax to be raised in a city is $4117136; the taxable property is valued at $162580364; find the rate of levy to one thousandth of a mill, and construct a tax table to $90000.

With the above table, find the amount of tax to be paid by:

10. Eli Wiggins, property $874.
11. Marion Thompson, property $194560.
12. Timothy Stewart, property $1418720.
13. Silas Burns, property $84.
14. John Shaw, property $848.
15. Jonas Newcome, property $8484.
16. Emmanuel Goldsmith, property $84848.

ARTICLE 211.—*Internal Revenue.*

1. The tax on proof spirits is 70 cents a gallon; what would be the tax on a barrel of 48 gallons?

2. What would be the tax on a barrel of alcohol containing 52 gallons, 50% above proof?

3. What would be the postage on a book weighing 1 lb. $7\frac{1}{4}$ oz., at the rate of 1 cent for each 2 ounces or fraction thereof?

4. What would be the postage on a letter weighing 1 lb. $7\frac{1}{4}$ oz., at the rate of 2 cents for every ounce or fraction thereof?

5. What would be the postage on a package weighing 1 lb. $7\frac{1}{4}$ oz., at the rate of 1 cent for each ounce, or fraction thereof?

6. What would be the postage on 15 letters, each weighing $\frac{1}{4}$ oz.?

7. What would be the postage on 15 packages, each weighing $\frac{1}{4}$ oz.?

8. What would be the postage on 15 books, sent separately, each weighing $\frac{1}{4}$ oz.?

9. What would be the postage on 2 dozen books, each weighing 2 lb.?

10. The tax on pencils is $3 per 1000; what must be paid for 216 boxes, containing 50 each?

11. The tax on small ornaments is 50 cents per 1000; what will be the tax on 100 bundles, containing 200 small ornaments each?

12. What will be the tax on 3 T. 13 cwt. of sugar, at 8 cents a pound?

13. A firm paid $30 postage on 2-oz. letters; how many were sent?

14. Paid $30 postage on 8-oz. books; how many were sent?

ARTICLE 212.—*Duties or Customs.*

1. What is the duty on 5 T. 3 cwt. of flour sulphur, at $20 per ton?

2. What is the duty on 23040 steel pens, at 12 ct. a gross?

3. Find the duty on 1000000 lb. of iron ore, at 75 ct. per ton.

4. Find the duty on 72000 shingles, at 35 ct. per 1000.

5. A cask of borax weighs 572 lb.; allowing 6% for tare, what will be the duty at 5 ct. per lb.?

6. Imported an invoice of silk, costing $3739.30; what was the duty at 50%?

7. Imported 450 boxes raisins: gross weight of each, 25 lb., tare 8%; find the duty at 2 ct. per lb.

8. What will be the duty on 2 dozen repeating rifles, costing in England £5 5 s. each, the duty being 25%, and the pound quoted at $4.88?

9. Find the duty on 46 T. Bessemer steel, at 45%; cost per ton, £6 10 s., and the pound being $4.84.

10. Imported 10 cases woolen cloths, weighing 272 lb. each; tare, 5%; cost, 90 ct. per lb. What is the duty, at 35 ct. per lb. and 40% ad valorem?

11. Find the duty on 72 crates of queensware costing £73 6 s. 8 d. per crate, commission $3\frac{1}{3}$%, duty 55%, the pound = $4.86.

12. Imported 100 cases German toys, costing 180 marks per case, commission $3\frac{1}{3}$%; find the duty at 35%, the mark being 23.6 ct.

13. Bought 100 dozen umbrellas at £3 6 s. per dozen; what was the duty at 50%, £1 = $4.868?

14. Bought 18 bales Turkey sponge, weighing 130 lb. each, at 5 s. 4 d. a lb.; find the duty at 20%, £1 = $4.86.

RATIO.

ARTICLE 214.

What is the ratio of:

1. 140 to 7?
2. $37\frac{1}{2}$ to $3\frac{3}{4}$?
3. 56 to $2\frac{1}{3}$?
4. 100 to 17?
5. 112 to $17\frac{1}{2}$?
6. 18 to 171?
7. $18\frac{3}{4}$ to $7\frac{1}{2}$?
8. $40\frac{4}{5}$ to $25\frac{1}{2}$?
9. $7\frac{3}{7}$ to 26?
10. 1000 to $35\frac{5}{7}$?
11. $88\frac{1}{2}$ to $19\frac{2}{3}$?
12. 87 to $23\frac{1}{5}$?
13. $41\frac{2}{3}$ to $6\frac{3}{4}$?
14. $7\frac{7}{9}$ to 175?
15. $\frac{8}{9}$ to 18?
16. $\frac{4}{7}$ to 100?
17. 4.2 to .07?
18. $13\frac{3}{11}$ to 4.5?
19. 9 A. to 18 sq. rd.?
20. 7 mi. 10 rd. to 30 rd.?
21. 1 bu. 1 pk. 1 qt. to 1 qt. 1 pt.?
22. 5 lb. 4 oz. to 7 cwt.?
23. 3 weeks to 9 hr.?
24. 4 sq. mi. to 13 A.?

ARTICLE 215.

Find the antecedent in the following:

1. Consequent, 35; ratio, 20.
2. Consequent, 280; ratio, 100.
3. Consequent, $17\frac{1}{2}$; ratio, 19.
4. Consequent, $\frac{8}{9}$; ratio, $\frac{2}{7}$.
5. Consequent, $8\frac{2}{5}$; ratio, $6\frac{1}{4}$.
6. Consequent, $3\frac{4}{5}$; ratio, 4.6.
7. Consequent, 4.3; ratio, $6\frac{1}{2}$.
8. Consequent, 15 sq. mi.; ratio, .008.
9. Consequent, 2 ft. 9 in.; ratio, $4\frac{2}{3}$.
10. Consequent, 3 wk. 3 da. 12 hr.; ratio, $1\frac{4}{7}$.

Article 216.

Find the consequent in the following:

1. Antecedent, 137.2; ratio, 7.
2. Antecedent, 3.4; ratio, .08.
3. Antecedent, $4\frac{1}{2}$; ratio, $6\frac{3}{4}$.
4. Antecedent, $\frac{2}{5}$; ratio, $\frac{8}{15}$.
5. Antecedent, 4 bu. 1 qt.; ratio, 6.
6. Antecedent, 13 gal. 3 qt.; ratio, .05.
7. Antecedent, 14 hr. 40 min.; ratio, 30.
8. Antecedent, 13.2 liters; ratio, .08.

Article 217.

Find the value of the following compound ratios:

1. $\left\{\begin{array}{l} 14 : 8. \\ 18 : 7. \end{array}\right.$

2. $\left\{\begin{array}{l} 14 : 4. \\ 16 : 6. \\ 18 : 8. \end{array}\right.$

3. $\left\{\begin{array}{lcl} 16 \text{ bu.} & : & 28 \text{ bu.} \\ 175 \text{ A.} & : & 180 \text{ A.} \end{array}\right.$

4. $\left\{\begin{array}{lcl} 27 \text{ da.} & : & 22 \text{ da.} \\ 77 \text{ horses} & : & 63 \text{ horses.} \end{array}\right.$

5. $\left\{\begin{array}{l} 1.2 : .3. \\ 3\frac{1}{3} : \frac{2}{3}. \end{array}\right.$

6. $\left\{\begin{array}{lcl} 1 \text{ wk.} & : & 8 \text{ hr.} \\ 16 \text{ men} & : & 2 \text{ men.} \end{array}\right.$

7. $\left\{\begin{array}{lcl} 6.4 & : & 8. \\ 4.5 & : & 9. \\ 396 & : & 7.2. \end{array}\right.$

8. $\left\{\begin{array}{lcl} 6 \text{ men} & : & 2 \text{ men.} \\ 8 \text{ da.} & : & 16 \text{ da.} \\ 12 \text{ yd.} & : & 2 \text{ yd.} \end{array}\right.$

Article 219.—*Reduction of Ratios.*

Reduce the following ratios to their lowest terms:

1. 80 : 64.
2. 259 : 111.
3. 77 : 33.
4. 999 : 99.
5. 9999 : 4545.
6. 648 : 486.
7. 388 : 1261.
8. 329 : 517.
9. 48 da. : 36 da.
10. 9 wk. : 2 da. 1 hr.
11. 22 gal.: 1 gal.: 1 qt.: 1 pt.
12. 8 oz. : 3 lb. Av.

ARTICLE 220.—*Clearing Ratios of Fractions.*

Clear the following ratios of fractions:

1. $7\frac{7}{8} : 4\frac{4}{5}$.

2. $16\frac{3}{4} : 2\frac{1}{3}$.

3. $6\frac{3}{4} : 2\frac{3}{5}$.

4. $4\frac{4}{9} : 3\frac{2}{7}$.

Express the following ratios in their simplest forms:

5. $5\frac{5}{9} : 7\frac{1}{2}$.

6. $9\frac{1}{3} : 8\frac{3}{4}$.

7. $16\frac{8}{9} : 6\frac{1}{3}$.

8. $11\frac{1}{5} : 9\frac{1}{3}$.

PROPORTION.

ARTICLE 223.—*To find Missing Terms.*

1. 9 : 12 : : 51 : what?

2. 12 : 16 : : what : 28?

3. 38 : what : : 57 : 12?

4. 36 : what : : 27 : 72?

5. $27\frac{1}{2} : 37\frac{1}{2} :: \text{what} : 18\frac{3}{4}$?

6. 8 : 9 : : 73 : what?

7. 8 : 9 : : what : 73?

8. 8 : what : : 9 : 73?

9. What : 8 : : 9 : 73?

10. 5 qt. : 2 pk. 2 qt. : : 24 : what?

11. $\left.\begin{matrix} 7 : \text{what} \\ 8 : 3\frac{1}{2} \end{matrix}\right\} :: 26 : 45\frac{1}{2}$?

12. $\left.\begin{matrix} 11\frac{1}{2} : 7\frac{2}{3} \\ 16\frac{2}{3} : \text{what} \end{matrix}\right\} :: 50 : 8$?

13. $5 \text{ gal.} : 2 \text{ gal. } 1 \text{ pt.} :: \left\{\begin{matrix} 8 : 6 \\ 18 : \text{what?} \end{matrix}\right.$

14. $\left.\begin{matrix} 3.4 : 5.1 \\ 8\frac{2}{5} : 4.9 \end{matrix}\right\} :: \text{what} : 3 \text{ cwt. } 1 \text{ lb.}$?

ARTICLE 224.—*Simple Proportion.*

1. If 17 A. cost $205, what will 85 A. cost?

2. If 46 bu. of wheat cost $37.20, what will 115 bu. cost?

3. If $1000 will buy 160 hogs, what will 1000 hogs cost?

4. What cost 210 brooms, at $2.60 per doz.?

5. Seventy horses cost $11000; at that rate, how many can be bought for $16500?

6. If a lot 46 feet front is worth $975, what would a lot 207 feet front be worth?

7. If 49 yd. of silk cost $50.40, what will 126 yd. cost?

8. If 27 gal. of milk cost $31.50, what will 84 gal. cost?

9. If a telegram of 40 words costs $1.70, what should be paid for a telegram of 76 words for the same distance?

10. If 15 dozen brooms cost $41.40, what will 800 brooms cost?

11. If $47 will buy 1750 lb. of iron, what will 2450 lb. cost?

12. If a car travels 506 mi. in 44 hr., how long would it require to go 1587 mi.?

13. A man has corn to feed 54 horses 38 weeks; how long would it last 57 horses?

14. A laborer works for $1.25 a day, and is paid in potatoes at 55 ct. a bu.; how many bushels will he receive for 50 days work?

15. Ten pipes fill a reservoir in 64 hr.; if 2 pipes were closed, how long would it take the others to fill it?

16. A man walks $\frac{4}{5}$ mi. in $\frac{4}{11}$ hr.; how far can he walk in $\frac{16}{33}$ da.?

17. If a gallon of vinegar costs as much as 1 gal. 2 qt. of milk, how much vinegar should be given for 1 gal. of milk?

18. A watch loses 1 min. 24 sec. in a week; how much will it lose in 4 da. 12 hr.?

19. If 2 T. 5 cwt. of hay cost $25.20, how much can be bought for $84?

20. A crew of 96 men have provisions for 72 days; how many men must desert, that the remainder may have enough for 108 days?

21. A man borrows 256 bu. of oats, worth 35 ct. a bu.; how much should he return, the price having fallen 3 ct. a bu.?

22. How many bu. of oats, at 53 ct., should be given for 940 bu. 3 pk. of wheat, at 71 ct.?

23. When flour is $10 a bl. the 10 ct. loaf weighs 1 lb. 12 oz.; what should it weigh when flour is $8 a bl.?

24. A man makes 5800 steps, of 33 in. each; if his son's steps are 4 in. shorter, how many steps must he make in walking the distance with his father?

25. If a locomotive burns 200 bu. 1 pk. of coal in running $44\frac{1}{2}$ mi., how far can it run with 227 bu. 1 pk.?

26. If a man can cut 12 C. of wood in 55 hr., how much can he cut in 22 days, working 10 hr. a day?

27. If 580 sheep can graze on 72 A. 80 sq. rd. of pasture, how much will be required for 850 sheep?

28. If a yard-stick casts a shadow 4 ft. long, when held upright, how high is the tree whose shadow is 220 ft. long?

29. Bought 120 chairs, at 70 ct. apiece; had the cost been 10 ct. more apiece, how many could I have bought?

30. Had the cost been 10 ct. less apiece, how many could I have bought?

31. Had I bought 30 more for the same money, what would each have cost?

32. Had I bought 20 less for the same money, what would each have cost?

33. If a man earns \$402 in $\frac{5}{8}$ of a year, how much can he earn in $\frac{5}{6}$ of a year?

34. What cost $37\frac{1}{2}$ yd. of cloth, if $\frac{3}{4}$ yd. is worth \$$\frac{4}{5}$?

35. How long should I lend a man \$880, to compensate for a loan of \$660 for 60 days?

36. If .68 yd. of cloth is worth \$1.16, find the value of .85 yd.

37. If the composition for a book of 336 pages cost \$450.52, what will be the cost of composition for a similar book of 504 pages?

38. If a hog weighing 325 lb. is worth \$23.40, what should be given for one weighing 425 lb.?

39. How many men can do in $5\frac{1}{4}$ days as much work as 364 men can do in $8\frac{1}{4}$ da.?

40. What sum will pay freight on 6 T. 15 cwt., as far as 3 cwt. 25 lb. can be carried for \$1.04?

41. A man was charged \$132 for silk, but discovered that it had been measured with a measure $34\frac{1}{2}$ inches long, instead of 1 yd.; what was the true bill?

42. Eight cu. ft. of water weigh 5 cwt.; what will be the capacity of a vessel containing 4 T. 7 cwt. 50 lb. of water?

43. A grocer's weights are deficient at the rate of 1 oz. in 2 lb.; what is the true weight of a parcel sold for 240 lb.?

44. At 10 ct. a lb. (false), what will he charge for sugar, the true weight of which is 155 lb.?

45. If $\frac{5}{6}$ ℥ make 160 pills, how many can be made from 3 ℥ 2 ℈?

46. A town of 4750 inhabitants increased in population 950 in one year; at the same rate, what will be the increase the next year?

47. If I sell my horses at a gain of 36%, I clear \$4560; what will be my profit if I sell at 63% gain?

48. If muslin $27\frac{1}{2}$ in. wide is worth 11 ct. a yd., how much should be paid per yd. for muslin 4 ft. $2\frac{1}{2}$ in. wide?

49. If a school with 750 pupils sends 80 to the high school, how many should a school of 1800 pupils send?

50. The fore wheel of a wagon is 17 ft. 6 in. in circumference; and the hind wheel, 20 ft. 5 in.; how many revolutions will the fore wheel make while the hind wheel makes 756?

51. How many revolutions will the hind wheel make while the fore wheel makes 756?

52. A mining company employed 580 miners, the weekly pay-roll of wages being $630.75; what would be the weekly wages after 40 men were discharged?

53. A man measuring a road gave the length at 840 yards, the true length being 825 yards; how much too short was his yard-stick?

54. A clock loses 1 min. 12 sec. in 48 hr.; how much will it lose in 6 da. 8 hr.?

55. A steamer goes 13 mi. 240 rd. per hour; a sailing vessel, $7\frac{1}{3}$ mi. per hour; how long will the latter be on a voyage which the steamer could perform in 73 hr. 12 min.?

56. If a county, having 350000 inhabitants, is entitled to 8 representatives, how many should be sent by a county whose population is 787500?

57. A man, whose farm is valued at $7930, is taxed $14.78 for a bridge; what will be levied upon his neighbor, whose farm is valued at $8947?

58. With a certain machine a power of 90 pounds can move a weight of 3 T. 6 cwt.; what weight can be moved by a power of 3 cwt. applied to the machine?

59. My gain on $4760 sales was $116.38; at the same rate, what will be my gain on $15928 sales?

ARTICLE 225.—*Compound Proportion.*

1. If 5 men in 6 da. earn $49.50, how much can 8 men earn in 9 da.?

2. If 6 men in 8 da. earn $78, how many men can be hired for 4 da. for $117?

3. If 8 men in 12 da. earn $120, how long can 14 men be hired for $210?

4. Twelve lots, each 15 rd. long and 12 rd. wide, cost $2400; at the same rate, what would be the price of 18 lots, each 12 rd. long and 10 rd. wide?

5. How many lots, 15 rd. by 7 rd., could be bought for $2800?

6. If lots are 9 rd. wide, how long should they be so that 22 lots should be worth $3960?

7. How wide must the lots be, so that 15, each 15 rd. long, may be worth $2700?

8. Interest for 6 mo. 10 da., at 6%, was $72.20; what would it have been for 3 mo. 24 da., at 8%?

9. A man bought 18 cows with his commission on $21600 sales, at $2\frac{1}{2}$%; how many could he buy with the commission on $44000 sales at $1\frac{1}{2}$%?

10. If 20 bu. of potatoes can be raised on a lot 20 yd. long and 20 yd. wide, how many bushels can be raised on another lot 10 rd. long and 10 rd. wide?

11. If a railroad carries 4500 pounds 1800 miles for $27, how far can 3000 pounds be carried for $11?

12. If 4000 books, of 384 pages each, require 200 reams of paper, how many similar books, of 324 pages each, can be printed from 216 reams of paper?

13. If 9 dogs catch 9 rabbits in 9 min., how many rabbits will 12 dogs catch in 12 min.?

14. If 10 cats catch 10 rats in 10 min., how many cats must be employed to catch 18 rats in 18 min.?

15. If a merchant's profits are \$7380 for 9 mo., when he is clearing 8% a year, what will be his gain for 7 mo., when he is clearing 10% a year?

16. If the 10 ct. loaf weigh 2 lb. 3 oz., when flour is \$9.75 per barrel, what should the 8 ct. loaf weigh, when flour is \$6.50 per barrel?

17. If carpets cost \$810 for a house of 12 rooms, each 15 by 18 feet, what will the same kind of carpet cost for a house of 10 rooms, each 12 by 15 feet?

18. What is the ratio of the glazing of two houses: the first contains 15 rooms, with four windows each; each window has 2 sashes; each sash, 6 panes, 11 by 16 in.; the second house has 11 rooms; each room, 3 windows; each window, 2 sashes; each sash, 2 panes, 15 by 32 in.?

19. A farmer sold his potatoes for \$147.84; the next year he planted a strip which was longer in the ratio of 5 to 4, but narrower in the ratio of 3 to 4; crops were more abundant in the ratio of 10 to 9, and prices were lower in the ratio of 7 to 8; what should he receive for his crop the second year?

20. A road 300 rd. long and 40 ft. wide, was dug 2 ft. 6 in. deep by 40 men in 5 days, of 10 hr. each; how many men must be employed to make a road 5 mi. long, 2 rd. wide, dug 3 ft. deep, in 16 days, of 11 hr. each?

21. If the freight of 20 hogsheads of sugar, each weighing 13 cwt. 20 lb., is \$44.88 for 65 miles, what should be the freight on 250 barrels of sugar, each weighing 2 cwt. 8 lb., for 66 mi.?

22. If a floor 33 ft. 9 in. by 26 ft. 8 in. cost \$22.50, what will be the cost of a floor 39 ft. 6 in. by 29 ft. 4 in.?

23. How many flag-stones, each 88 in. long and 20 in. wide, will be required to replace a pavement containing 8800 bricks, each 8 in. long and 4 in. wide?

24. If 5 men can dig a cellar 48 ft. long, 20 ft. wide, and 9 ft. deep, in 8 da., of 8 hr. each, how many men must be employed to dig a cellar 60 ft. long, 27 ft. wide, and 10 ft. deep, in 10 days, of 10 hr. each?

25. If an engine, running 18 mi. 240 rd. in 40 min., can carry a train from one station to the next in 2 hr. 27 min., how long would the same distance take a freight train moving 8 mi. 240 rd. in 1 hr. 40 min.?

26. If the interest of a certain sum for 3 yr. 6 mo., at 6%, is $266.70, what will be the interest of a sum $\frac{6}{5}$ as large, for 6 yr. 3 mo., at 10%?

27. A certain excavation costs $75. What would be the cost of an excavation 20% wider, 25% deeper, and 50% longer?

ARTICLE 226.—*Partnership.*

1. Two partners put in $7500 and $4500; they lose $1500; how should this loss be apportioned?

2. A's capital was $850; B's, $750. At the end of one year they have $2000; how should it be divided?

3. A contributes $90; B, $80; C, $130; they lose $210; what is the loss of each?

4. Divide 3948 into 2 parts, which shall be to each other as 3 to 4.

5. Divide 3948 into 2 parts, which shall be to each other as $\frac{1}{3}$ to $\frac{1}{4}$.

6. Divide 3948 into 3 parts, which shall be to each other as 3, 4, and 5.

7. Divide 3948 into 3 parts, which shall be to each other as $\frac{1}{3}$, $\frac{1}{4}$, and $\frac{1}{5}$.

8. Divide 19.56 into 2 parts, which shall be to each other as 7.9 and 8.4.

9. Divide 3.925 into 2 parts, which shall be to each other as 28 and $\frac{1}{28}$.

10. A has 60 A. 120 sq. rd.; B, 81 A. They join these for a pasture, for use of which they receive $75.60; how should this be divided?

11. A father left his three sons the following sums: $750, $675, and $375; but his property amounts to only $1440; how should this be divided?

12. A society of 55 musicians charter a car for $44, to carry them to Columbus. If they receive a second society of 33 to go with them, how should the expense be divided?

13. A's lot is 80 ft. front; B's, 75 ft.; C's, 100 ft.; D's, 55 ft.; and E's, 85 ft. How much should each contribute, to raise $50, to pay for watering the street?

Article 227.—*Bankruptcy.*

1. A bankrupt owes $46000; his property sells for $20470, and the expenses are $1150; how much will he pay on the dollar?

2. A bankrupt's assets are $16800, his liabilities are $55000, and the expenses of settlement are $2500; how much will he pay on the dollar?

3. A speculator fails, owing $250000; the assignee sells his real estate for $23000, and his personal property for $18000, and charges $3500 for fees and expenses; what will a creditor receive for a claim of $940?

Article 228.—*General Average.*

1. A ship is valued at $63000; and its cargo, at $32000; what will be the general average on a loss of $1140?

2. A shipped 300 barrels of flour; B, 240; and C, 100 barrels; 160 barrels were lost in a storm. How much of this loss will fall on each?

3. Goods valued at $800 were thrown overboard from a ship valued as $10000, with a cargo valued at $15600: how much will A lose, his shipment being valued at $800?

4. A ship is valued at $40000; and the cargo, at $35600. During a storm, A's shipment, valued at $1890, is washed overboard; how much will he receive for it?

ARTICLE 229.—*Partnership with Time.*

1. A invested $400 for 4 mo.; B, $600 for 6 mo.; how should they divide the $780 gained?

2. A and B were to receive $152.10 for removing a bank of earth. A furnished 10 carts 8 days; and B, 12 carts 6 days. How much should each receive?

3. A and B each put in $1000 at the beginning of the year, but at the end of 6 mo. A took out $500; they gained $2310 during the year. How should it be divided?

4. A put in $500 for 4 mo.; B, $600 for 3 mo.; C, $250 for 4 mo.; they lose $576. What will be the loss of each?

5. A and B were in partnership 4 mo. A had $2000 in the whole time; B put in $1000 at the beginning of each month; the gain was $414. How should it be divided?

6. A pastured 30 cows 7 mo.; B, 50 cows 9 mo.; the expense was $217.80; How should it be divided?

7. A commenced business with $3000; 6 months after, B joined him with $3600; 4 years from commencement, they had gained $4305. What was the share of each?

8. A and B were partners for 10 mo. A put in $700 at first, and two months afterward $200 more; B put in $500 at first, and three months afterward $500 more. A's loss was $215; what was B's loss?

ARTICLE 230.—*Equation of Payments.*

Find the average time in the following:

1. $600, due in 3 mo.; $400, in 5 mo.; and $500, due in 2 mo.

2. $750, in 3 mo.; $750, in 5 mo.; and $750, in 7 mo.

3. $30, in 8 mo.; $20, in 4 mo.; and $40, in 10 mo.

4. $60, due now; $60, in 3 mo.; and $60, in 9 mo.

5. $700, due now; $500, in 10 da.; and $700, in 20 da.

6. $60, due in 60 da.; $90, in 90 da.; and $60, due in 120 da.

7. $200, due in 4 da.; and $5000, due in 30 da.

8. $70, due in 7 da.; $80, due in 8 da.; and $90, in 9 da.

9. Bought goods as follows: May 7, $10; May 9, $15; May 20, $34. Find the equated time.

10. Bought $420 worth of goods: 1 seventh cash, 2 sevenths in 7 mo., balance in 14 mo. Find the equated time.

11. Bought the following bills: July 17, $300; Aug. 26, $700. Find the equated time.

12. Bought: April 13, $400; May 1, $550; May 7, $350; May 14, $700. Find the equated time.

13. Bought: Aug. 7, $300; Aug. 28, $900; Sept. 7, $900; Sept. 28, $300. Find the equated time.

14. Bought: March 5, $500; April 1, $400; April 14, $200; May 1, $600. Find the equated time.

15. $700 was due Jan. 1; $900, May 1; and $400, July 1. Find the equated time.

16. Bought goods as follows: May 19, 1884, at 6 mo., $1360; June 12, 1884, at 4 mo., $2168; July 25, 1884, at 6 mo., $988; Aug. 3, 1884, at 4 mo., $1650. Find the equated time.

Article 232.—*Average.*

Find the average of the following:

1. 15 lb. of sugar, at 9 ct. a lb.; and 10 lb., at 14 ct. a lb.

2. 10 oz. of gold, at \$18½ an oz.; and 20 oz. of silver, at 95 ct. an oz.

3. 15 lb. of honey, at \$.40 a lb.; and 10 lb. of sugar, at 5 ct. a lb.

4. 30 gal. of syrup, at \$2.22 a gal., diluted with 7 gal. of water.

5. 7 gal. of citrus juice, at \$2.40 a gal.; 2 qt. of corn syrup at 15 ct. a qt.; and 2 gal. of water.

6. A man walked 2 mi. in 20 min. 35 sec., and then 4½ mi. in 40 min. 30 sec.; find the average time for 1 mile.

7. The barometer, at 5 observations, stood 29.81 in., 29.87 in., 29.83 in., 29.91 in., and 29.93 in.; what was the average height?

8. In a regiment, 230 men averaged 5 ft. 4 in.; 280 averaged 5 ft. 8 in.; and 205 averaged 5 ft. 9 in. What was the average height?

9. A steamer went 13 mi. 160 rd. per hour, for 7 hr.; and then 12 mi. 30 rd. per hour, for 11 hr. What was the average speed?

10. 13 members of a council were present at 11 meetings, 2 at 12, 2 at 14, and 3 at 15; what was the average number of meetings attended by each of the 20 members?

11. What was the average number of members present at each of the 15 meetings?

12. In a dwelling, 3 floors are each 15 by 17 ft.; 3 are 14 by 18 ft.; and 3 are 19 by 24 ft. What is the average surface?

INVOLUTION.

Article 234.

Find the following:

1. Second power of 81.
2. Third power of 32.
3. Fourth power of 25.
4. Fifth power of 3.1.
5. Second power of 69.3.
6. Third power of 5.5.
7. Fourth power of $6\frac{1}{2}$.
8. Third power of $16\frac{1}{10}$.
9. Second power of $99\frac{1}{9}$.
10. Sixth power of $1\frac{1}{4}$.

Find the square of:

11. 309.
12. 54.03.
13. $60\frac{3}{5}$.
14. $\frac{10}{21}$.
15. $1\frac{10}{21}$.
16. $15\frac{1}{9}$.
17. $30\frac{1}{4}$.
18. $6\frac{1}{40}$.
19. $44\frac{1}{44}$.

Find the cube of:

20. 36.
21. 125.
22. 105.
23. $13\frac{1}{3}$.
24. 19.1.
25. 347.
26. $\frac{17}{35}$.
27. 10.4.
28. $10\frac{1}{4}$.

Find the fourth power of:

29. 91.
30. 6.2.
31. $10\frac{1}{2}$.
32. $33\frac{1}{3}$.
33. 8.4.
34. 28.
35. $\frac{13}{14}$.
36. $15\frac{1}{3}$.
37. $3\frac{3}{7}$.

Find the fifth power of:

38. 11.1.
39. $27\frac{3}{4}$.
40. 105.

Reduce the following:

41. 22^3.
42. 16.5^2.
43. $(17\frac{1}{3})^4$.
44. 19.1^3.
45. 11^4.
46. $(1\frac{1}{2})$

EVOLUTION.

ARTICLE 238.—*Square Root.*

Find the square root of:

1. 144.	**10.** 1.21.	**19.** $50\frac{1}{196}$.
2. 1444.	**11.** 15.21.	**20.** $\frac{3025}{3969}$.
3. 7744.	**12.** 10609.	**21.** $12\frac{1}{2}$.
4. 625.	**13.** 9409.	**22.** 1000.
5. 5625.	**14.** 576.	**23.** $5\frac{1}{5}$.
6. 15625.	**15.** 5476.	**24.** 16.1.
7. 30625.	**16.** $96\frac{1}{25}$.	**25.** 257.
8. 50625.	**17.** $215\frac{1}{9}$.	**26.** 25.7.
9. 180625.	**18.** $1235\frac{1}{49}$.	**27.** 12.09.

ARTICLE 239.—*Square Root by Factoring.*

Find, by factoring, the square root of:

1. 1225.	**4.** 11025.	**7.** 50×450.
2. 2304.	**5.** 5184.	**8.** 125×1125.
3. 4096.	**6.** 18225.	**9.** 125.44.

ARTICLE 240.—*Applications of Square Root.*

1. The base of a right-angled triangle is 60; perpendicular, 45; find the hypotenuse.

2. The hypotenuse is 41 ft.; the base, 40 ft.; find the perpendicular.

3. A ladder 53 ft. long reaches a window 45 ft. from the ground; how far is the foot of the ladder from the bottom of the wall?

4. A well is 63 ft. deep and 16 ft. wide; what is the length of the longest pole that can be placed entirely within the well?

5. A mast, 77 ft. high, stands in the middle of ship 72 ft. wide; how long is the rope ladder from the ship's side to the mast-head?

6. A tree, 72 ft. high, is broken 20 ft. from the ground; how far from the foot will the top reach?

7. A pole, 45 ft. high, stands in the center of a circular ring 56 ft. in diameter; what is the length of the rope from the top of the pole to the edge of the ring?

8. A rope, 73 ft. long, reaches from the edge of a ring to the top of a center pole 55 ft. high; how wide is the ring?

9. Base and perpendicular each 60 ft.; how long is the hypotenuse?

10. If the hands of a clock were 3 in. and 4 in. long, how far apart would the points be at 3 o'clock?

11. A boy is due south from his home 144 mi.; he travels due west 165 mi.; how far is he then from home?

12. A stream is 120 feet wide; how long must a bridge be, if it rises in the center 11 feet above its height at the end piers?

13. Hypotenuse, 80 ft.; base and perpendicular equal; find them.

14. A is 60 mi. north of B, and 70 mi. west of C; how far apart are B and C?

15. If Cleveland is 225 mi. further north than Cincinnati, and 120 mi. further east, how far apart are the two cities?

Article 241.

1. A square farm contains 360 A.; how long is it?

2. A field is 12 rd. square; what is the side of another square field containing 1 sq. rd. more than twice as much as the first?

3. A farmer has a field 87 rd. square, which he exchanged even with his neighbor for two square fields, one 63 rd. long; how long was the other?

4. How much more fence will be required for a field 80 rd. long and 20 rd. wide, than for a square field of equal area?

5. Find the side of a square field equal to 4 fields 5 rd., 12 rd., 84 rd., and 3612 rd. square.

6. There are 3 square fields: the first is 120 rd. sq.; the second contains $3\frac{1}{16}$; and the third, $5\frac{1}{16}$ as much land as the first. What is the difference in the length of the two latter fields?

Article 244.—*Cube Root.*

Find the cube root of:

1. 13824.
2. 79507.
3. 250047.
4. 405224.
5. 314432.
6. 59319.
7. 8615125.
8. 135005697.
9. 746142643.
10. 620650.477.
11. 282.300416.
12. .030664297.
13. 3.
14. 300.
15. .009663597.
16. .000002146689.
17. $\frac{64}{226981}$.
18. .4.
19. .04.
20. .004.
21. $592\frac{88}{125}$.
22. $\frac{5}{8}$.

Article 245.

1. What is the side of a cubical box which contains 7 cu. ft. 71 cu. in.?

2. What is the side of a cubical tank which contains 2744 cu. ft.?

3. How many cubical blocks, 3 in. long, can be cut from a cubical block 15 in. long?

4. How many cubical blocks, $\frac{1}{3}$ in. long, can be cut from a cubical block 15 in. long?

5. What is the side of a cube which weighs $12\frac{1}{2}\%$ as much as a cube 11 in. in diameter?

6. What is the side of a cube which contains 2 cu. ft.?

MENSURATION.

ARTICLE 247.—*Areas of Parallelograms.*

Find the surface of:

1. A pavement, 20 yd. long and 6 ft. 9 in. wide.
2. A meadow, $\frac{3}{4}$ mi. long and 40 rd. wide.
3. A floor, 18 ft. 9 in. long and 13 ft. 4 in. wide.
4. A canal, 45 mi. long and 30 ft. 3 in. wide.
5. A park, 990 ft. by 440 ft.
6. A pasture, 20 ch. by 16 ch.
7. A wall, 8 ft. high and 30 yd. long.
8. A canvas, 5.4 m. by 7.5 m.
9. A roof, each side being 16 ft. 6 in. by 40 ft.
10. A street, 2 mi. 240 rd. long and 66 ft. wide.

11. How many bricks, 4 in. by 8 in., will be required for a pavement 40 ft. by 8 ft.?

12. How many acres in a field 120 rd. square?

13. How many yards of carpet, $\frac{3}{4}$ yd. wide, will be required for a floor 15 by 18 ft.?

14. A floor, 16 ft. long, requires 24 sq. yd. of carpet; how wide is the floor?

15. A man has a lot 54 yd. long and 24 yd. wide, which he exchanged for a square lot of equal surface; how much more fence would the first lot require than the last?

ARTICLE 248.—*Area of Trapezoid.*

1. A sky-light is 20 ft. long, and the two ends are 17 ft. and 10 ft. wide; what is the surface?

2. Find the surface of a field in the form of a trapezoid, the parallel sides being 73 rd. and 35 rd., and lying 32 rd. apart.

3. A lot is bounded by four streets: two of these are parallel, and measure 70 ft. and 90 ft. along the lot, and are 135 ft. apart; what is the surface of the lot?

ARTICLE 249.—*Area of Triangles.*

Find the area of:

1. A triangle, 40 ft. long and 20 ft. high.

2. A triangle, 96 yd. long and 55 ft. high.

3. A triangle, 10 ft. 8 in. long and 6 ft. 9 in. high.

Find the area of a right-angled triangle:

4. The base, 80 ft.; perpendicular, 60 ft.

5. The base, 60 ft.; perpendicular, 80 ft.

6. The base, 88 rd.; perpendicular, 25 rd.

Find the area of the following triangles:

7. The sides are 51 yd., 68 yd., and 85 yd.

8. The sides are 51 yd., 52 yd., and 53 yd.

9. The sides are 52 rd., 56 rd., and 60 rd.

ARTICLE 250.—*Area of Trapezia.*

1. Find the area of a trapezium, one diagonal being 120 rd., and the perpendiculars to the diagonal from the opposite angles being 45 rd. and 55 rd.

2. Diagonal measures 70 ft., and the two perpendiculars on the diagonal, 30 ft. and 40 ft.; find the area of the trapezium.

3. A man has a four-sided lot: the line between two opposite corners is 132 ft. long, and the other corners are 88 ft. and 110 ft. perpendicularly distant from that line; find the area.

4. Diagonal, 100 rd.; perpendiculars on it from opposite corners, 50 rd. and 70 rd.; find the value of the trapezium, at $960 per acre.

ARTICLE 251.—*Diameter and Circumference of a Circle.*

1. Diameter, 20 ft.; find the circumference.

2. Circumference, 20 ft.; find the diameter.

3. Radius, 26 ft.; find the circumference.

4. The diameter of a circular plat is 90 feet; what is the length of the fence around it?

5. What is the thickness of a tree, if it measures 4 ft. 8 in. around?

6. What is the distance across a circular field, if it is 170 rd. around it?

7. What is the distance around a circular field, if it is 170 rd. across it?

8. What length of tyre would be required for the wheels of a wagon, the front ones being 5 ft. 4 in. in diameter, and the hind ones 5 ft. 11 in. in diameter?

ARTICLE 252.—*Area of a Circle.*

Find the area of:

1. A circle whose radius is 25 ft.

2. A circle whose diameter is 20 ft. 10 in.

3. A circle whose diameter is $3\frac{1}{2}$ in.

4. A man lays out a lawn with a rope 60 ft. long, fastened to a stake at the center; how much land in the lawn?

5. What is the diameter of a circle that is equal to a square whose side is 30 ft.?

6. What is the side of a square that is equal to a circle whose diameter is 30 ft.?

7. A lot, 120 feet in diameter, has a gravel walk 20 feet wide just within its circumference; what is the surface of the grass plat inside the gravel walk?

8. A lot, 18 rd. in diameter, has around its center a grass plat 12 rd. in diameter; what is the area of the paved ring covering the rest of the lot?

MENSURATION OF SOLIDS.

ARTICLE 254.—*Surface of Prism or Cylinder.*

1. Find the surface of a right prism 16 ft. high, standing on a triangular base whose sides are 6 ft., 8 ft., and 10 ft.

2. Find the surface of a rectangular prism 4 ft. high, standing on a base 2 ft. square.

3. Find the surface of a rectangular prism 2 ft. high, standing on a base 4 ft. square.

4. Find the entire surface of a cylinder 10 ft. high and 15 in. in diameter.

5. Find the convex surface of a cylinder 13 in. high, with a radius of 2 in.

6. Find the entire surface of a cylinder 13 ft. 2 in. high, and 6 ft. 6.54 in. in circumference.

ARTICLE 255.—*Volume of Prism or Cylinder.*

1. How many cu. in. in a prism 10 in. high, on a base 2 in. square?

2. How many cu. in. in a prism 2 in. high, on a base 10 in. square?

3. Find the volume of a flag-stone 10 ft. long, 3 ft. 9 in. wide, and 8 in. thick.

4. A sill is 40 ft. long and 9 in. wide; how thick must it be to contain 25 cu. ft.?

5. Find the volume of a cylinder 20 in. high, whose circumference is 39.27 in.

6. A cylinder 10 in. in diameter contains $1963\frac{1}{2}$ cu. in.; what is its height?

Article 256.—*Surface of Pyramid or Cone.*

1. Find the convex surface of a right pyramid, the base being 18 in. square, and the slant height 4 ft.

2. Find the convex surface of a cone, the radius of the base being 6 in., and the slant height 8 in.

3. Find the entire surface of a cone, the diameter of the base being 20 in., and the slant height 40 in.

4. Find the entire surface of a cone, the diameter of the base being 40 in., and the slant height 20 in.

Article 257.—*Volume of Pyramid or Cone.*

1. Find the volume of a pyramid 48 ft. high, on a base 18 in. square.

2. The height of a pyramid is 8 ft., and the base is a triangle whose sides are 6, 8, and 10 in.; find the volume.

3. Find the volume of a cone whose altitude is 20 ft., and the diameter of the base 4 ft.

4. Find the volume of a cone, the altitude being 12 ft., and the radius of the base being 3 ft. 4 in.

5. The altitude of a cone is 2 ft., and the circumference of the base is 2 ft.; find the volume.

ARTICLE 258.—*Surface of a Sphere.*

Find the surface of:

1. A sphere whose diameter is 22 in.

2. A sphere whose radius is 4 ft.

3. A planet whose diameter is 2465 mi., supposing it to be a sphere.

4. If a base ball is $2\frac{7}{8}$ in. in diameter, how much leather will be required to cover 1600 balls, adding 10% for waste?

ARTICLE 259.—*Volume of a Sphere.*

Find the volume of:

1. A sphere 8 ft. 2 in. in diameter.

2. A globe whose radius is 20 in.

3. A planet whose diameter is 2240 miles, supposing it to be a sphere.

4. Find the weight of 500 cannon-balls, each 2 ft. in diameter, a cubic foot of iron weighing 430 lb.

ARTICLE 260.—*Applications of Mensuration.*

1. What will it cost to sod a yard 40 ft. by 32 ft., at 11 ct. a sq. yd.?

2. A room is 18 ft. long, 15 ft. wide, and 10 ft. high: what will the plastering cost, at 5 ct. a sq. yd., deducting 1 opening, 6 ft. square; 2 openings, 3 ft. 6 in. by 8 ft.; and 3 openings, 4 ft. by 7 ft. 6 in.?

3. What will it cost to paint both sides of a fence 78 ft. long and 5 ft. 6 in. high, at 14 ct. a sq. yd.?

4. A fish pond, 80 ft. in diameter, is surrounded by a tight fence 5 ft. $10\frac{1}{2}$ in. high; what will it cost to paint that fence, at 15 ct. a sq. yd.?

5. A museum room is 70 ft. long, 40 ft. wide, and 22 ft. high; what will it cost to paint the walls and ceiling at 29 ct. a sq. yd., deducting 1 sky-light, 14 ft. sq.; 4 doors, 5 ft. 3 in. by 10 ft.; and 12 windows, 6 by 9 ft.?

6. What will it cost to plaster a concert hall 100 ft. long, 70 ft. wide, and 26 ft. high, at $22\frac{1}{2}$ ct. a sq. yd.; deducting 8 openings, 8 by 12 ft., and 3 openings, 7 by 14 ft.?

Article 261.—*Board Measure.*

1. How many feet in an inch board 20 ft. long and 9 in. wide?

2. How many feet in a 3 in. plank 16 ft. long and 14 in. wide?

3. How many feet in a sill 30 ft. long, 10 in. wide, and 5 in. deep?

4. One sixth of the thickness being lost in sawing, how many feet of 2 in. plank can be made from a stick 2 ft. square and 20 ft. long?

5. One third of the thickness being lost in sawing, how many feet of $\frac{1}{2}$ in. boards can be made from a stick 2 ft. square and 14 ft. long. (All boards less than 1 in. thick are counted and measured as if 1 in. in thickness.)

6. How many feet in a plank 2 in. thick, which is 18 ft. long, 16 in. wide at one end, and 10 in. wide at the other end?

Article 262.—*Masons' and Bricklayers' Work.*

1. How many perches in a pile of stone 450 ft. long, 440 ft. wide, and 4 ft. high?

2. A cellar is 9 ft. deep, 39 ft. long, and 24 ft. wide inside: if the walls are 18 in. thick, how many perches of stone will they require?

3. A cellar is 10 ft. deep, 48 ft. long, and 19 ft. wide, measuring the outside; the walls are 2 ft. thick; what will the stone cost, at \$4.12½ a perch?

4. A pile of stone is in the form of a cone, 45 ft. in diameter at the bottom, and 17 ft. high; what is it worth, at \$1.75 a perch?

5. How many bricks in a wall 160 ft. long, 7 ft. high, and 2 ft. thick, allowing 20 bricks to 1 cu. ft.?

6. The bricks in a wall are 9 in. by 4 in., and 2¼ in. thick; what will they cost, at \$7.50 per 1000, the wall being 72 ft. long, 12 ft. 6 in. high, and 2 ft. 6 in. thick?

Article 263.—*Measurement by Bushels or Gallons.*

1. How many bushels in a bin 16 ft. long, 10 ft. 6 in. high, and 4 ft. 4 in. wide?

2. How many bushels in a crib 15 ft. square and 8 ft. high?

3. A pit is 10 ft. square and 28 in. deep; how many bushels of potatoes will it hold?

4. How many bushels of lime can be made in a kiln in the form of a cone, 14 ft. high, the diameter of the base being 11 ft. 8 in.?

5. How many bushels of barley can be put in a cylindrical tub 16 ft. in diameter and 4 ft. deep?

6. How many gallons are equal in volume to 55 bu.?

7. How many bushels are equal in volume to 1536 gal.?

8. How many gallons in a tank 7 ft. in diameter and 11 ft. deep?

9. How many barrels (31½ gal. each) in a reservoir 63 ft. square and 5 ft. 6 in. deep?

10. A cistern is made 8 ft. 4 in. in diameter and 11 ft. deep; what will it cost, at 80 ct. a barrel?

PROGRESSIONS.

ARTICLE 265.—*Arithmetical Progression. Case I.*

1. The first term is 770; the common difference, 10; what would be the 20th term of an increasing series?

2. The first term is 770; the common difference, 10; what would be the 20th term of a decreasing series?

3. A new house rents for $900 per year; if the rent is reduced $30 each year, what will be the rent the 15th year?

4. The houses on an avenue are numbered regularly, beginning with 720; what will be the number of the 63d house?

5. If lots, 20 ft. wide, are numbered in regular order along a line, how far will the 36th lot be from the starting point?

6. What is the 100th term of a decreasing series, the 1st term being .004, and the common difference .000004?

ARTICLE 266.—*Case II.*

1. The extremes are 7 and 70; the number of terms, 10; find the common difference.

2. The 1st term is 18; the 8th term, 900; find the common difference.

3. The extremes are 1 and 1000; the number of terms, 28; find the common difference.

4. If boys are paid according to their ages, and a boy 13 years old earns $3.70 a week, while a boy 19 years old earns $7.30 a week, how much is the increase for each year?

5. The 1st term is 721; the 12th term, 127; find the common difference.

ARTICLE 267.—*Case III.*

1. The extremes are 4 and 80; the number of terms 20; find the sum of the series.

2. A man earned $370 the first year, and his salary was regularly increased, so that in the 9th year he received $1130; what were his total earnings in 9 yr.?

3. The extremes are 6 and 100, and the number of terms 10; find the sum of the series.

4. Extremes, 10 and 100; number of terms, 6; what is the sum of the series?

5. The 1st term is 450; common difference, 7; what is the sum of 10 terms of an increasing series?

6. The 1st term is 450; common difference, 7; what is the sum of 10 terms of a decreasing series?

7. The 15th term of an increasing series is 972; the common difference, 9; what is the sum of the 15 terms?

8. The 1st term is 11; the 8th term, 67; what is the sum of the series, there being 12 terms?

ARTICLE 269.—*Geometrical Progression. Case I.*

1. The 1st term of an increasing geometric series is 5; the ratio, 3; what is the fourth term?

2. The 1st term of an increasing geometric series is 3; the ratio, 5; find the fourth term.

3. The 1st term of a decreasing geometric series is 6; the ratio, 2; find the fifth term.

4. The 1st term of a decreasing geometric series is 2; the ratio, 6; what is the fifth term?

5. What is the 8th term of an increasing geometric series, the first term being 40, and the ratio 3?

ARTICLE 270.—*Case II.*

1. Find the sum of 10 terms of the series whose first term is 6, and ratio 2, the series being increasing.

2. Find the sum of 8 terms of the geometric series 3, 6, etc.

3. Find the sum of 8 terms of the geometric series 6, 2, etc.

4. Find the sum of the infinite decreasing series, of which the first term is $\frac{3}{4}$, and ratio $\frac{4}{3}$.

5. Find the sum of the infinite geometric series 3, 2, etc.

6. Find the sum of the infinite geometric series, whose first term is .148, and ratio 1000.

MISCELLANEOUS EXAMPLES.

1. Reduce $\frac{245632}{399152}$ to its lowest terms.

2. What is $27\frac{1}{2}\%$ of $\frac{8}{9}$?

3. What is the value of the ratio, $2\frac{1}{2}$ pk. : 4 bu.?

4. What is the interest of $745.20 for 2 yr. 7 mo. 6 da., at 5%?

5. What cost 6 bu. 6 qt. of cherries, at 60 ct. a peck?

6. What is the equated time of the following: $750, in 34 da.; $800, in 40 da.; and $950 in 50 da.?

7. An agent sent the owner $804.20 for rent of house 28 months, retaining 5% commission and $47 expenses; what was the monthly rent?

8. How much would be received for 24 bu. 3 pk. of peaches, packed in baskets containing 2 pk. 6 qt. each, and sold at $1.70 per basket?

9. What will be the proceeds of a note of $475, dated May 29, 1860, at 90 da., and discounted in bank July 1, at $4\frac{1}{2}\%$?

10. What will be the cost of a pile of wood 8.5 m. long, 6.8 m. wide, and 3.2 m. high, at 19 fr. per stere?

11. What cost 420 boards 16 ft. long, 9 in. wide, and 1 in. thick, at $3\frac{1}{2}$ ct. per ft.?

12. If $5\frac{1}{2}$ yd. cost $\$42\frac{1}{3}$, what will $8\frac{1}{4}$ yd. cost?

13. What cost 7707 lb. of wheat, at $1.20 per bu.?

14. Find the convex surface of a cone whose slant height is 16 ft., and base 12 in. in diameter.

15. What is the present worth of a debt of $320, due in 7 yr., money being worth 4%?

16. A has 275 bu. wheat; B, 405 bu. corn; C, 205 bu. oats; what would be the contents of the largest basket with which each one could exactly measure his grain?

17. A cistern is 4 ft. in diameter, and 3 ft. deep; what will it cost to line it with sheet lead weighing 5 lb. to the square foot, and costing 13 ct. per lb.?

18. What would be the amount of $333.33, at interest 3 yr. 3 mo. 3 da., at $3\frac{1}{3}$%?

19. What cost 7381 lb. of hay, at $17.50 per ton?

20. I invested $16170 in bonds, at 5% premium, and sold at 8% premium; find my gain.

21. In 14 meters, how many yards?

22. What principal, in 2 yr. 8 mo., at $7\frac{1}{2}$%, will earn $69.68 interest?

23. At 7 ct. a yd., what will a strip of canvas cost, extending along the four fences of a lot 42 rd. square?

24. Invested $23100 in bonds, at 5% premium, and sold at 5% advance; find my gain.

25. A invested $5400 for 7 mo.; B, $5600 for 9 mo.; they gained $546. Divide it.

26. Find the cost of a lot 100 rd. sq., at $100 per A.

27. Reduce $\frac{4}{15}$, $\frac{4\frac{1}{2}}{6}$, $\frac{3\frac{1}{3}}{5}$ to fractions having the least common denominator.

28. A debt of $420 will be due in 5 yr.; what should be the discount for cash, if money is worth 4%?

29. The first term of an increasing arithmetical progression is 735; the common difference, $4\frac{1}{2}$; find the 119th term.

30. Find the value of a cubical pile of wood 14 ft. long, at $2.40 a cord.

31. A vat is 11 ft. long, 7 ft. wide, and 9 in. deep; what is its capacity in gallons?

32. In $2\frac{1}{2}$ Ha. how many acres?

33. A man bought stock at 22% discount, and sold it at 4% premium; what % did he gain?

34. If 8 drivers receive $16.20 for 9 trips, of 1 hr. 30 min. each, how much should 12 drivers receive for 10 trips, of 2 hr. each?

35. 18 is what % of $33\frac{1}{3}$?

36. Reduce 11111111 sq. in. to A.

37. What is the square root of 5313025?

38. A fly-wheel is 10 ft. in diameter; what distance does a point in the circumference move in 16 revolutions?

39. After 22% of my flock died, I had 273 remaining; how many died?

40. How many bushels in a box 3 ft. long, 28 in. wide, and 16 in. deep?

41. How many minutes in the first four months of the year 1888?

42. Find the area of a triangle whose base is 4 rd., and height 4 yd.

43. What cost 1040 pwt. of silver, worth $91\frac{2}{3}$ ct. per oz.?

44. If a sidewalk, 1 mi. 120 ft. long, cost $487.60, what will one 90 rd. long cost?

45. A note for $940, dated Jan. 23, payable in 3 months, was discounted in bank March 20, at 5%; what was the discount?

46. What cost 56 three-inch planks, 30 ft. long and 12 in. wide, at 2 ct. per foot?

47. What is the least quantity of iron that would make an exact number of 25 lb. balls, or 30 lb. plates, or 35 lb. bars, without remainder in either case?

48. What debt, due in 6 years, is now worth $375, money being worth 5%?

49. What % would be lost by buying an article 20% above its value, and selling it 10% below its value?

50. In 50 kilograms how many pounds?

51. What would be the compound interest of $300 for 4 yr., at 6%?

52. How many bushels of cranberries can be bought for $39.90, at 10 ct. 5 m. a pt.?

53. A foundry building and patterns are valued at $18000; what would be the premium for insuring $\frac{3}{4}$ of this value, at $1\frac{1}{2}$%?

54. Find the side of a cubical box that will hold as much as another box 80 in. long, 75 in. wide, and 1 yd. high (inside measures).

55. What cost 49.3 meters of broadcloth, at 17 francs per meter?

56. A steamer is worth $105000, and a man sells $\frac{3}{4}$ of his interest for $14700; what part of the ship did he own?

57. A man gained 5% the first year, and 8% the second year, at the end of which he was worth $15876; what capital had he at first?

58. How many hours per day must 42 men work, for 8 da., to do as much as 56 men can do in 6 da., of 9 hr. each?

59. A debt having run 4 yr. 6 mo., at 8%, the interest was $44.10; what was the amount?

60. What cost 7000 qt. bags of salt, at 36 ct. a bu.?

61. At $16\frac{2}{3}$ ct. per doz., how many lemons can I buy for $50?

62. How many bushels will a bin hold, if it costs $189 more to fill it with wheat, at $1.05 a bu., than with corn, at 60 ct. a bu.?

63. What is the equated time of the following purchases: June 25, $470; July 3, $720; Aug. 1, $860?

64. Find the entire surface of a cone, the slant height being 20 in., and the diameter of the base 10 in.

65. Reduce $\frac{17}{18}, \frac{14}{15}, \frac{2\frac{1}{4}}{3\frac{1}{8}}, \frac{7}{10}$ to least common denominator.

66. A bottle of milk contains 1 pt. 3 gi.; how many dozen bottles can be filled from a tierce containing 42 gal. of milk?

67. A note is given May 15, 1885, for $500, with interest at 6%, payable annually; no interest having been paid, what is due May 15, 1890?

68. If I sell $\frac{8}{9}$ of an article for what $\frac{9}{10}$ of it cost, what % do I gain or lose?

69. A square field containing $2\frac{1}{2}$ A. is enclosed by a close fence 6 ft. high; what did the fence cost, at 2 ct. per sq. ft.?

70. In 40 yd., how many meters?

71. What is the fifth term of the increasing geometrical progression, whose first term is 7, and ratio 3?

72. Add all the odd numbers below 25, and find the square root of the sum.

73. What cost 7 T. 14 cwt. 67 lb. of Muscovado sugar, at $4\frac{3}{4}$ ct. per lb.?

74. An agent kept $560 commission on sales, and sent his principal $15440; what was his rate % commission?

75. Find the weight of 8 doz. boxes of fruit, each weighing 15.4 Kg.

76. What must I mark cloth that cost $8 a yard, so that I can deduct 20% and still gain 20%?

77. What cost a sight draft on New Orleans for $2370, at $\frac{1}{10}$% discount?

78. I bought vinegar at $1.25 per gal.; $33\frac{1}{3}$% leaked out; at what rate per gal. must I sell the remainder to gain $33\frac{1}{3}$%?

79. What cost 10000 feet of canvas cloth, at $18\frac{3}{5}$ ct. per yd.?

80. A contributed \$7500; B, \$5700; they gain \$3872; how should they divide it?

81. A sum of money was borrowed May 22, 1884, at 4%, and \$661.38 was paid in full Jan. 5, 1890; how much of this was interest?

82. Reduce $\frac{1554}{4107}$ to its lowest terms.

83. What will be the cost of a sight draft on Philadelphia for \$1700, at $\frac{1}{8}$% premium?

84. How many times will a wagon wheel, 18 ft. 4 in. in circumference, revolve in going 4 miles?

85. How much will the ground cost on which a man can raise 728 bu. of potatoes, if each bu. requires $1\frac{1}{2}$ sq. rd., and land costs \$7.50 per A.?

86. Invested \$7840 in bonds, at 2% discount, and sold at 4% advance; find my gain.

87. How many perches in a wall 55 yd. long, 15 ft. high, and 3 ft. 3 in. thick?

88. What is the largest measure that could be used to measure out 81 gal., 120 gal., and 150 gal.?

89. A horse is fastened by a rope, 60 ft. long, to a stake in the center of a field; over what space can he graze?

90. The first term of a decreasing arithmetical progression is 873; the common difference, $2\frac{1}{3}$; find the 200th term.

91. How many cords in a pile of wood 56 ft. 3 in. long, 53 ft. 4 in. wide, and 5 ft. 4 in. high?

92. Find the hypotenuse of a right-angled triangle, the other sides being 90 and 56.

93. What is the solidity of a globe whose diameter is 12 in.?

94. What will it cost to plaster a wall for blackboard use, it being 11 ft. 3 in. by 5 ft. 4 in., the price being 50 ct. per sq. yd.?

95. What is $\frac{5}{6}\%$ of $\frac{5}{6}$?

96. If 27 oxen require 33 A. 120 sq. rd. of pasture, how much will 13 oxen require?

97. At $1\frac{3}{8}\%$ premium, what must be paid for insuring $\frac{2}{3}$ of the value of a house worth $7200?

98. Bought stock at 12% discount, and sold at 9% advance; what % did I gain?

99. At $1.94 a cu. ft., what must be paid for a granite block 28 in. long, 27 in. wide, and 32 in. high?

100. An agent bought cotton for a manufacturer, charging $\frac{1}{2}\%$ commission; the total bill was $17487; what was the agent's commission?

101. Find the value of the stamps required for 75 boxes of pencils, containing 100 each, the taxes being $3 per thousand.

102. Reduce .50625 to a common fraction.

103. What sum at interest 3 yr. 6 mo. 20 da., at $6\frac{1}{4}\%$, will amount to $532.40?

104. What cost 41 gal. 1 gi. of vanilla, at $5 per gal.?

105. Invested $7840 in bonds, at 2% discount, and sold them at 4% decline; find my loss.

106. What will it cost to plaster a room 18 ft. long, 15 ft. wide, and 12 ft. high, at 18 ct. per sq. yd., deducting 2 openings, each 4 ft. by 8 ft.; and 2 others, each $3\frac{1}{2}$ ft. by $8\frac{1}{2}$ ft.?

107. What will be the cost of a sight draft on Chicago for $847.30, at $\frac{1}{4}\%$ premium?

108. What would be the largest baskets in which either 350 bu. 1 pk. of peaches, or 250 bu. 2 pk. of plums could be packed without leaving any remainder in either case?

109. Find the convex surface of a cylinder 20 in. in diameter and 40 in. long.

110. In 50 gallons how many liters?

111. In what time time will any principal double itself at $3\frac{1}{5}\%$?

112. Find the surface of a sphere, the diameter being 14 in.

113. What cost 125 T. 7 cwt. 9 lb. of coal, at $4.50 per T.?

114. What is the diameter of a circle containing 3 A.?

115. A man realizes $1800 per annum on $24000; what is his rate of gain?

116. How many medals, each weighing 3.3 Dg., can be made from 2442 Kg. of silver?

117. What is the difference between the square of 625 and the square root of 625?

118. How many acres in a square field enclosed with 6 miles of fence?

119. What cost 1000000 in. of twine, at 4 m. per rd.?

120. A note dated Aug. 21, at 90 da., was discounted in bank Oct. 29, at 7%, and $2612.75 given for it; find the face of the note.

121. A co-operative company has 15000 shares, of $50 each; A holds 73 shares; what will be his assessment for a loss of $7920 by fire?

122. Received $51.51 interest on a loan of $367.20, at 5%; how long had it been loaned?

123. Reduce $\frac{18225}{50625}$ to its lowest terms.

124. If a stream flows 3 mi. 20 rd. in 1 hr. 4 min., how far will it flow in 3 hr. 44 min.?

125. How many perches in a breakwater 800 yd. long, 11 yd. high, and 5 yd. thick?

126. What must be paid for a fence around a lot 60 rd. square, the fence being made of four horizontal strips, each 9 in. wide, and costing $1\frac{1}{4}$ ct. per sq. ft.?

127. What is the ratio of 7.36 to $7\frac{2}{3}$?

128. $5\frac{3}{5} + 4\frac{5}{6} + 7\frac{7}{8} + 3\frac{5}{12} = ?$

129. Imported 50 casks of cologne, 45 gal. each, invoiced at 10 fr. per gal. ($1 = 5.18 fr.) Find the duty, at $2 per gal. and 50% ad valorem.

130. What must be paid for 5 sills, each 40 ft. long, 8 in. wide, and 9 in. high, at 60 ct. a cu. ft.?

131. What will it cost to fresco the ceiling of a room 36 ft. long and 22 ft. 3 in. wide, at 50 ct. per sq. yd.?

132. $6\frac{1}{4}$ is what % of 1000?

133. Find the volume of a sphere whose diameter is 44 in.

134. What is the compound interest of $500, for 4 yr., at 8%?

135. What is the least number of books that would make an exact number of either scores or gross?

136. If a man walks $4\frac{1}{2}$ miles in 1 hr., how far can he walk in 5120 sec.?

137. A debt, due in 5 years, was discounted at 7%, $420 being taken off; what was the face of the note?

138. How much grain must I take to mill, to have 154 bushels after the miller has taken out his toll of 4 qt. to the bu.?

139. Find the base of a right-angled triangle, the hypotenuse being 117, and the perpendicular 45.

140. A bill of exchange on London for £86 8 s., cost $420.12; what was the rate of exchange?

141. A man sold 520 sheep, and had 35% of the flock remaining; how many had he at first?

142. If 4 men, in 6 da., dig a cellar 45 ft. long, 16 ft. wide, and 9 ft. deep, how many men will be required to dig a cellar 75 ft. long, 18 ft. wide, and 12 ft. deep, in 3 days?

143. Reduce 50000 minutes to weeks.

144. A's money is 65% more than B's, and together they have $54325; how much has each?

145. \$552.96 was loaned July 21, 1810, at $4\frac{1}{6}\%$, and \$666.56 was paid on settlement; find the date of settlement.

146. What is the diameter of a circle containing 785 A. 64 sq. rd.?

147. How deep must a box be made, to hold 90 bu., if it is 7 ft. long and 6 ft. wide?

148. If 35 castings weigh 48 T. 4 cwt. 25 lb., what is the weight of each?

149. Consequent, $22\frac{3}{4}$; ratio, $1\frac{6}{7}$; find antecedent.

150. 24% of my land is in corn, leaving 266 A. otherwise planted; how much is cultivated?

151. What cost an abutment 66 ft. long, $22\frac{1}{2}$ ft. high, and 4 ft. thick, at \$2.25 a perch?

152. Money loaned at $4\frac{1}{2}\%$, and \$709.20 paid, of which \$69.20 was interest; how long was it loaned?

153. What cost 475 gal. 3 qt. 1 pt. of molasses, at 18 ct. a qt.?

154. If 800 men, in 30 da., can build a pier 240 ft. long, 8 ft. thick, and 12 ft. high, how long must 240 men be employed to build a pier 360 ft. long, 10 ft. thick, and 8 ft. high?

155. What would be the equated time of paying the following bills: May 5, \$230, at 6 mo.; June 1, \$250, at 4 mo.; July 5, \$320, at 5 mo.; Aug. 1, \$420, at 3 mo.

156. Bought lemons 5% below quotations, sold them at 10% above quotations, and gained \$24 on 40 boxes; what was the price per box?

157. A has 350 eggs; B, 525; C, 280; they have boxes made, in which each can exactly pack his eggs; if the boxes are the largest possible, how many eggs will each hold?

158. What cost a farm 180 meters square, at 7000 fr. per Ha.?

159. What cost a sight draft on Charleston for \$950, at $\frac{1}{2}\%$ discount?

160. What cost 4 cwt. 59 lb. 7 oz. of beef, at 13 ct. a lb.?

161. Find the solidity of a sphere whose radius is 11 in.

162. The time past noon is $\frac{1}{15}$ of the time to midnight; what is the time?

163. A man had 450 A. of land, and sold 162 A.; what % of his farm has he still?

164. What will it cost to pave a circular court 80 ft. in diameter, at 55 ct. a sq. yd.?

165. The last term of a decreasing arithmetical progression of 19 terms is 999; common difference, 7; find the sum of the terms.

166. Reduce $\frac{19}{32}$ bu. to integers.

167. A debt was paid 8 yr. before due, and \$420 deducted, at 7% discount; how much was the debt?

168. What cost 4355 gal. 1 pt. 2 gi. of ink, at 70 ct. per gal.?

169. A note dated May 19, at 90 da., was discounted June 15, at 4%, and \$2.31 deducted; what was the face of the note?

170. I invested \$7840 in bonds, at 2% discount, and sold them at 4% premium; find my gain.

171. At 16 fr. per meter, how many kilometers of cloth can be bought for 100000 fr.?

172. Divide $\frac{4}{15}$ of $\frac{3\frac{3}{7}}{2\frac{2}{3}}$ by $\frac{3}{10}$ of $\frac{2\frac{2}{3}}{1\frac{4}{5}}$.

173. What date 4 mo. 20 da. after Dec. 11, 1885?

174. If a man can walk 3 mi. 240 rd. in 1 hr. 12 min., how far can he walk in 2 hr. 48 min.?

175. A note is given June 10, 1870, for \$480, with interest at 5%, payable semi-annually; interest having been paid for two years, what is due Aug. 25, 1876?

176. An agent bought wool at 37 ct. per lb.; commission, $\frac{3}{4}\%$; expenses, \$97.20; the total cost to the principal, \$8000.03; how many pounds were bought?

177. $3\frac{3}{5} + 13\frac{3}{4} + 23\frac{5}{6} - 33\frac{2}{3} = ?$

178. At what rate must \$450 be loaned for 2 yr. 2 mo. 20 da., to amount to \$540?

179. How many panes of glass, 10 in. by 16 in., are in a half-box containing 50 sq. ft.?

180. The base and perpendicular of a right-angled triangle are each 58; find the hypotenuse.

181. A man lost 14% of his weight by sickness, and then weighed 129 lb.; how much had he lost?

182. A rectangle 15 ft. wide contains 10 sq. rd.; how long is it?

183. The longitude of one place is 20° 10′ E.; of another, 70° 20′ W. When it is 1 o'clock P. M. at the former place, what is the time at the latter?

184. The stamps on letters are 2 cents for every half-ounce or fraction thereof; what will stamps cost for 730 letters, each weighing $1\frac{1}{5}$ oz.?

185. A box is 8 dm. high and 62.5 cm. wide; how long must it be to contain 1 m^3?

186. A invests \$5000 Jan. 1, and draws out \$1000 May 1; B invests \$4000 Jan. 1, and puts in \$1000 more May 1; July 1, they dissolve, having gained \$1350; how should the gain be divided?

187. What cost 4 T. 9 cwt. of cheese, at 12 ct. 4 m. per lb.?

188. A mill is valued at \$28000; the stock, \$36000; what would be the cost of insuring $\frac{3}{5}$ of the value of the mill at $1\frac{1}{2}\%$, and $\frac{3}{4}$ of the value of the stock at $1\frac{1}{4}\%$?

189. A note \$4800, dated June 23, 1846, payable in 90 da., was discounted at 6%, and \$23.20 was taken off; when was it discounted?

190. What cost a 30-day draft on New York for $2517, exchange being $\frac{1}{8}\%$ premium?

191. A note given June 7, 1888, for $600, with 9% interest, was endorsed as follows: Dec. 5, 1888, $25; July 20, 1889, $95.45; May 7, 1890, $20; June 20, 1890, $139.60. What was due May 7, 1892?

192. What will it cost to paper the walls of a room 20 ft. long, 14 ft. wide, and 12 ft. high, at 22 ct. per sq. yd., no allowance being made for openings?

193. How long will it take a man to walk 990000 in., if he can walk a mile in 16 min.?

194. What sum at compound interest for 2 yr., at 6%, will amount to $842.70?

195. What cost 450 boards, 12 in. long, 3 in. wide, and $\frac{1}{2}$ in. thick, at 4 ct. per ft.? (Count all boards thinner than 1 in. the same as if 1 in. thick.)

196. 28% of the pupils enrolled in a school withdrew, and 1224 remained; how many withdrew?

197. A note of $5040, dated May 23, 1856, payable in 60 da., was discounted at 5%, the proceeds being $5013.40; when was it discounted?

198. Reduce $\frac{17\frac{1}{7}}{250}$ to a decimal.

199. The antecedent is 10 hr. 40 min.; the ratio, $5\frac{1}{3}$; find the consequent.

200. A lot is 80 rd. sq., and worth $560; what would it be worth, if a strip 4 rd. wide is taken off all around the outside?

201. What cost a 60-day draft on San Francisco for $3913.25; exchange, $\frac{1}{2}\%$ premium, reckoning money at 6%?

202. A coin is 2 centimeters in diameter; how far would 800 such coins extend if laid in a straight line?

203. $500 was borrowed Jan. 1, at 6%, and $100 was paid on the first day of each of the next four months. What was due July 1?

204. What must be paid for insuring a hotel building and furniture: the house, valued at $130000; and furniture, at $74000; both insured at $\frac{3}{5}$% on three fourths of the valuation?

205. A ship's chronometer is set to Greenwich time; in what longitude will the ship be when the chronometer is 9 hr. 10 min. fast?

206. A sum at interest for 3 yr. 5 mo. 18 da., amounted to $95.80, of which $20.80 was interest; find the rate %.

207. What would be the equated time of the following purchases: July 1, $140; July 8, $150; July 15, $160; July 22, $170; July 29, $180; and Aug. 5, $190?

208. How many octavo books, of 240 pages each, can be printed on 100 reams of paper?

209. If a dairy furnishes 2631 gal. 1 qt. of milk in 3 wk. 4 da., how much would that be for 4 wk. 3 da.?

210. Bought 60 $100 bonds at 5% discount, and sold at 5% profit; find my gain.

211. 5 C. 23 cu. ft. is what fraction of 34 cu. yd.?

212. A field is 40 rd. square; what is the distance between opposite corners?

213. A put into the firm $7500, for 11 mo.; B, $6600 for 10 mo.; on closing business, they had $12615; how much would each lose?

214. A pillar, 8 ft. 3 in square, cost $519.75, at $3.15 a perch; how high was it?

215. The assessment for paving a street being $2.0592 per foot, what must A pay, whose lot extends along that street 3 rd. 5 ft. 8.03 in.?

216. A debt of $900 is due in 2 yr. 6 mon.; the discount for paying now is $150; what rate % is that?

217. Find the surface of a sphere whose radius is 13 inches.

218. Reduce $\frac{51821}{80087}$ to its lowest terms.

219. Find the solidity of a prism 20 ft. high, standing on a base 4 ft. 6 in. square.

220. Bought stock at 6% discount, and sold it at 5% gain; at what rate did I sell it?

221. What date is 3 mo. 22 da. before June 22, 1873?

222. What sum, at compound interest for 3 years, at 5%, will amount to $926.10?

223. A field 60 rd. long contains 15 A.; what would the fence cost, at 30 ct. a rod?

224. How many coins, weighing 5 g. each, can be made from 1 quintal of bronze?

225. $31.50 was deducted from a note having 3 yr. 9 mo. to run, leaving the present worth $140; what was the rate %?

226. How much would be realized from a lot 10 rd. long and 7 rd. wide, sold for graves, the graves being 7 ft. long and 2 ft. 6 in. wide, and costing $4.50?

227. What cost a bill of exchange on London for £138 15 s., exchange at $4.84?

228. Find the total surface of a cylinder 30 in. in diameter and 50 in. long.

229. A bankrupt owes A $500, and B $360, and pays A $77 more than B; how much does he pay each?

230. A horse is fastened to a fence by a rope 90 ft. long; over what space can he graze?

231. Reduce .065625 to a common fraction.

232. The list price is 96 ct. per gross, with 20, 25, and $37\frac{1}{2}$% off; what is the cost per gross?

233. A fruit seller found that whether he counted his pine-apples by 4's, 5's, 6's, or 8's, there was no remainder; what was the least number he could have had?

234. \$480 was loaned for 5 yr. 15 da., and \$108.90 was received for interest; what was the rate %?

235. What sum would be received for 2 ℥ 2 ℈ of medicine, made in 5 gr. pills, sold 20 in a box, at 25 ct. per box?

236. An agent affects an exchange of a house, at \$4600, for a farm, the owner of the house receiving \$1100 difference; what is the agent's commission on the two pieces of property, at $\frac{3}{4}$%?

237. A lot lies between two parallel roads $\frac{1}{2}$ mi. apart; it is 90 rd. on one road and 75 rd. on the other; what is the lot worth, at \$80 an acre?

238. 44% of the workmen were discharged, and 98 remain; how many were employed at first?

239. What is the square root of 40?

240. The hypotenuse is 74 ft., and the base and perpendicular are equal; how long is the base?

241. How many lots, 50 meters long and 10 meters wide, can be made from 50 Ha. of land?

242. A crib is 18 ft. long and 4 ft. high; how wide must it be to contain 540 bu.?

243. Bought 125 bonds (\$100 each) at $2\frac{1}{2}$% discount, and sold them at $6\frac{1}{4}$% premium; what was the gain?

244. A man bought 40 sheep the first year, and each succeeding year 3 more than the year before; how many did he buy in 6 years?

245. A note of \$5760, dated Oct. 19, payable in 60 da., was discounted Nov. 10, and \$29.52 deducted; find the rate.

246. A note is given Aug. 13, 1890, for \$730, with interest at 9%, payable annually; no interest having been paid after the first year, what was due Dec. 6, 1893?

247. Reduce $\frac{397}{560}$ to a decimal.

248. The list price is \$1.50 per gross, with 20 and 25 off; what is the cost per gross?

249. A draft on Dublin for £7 3 s. 4 d. cost $34.83; what was the rate of exchange?

250. Find the diameter of a sphere whose solidity is 7238.2464 cu. in.

251. A put in $850; B, $680; A's gain is $150 more than B's; what did each gain?

252. $560 was loaned Feb. 18, 1889, at 9%, and amounted to $770; when was it paid?

253. A man sent an agent 4010 barrels of pork to sell, and invest proceeds in wheat, commission $\frac{1}{4}$% in each case; pork sold at $8.80 per bbl., and wheat cost $1.33 per bu.; how many bu. were bought?

254. One city is in E. longitude 40° 17′; another, in W. longitude 30°, 13′; if a man travels from the first to the second, should his watch gain or lose time, and how much?

255. Bought bonds at 2% discount, and sold at $1\frac{1}{2}$% premium, and gained $94.50; what was the par value?

256. 150 castings weigh 17 T. 11 cwt.; find the weight of each.

257. The tax levy is 7.38 m. on the dollar; what tax must be paid on $107524?

258. What is the cube root of the square of 4096?

259. What is the area of a square field, in which a circular track containing 1256.64 A. can be made?

260. What debt, due in 3 mo., together with $800, due in 9 mo., could be paid in 7 mo. without loss to either?

261. A man insures his life for $16000 in favor of his wife; premium, $29.47 per $1000; if he dies during the seventh year thereafter, how much will his widow receive in excess of the amount paid out?

262. A put in $7000 for 6 mo.; B put in $5000, and received $\frac{5}{11}$ of the profit; how long was his money invested?

263. What is the cube of .043?

264. Divide $\frac{5}{16}$ of $\frac{4\frac{2}{3}}{7\frac{1}{5}}$ by $\frac{7}{8}$ of $\frac{6\frac{1}{4}}{10\frac{4}{5}}$.

265. A note is given Aug. 18, 1884, for $840, with 8% interest, endorsed as follows: May 9, 1885, $30.50; Dec. 15, 1885, $238.54; June 3, 1887, $137.44. What was due Oct. 20, 1888?

266. A cistern is 20 ft. in diameter and 14 ft. deep; how many barrels ($31\frac{1}{2}$ gal.) will it hold?

267. Find the diameter of a sphere whose surface is 7854 sq. in.

268. The first and fourth terms of a proportion are 38 and 152, and the second and third terms are equal to each other; find them.

269. A note is given Oct. 31, 1883, payable in 4 mo.; when is it legally due?

270. The sides of a triangle are 102, 104, and 106 ft.; find the area.

271. 31 gal. 2 qt. is what decimal part of 65 gal. 2 qt. 1 pt.?

272. What principal, loaned Nov. 18, 1880, at $4\frac{1}{2}$%, will gain $37.52 interest on settlement Aug. 28, 1888?

273. Find the volume of a column 30 ft. high, standing on a triangular base, whose sides are 3, 4, and 5 ft.

274. $13\frac{3}{4} - 4\frac{7}{9} + 15\frac{5}{8} - 7\frac{5}{6} = ?$

275. What will be the cost of a wall 440 ft. long, 30 ft. high, and 3 ft. thick, at $3.30 per perch, if a wall 450 ft. long, 33 ft. high, and 4 ft. thick, cost $9000, at $3.75 per perch?

276. At what rate % of discount will a debt of $413, due in 4 yr. 6 mo., be now worth $350?

277. A field is 40 rd. by 100 rd.; what would be the area of a square field that could be enclosed with the same length of fence?

278. Bought stock at 16% discount, and sold at 9% discount; what % did I gain?

279. The two parallel ends of a lot measure 15 rd. and 15 yd., and are 500 ft. apart; find the area.

280. If 48 pencils cost $1, how many can be sold for $1 at a gain of 20%?

281. What cost a draft on Bordeaux for 4827.3 fr., exchange at 5.18 fr.?

282. Find a number whose square is contained 162 times in 20000.

283. The slant height of a conical hill is 440 ft., and the circumference of its base $\frac{1}{2}$ mi.; how much land on its sides?

284. Reduce $\frac{8\frac{8}{9}}{10}, \frac{7}{5\frac{1}{4}}, \frac{9\frac{1}{3}}{14}$ and $\frac{7}{12}$ to the least common denominator.

285. Find the volume of a cylindrical log, 15 in. in diameter and 40 ft. long.

286. If each of the four sides of a square field were 20% longer, how much greater would be the surface of the field?

287. What is the square of that number of which 16 is the cube root?

288. A and B were in partnership; A's capital was $8400, and he received $720 out of $1500 profit; what was B's capital?

289. If a field of 15 A. 100 sq. rd. requires 18 bu. 3 pk. of seed, how much seed would be needed for 18 A. 120 sq. rd.?

290. What sum must I pay for a house, so that after spending $50 for repairs I can gain 5% by selling for $4830?

291. What is the value of the compound ratio: $2\frac{1}{2}$ bu.: 3 pk. 15 men : 25 men. 27 da. : 6 da.

292. What date is 5 mo. 27 da. before May 27, 1885?

293. How large a draft on London can be bought for $5000, exchange at $4.87?

294. A note was dated Feb. 13, 1866, and had accumulated $21.84 on settlement, Sept. 19, 1867; what was the amount then due?

295. A could plow a field in 7 da., working 8 hr. per da.; B, in 14 da., working 6 hr. per da.; how long would it require both, working 9 hr. per da.?

296. $5000 was borrowed July 1, at 5%; paid July 28, $1000; Sept. 10, $800; Oct. 9, $850. What was due Nov. 6?

297. A tank is 21 in. sq.; how deep must it be to contain 21 gal.?

298. After losing $2600, A and B dissolve partnership, A receiving $25200; B, $11200; how much had each at first?

299. Bought bonds at 4% premium, and sold at a decline of $1\frac{1}{2}$%; what % did I lose?

300. A put in $7000 for 6 mo.; B put in $5000, and received $\frac{5}{11}$ of the profit; how long was B's money invested?

301. A ring, 100 ft. in diameter, was made in a square field 100 ft. long; how much land was left in the four corners?

302. A man has goods costing him $11200, and gained 5% by selling them through an agent, whose commission was 2%; what did the agent receive as commission?

303. If 10 horses can haul 50000 lb. 2 mi. in 4 hr., how many horses will be required to haul 70000 lb. 5 mi. in 5 hr.?

304. A debt was contracted Jan. 19, 1888, with 9% interest; debt, $375. On settlement, $141 interest was paid; find the date of settlement.

305. What is the side of a square which is equal to a right-angled triangle whose base is 30 ft. and hypotenuse 78 ft.?

306. Reduce $\frac{59085}{133926}$ to its lowest terms.

307. What is the cube of that number of which 53 is the square root?

308. A malt tub is 18 ft. in diameter and 6 ft. deep; how many gallons will it contain?

309. A note at 60 days was discounted July 13, at 8%, and $18.36 was deducted for bank discount, and $2411.64 paid the holder; what was the date of the note?

310. A pile of stone is 22 ft. long and 18 ft. wide; how high must it be to contain 96 perches?

311. Take the cubes of all the even numbers under 20; add them, and extract the square root of half the sum.

312. The tax levy being 23.64 m. on the dollar, what tax must a man pay, whose property is assessed at $43246?

313. $512 was loaned at $7\frac{1}{2}$%, and $228.80 interest was due April 7, 1886; when was the money loaned?

314. The fence was removed from a square field containing 40 A.; what would be the area of a field 20 rd. wide, which the same fence would exactly inclose?

315. A debt of $732 is now worth $600, reckoning money at 8%; how long before it is due?

316. If 15 men earn $427.50 in 19 da., of 10 hr. each, how many days, of 8 hr. each, must 38 men be employed to earn $592.80?

317. The list price is 40 ct., with $\frac{1}{3}$ and 10 off; what is the cost?

318. An agent bought, for a capitalist, ground 400 ft. along a street, charging 2% commission, and drawing on his principal for $18360 in full; what was the price per front foot?

319. A bin is 6 ft. wide and 4 ft. 8 in. high; how long must it be to contain 240 bu.?

320. A note of $600, with interest at 6%, was dated Nov. 13, 1870, and endorsed as follows: July 10, 1871, $100; May 7, 1872, $100; April 4, 1873, $100. What was due May 1, 1874?

321. I sold two farms, at $1920 each; on the first I gained 20%, and on the second lost 20%; what % did I gain or lose on the two?

322. A man saved $124 the first year, and each succeeding year $11 more than the year before; how much did he save in 20 yr.?

323. $323\frac{5}{8} - 138\frac{3}{5} + 217\frac{3}{4} - 401\frac{5}{6} = ?$

324. What % does a dealer gain who buys 450 bu. apples, at 60 ct. a bu., and sells them at 24 ct. a pk., if $\frac{1}{4}$ are lost by spoiling?

325. The list price was 72 ct. per gross, with 20, 25, and $16\frac{2}{3}$ off; find the cost per gross.

326. I paid $75.60 for insuring $\frac{2}{3}$ of the value of my factory, at $\frac{7}{8}$%; what was the factory worth?

327. A square field contains 160 A.; what would be the area of a circular field with the same length of fences?

328. When it is 6 hr. 3 min. A. M. at a place in 100° E. long., what is the time at a place in 40° W. long.?

329. Find the radius of a sphere whose surface is 380.1336 sq. in.

330. Find the cube root of the sum of the cubes of 27, 36, and 45.

331. At $1\frac{1}{2}$ ct. a sq. ft., what will lumber cost for a platform 200 ft. long, 70 ft. wide at one end, and tapering to 40 ft. at the other end?

332. Money loaned Dec. 24, 1882, at $3\frac{1}{2}$%, amounted to $600.99, June 6, 1887; how much of this was interest?

333. An arithmetical progression has 10 terms; the third term is 29, and the seventh 73; find the sum of the terms.

334. The sides of a triangle are $25\frac{1}{2}$, 26, and $26\frac{1}{2}$ in.; what is the surface?

335. A log is 20 in. in diameter; how long must it be to contain 1 C. of wood?

336. A man marks his goods at 20% above cost; in selling at wholesale he takes off 10 and 5%; what is his gain %, at wholesale?

337. If a man walks 6 kilometers in an hour, how far is that in 15 sec.?

338. By selling at 64 ct. a yd., twice as much is gained as by selling at 57 ct.; what % would be gained, at 70 ct. a yd.?

339. How large a draft on Berlin can be bought for $500, when exchange is $.965 for 4 reichsmarks?

340. A note, due June 6, 1879, was discounted at 4%, the discount being $69.60, and the present worth $480; when was it discounted?

341. What number, added 3 times to $287\frac{5}{12}$, will make the sum $352\frac{1}{4}$?

342. $700 was borrowed May 19, at 7%. There were paid: June 2, $75; June 20, $100; July 15, $90; Aug. 7, $120; what was due Sept. 7?

343. 500 bolts, each containing 8 meters of ribbon, cost 560 fr.; how much would 375 dm. cost at the same rate?

344. A note of $1600, dated Sept. 17, 1888, at 50 da., was discounted in bank Sept. 25, 1888, and $15 deducted; what rate % was that?

345. Bought bonds at 4% discount, and sold at a profit of $12\frac{1}{2}$%; at what premium were they sold?

346. What % is gained by selling $\frac{5}{9}$ of any purchase for what $\frac{4}{5}$ of it cost?

347. Divide 31 lb. 1 oz. 10 pwt. by 120.

348. A note is given Dec. 12, 1879, for $1000, with interest at 6%, endorsed as follows: June 19, 1881, $41.17; Dec. 6, 1881, $177.83; Aug. 21, 1882, $138.25; May 12, 1883, $30.17. What was due Oct. 15, 1884?

349. Bought goods at 20 and 10 off, and sold them at 10 and 10 off; what % did I gain?

350. If a field 50 rd. long and 30 rd. wide produces 27 bu. of wheat, what will a field 75 rd. long and 60 rd. wide produce in another year when crops are greater in the proportion of 7 : 6?

351. Reduce $\frac{6\frac{2}{5}}{6\frac{6}{7}}$, $\frac{3\frac{3}{5}}{3\frac{3}{11}}$, $\frac{7}{8}$, and $\frac{9}{14}$ to the least common denominator.

352. In 10 T. how many metric tons?

353. Goods were sold at $\frac{1}{4}$ and 10 off; the cost was 30 ct. per gross; what was the list price per gross?

354. What sum, at compound interest for 2 yr. 6 mo., at 10%, will amount to $431.97?

355. A bill of exchange on Bordeaux for 8600 fr. cost $1694.20; what was the rate of exchange?

356. Two men exchanged 60-day notes, and immediately discounted them in bank; the first, at 6%, receiving $2572.70; the second, at 5%; what did he receive?

357. What is the difference between annual and compound interest of $10000 for 3 yr., at 10%?

358. A pole 40 ft. high stands in the center of a circular pond, whose area is 314.16 sq. yd.; what is the length of a line from the top of the pole to the edge of the pond?

359. The discount, at 6%, on a debt due in 3 yr., is $20.16; what would be the discount on it 16 mo. before due, at 9%?

360. The square of a certain number is 2209; what is the fourth power of the same number?

361. Bought at 40 and 5 off, and sold at 40 off the same list; what % did I gain?

362. Reduce $\frac{13\frac{1}{8}}{25\frac{1}{5}}$ to a decimal.

363. Find the surface of a sphere whose solidity is 11494.0672 cu. in.

364. Three men bought a horse for $150, and sold him for $210, by which A gained $30, and B $18; what had each paid for the horse?

365. What is the difference between simple and annual interest of $100, due in 10 yr., with 10%?

366. Complete the proportion of which the first, third, and fourth terms are $5\frac{5}{7}$, $16\frac{3}{8}$, and $8\frac{3}{4}$.

367. How many ft., board measure, in a plank 20 ft. long, 3 in. thick, 18 in. wide at one end and 16 in. wide at the other end?

368. What is the equated time of paying the following bills: Aug. 5, $290, at 3 mo.; Sept. 7, $410, at 30 da.; Sept. 29, $500 cash; Oct. 4, $600, at 60 da.?

369. A cubical block contains 3 cu. ft. 648 cu. in.; what will it cost to gild 5 sides, at 84 ct. a sq. ft.?

370. A prism stands on a triangular base, whose sides are 9, 12, and 15 ft. long; how high must it be to contain 80 cu. yd.?

371. How many ars in a lot 450 m. long and 49 dm. wide?

372. A man made a 60-day note, which he discounted in bank at 8%, and received $19261.51; it being due, for what sum must he give a 90-day note to redeem it, bank now discounting at 9%?

373. A debt of $660, with 5% interest, amounted to $807.40, May 20, 1873; when was the debt contracted?

374. Goods were listed at 40 ct. per gross, and sold at $\frac{1}{4}$, 20 and 5% off; what did 150 gross cost?

375. A man took out a life insurance policy for $6000, the rate being $32.65; how much will he pay in premiums in 30 years, if he lives that time?

376. What will be the length of a cubical box containing 512 liters?

377. If 6 men, in 5 mo., have $450 by saving 30% of their wages, how much will 9 men save in 4 mo., if wages have been raised 20%, and they save 40% of their wages?

378. A railroad, with 280000 $100 shares, wishes to make an extension costing $198000; what will be assessed on a man holding 1197 shares?

379. Find the volume of a cone, the altitude being 40 in., and the diameter of the base 18 in.

380. A debt of $806 was paid July 25, 1886, less $156, deducted for discount, at 5% ; when was the debt due?

381. Reduce .013824 to a common fraction.

382. A note was given Dec. 10, 1885, for $700, with interest at 8%, payable semi-annually, and interest was paid for 18 months: what was due May 2, 1892?

383. A horse is fastened by a rope, 120 ft. long, to a post in the corner of a square field; over what space can he graze?

384. At $4\frac{1}{2}$ ct. per ft., how many boards 16 ft. long, 5 in. wide, and $1\frac{1}{2}$ in. thick, can be bought for $17.10?

385. The longitude of Cincinnati is 84° 20′ W.; at what place on the earth's surface is it 1 hr. 4 min. P. M., when it is half past 6, A. M., at Cincinnati?

386. A note is given May 1, 1880, for $720, with 5% interest, and endorsed as follows: May 1, 1881, $30; Nov. 1, 1881, $20; July 1, 1882, $148. On settlement, $640 was due; what was the date of settlement?

387. Bought bonds at 4% premium, and sold at a loss of $12\frac{1}{2}$% ; at what discount did I sell?

388. A dealer imported 24 cases German toys, at 250 marks per case, commission 2%; find duty at 35%, exchange being 95 ct. 2 m. for 4 marks.

389. In a four-sided lot the line between two opposite corners measures 66 yd., and the other two corners are distant from that line 50 yd. and 60 yd.; what is the area of the lot?

390. How much iodine, at 1.3 fr. per Hg., can be bought for 2210 fr.?

391. A ladder 65 ft. long rests against a house, with its foot 16 ft. from the house: if the foot is drawn out 17 ft. further from the house, how far will the top of the ladder slide down the wall?

392. A debt, contracted June 30, 1882, amounted, when paid, to $467.50, of which $55 was interest, at 6%; when was the debt paid?

393. Goods were bought at $\frac{1}{3}$, 20, and 10 off, and sold at $\frac{1}{4}$, 15 and 5 off; what % was gained?

394. A put in $9000 for 6 mo.; B, $10000 for 5 mo.; at settlement, A had $9270; how much had B?

395. What is the sixth term of the geometrical progression 9, 12, 16, etc.?

396. What cost 55 metric tons of sal soda, at .15 fr. per kilogram?

397. A man has a note dated Aug. 25, at 90 da., which he wishes to have discounted Oct. 10, and finds that he will receive $9.40 more if discounted at 5% than if discounted at 6%; what was the face of the note?

398. A merchant, in selling at wholesale, takes off 5% from his retail prices, and gains 14%; what is his retail profit?

399. What sum at 6%, payable annually, would amount to $935.20 in 5 years, if no interest is paid before that time?

400. Find the volume of a sphere whose surface is 31416 sq. mi.

401. Two men were employed 3 days to lay a stable floor, 70 ft. long, 30 ft. wide, and 3 in. thick; wages, $2.25 per day; lumber, $23 per thousand ft.; what was the total cost?

402. If a man can fence a lot 100 rd. in diameter in 4 days, how long will he be employed to fence a lot 200 rd. in diameter?

403. If a man can plant a lot 100 rd. in diameter in 4 days, how long will he require to plant a lot 200 rd. in diameter?

ANSWERS.

Article 19.—**1.** 2019. **2.** 3625. **3.** 3289. **4.** 3479. **5.** 3213. **6.** 4117. **7.** 29595. **8.** 31980. **9.** 33960. **10.** 39372. **11.** 47467. **12.** 408028. **13.** 292002. **14.** 489641. **15.** 500081. **16.** 485558. **17.** 4009575. **18.** 4066552. **19.** 4125789. **20.** 4246920. **21.** 4929077. **22.** 4571993. **23.** 4627806. **24.** 3894072. **25.** 59682383. **26.** 63954128. **27.** 76129904. **28.** 59356529. **29.** 44609196. **30.** 33485205. **31.** 22253849. **32.** 39479884. **33.** 33537. **34.** 367958. **35.** 318042. **36.** 258677. **37.** 277670. **38.** 304267. **39.** 343207. **40.** 345280. **41.** 237957. **42.** 341390. **43.** 1045358. **44.** 3840490. **45.** 2077898. **46.** 64138. **47.** 44467. **48.** 72527. **49.** 27803. **50.** 27810. **51.** 334834. **52.** 2126906. **53.** $50421. **54.** 13602. **55.** 1325 pounds. **56.** 108410. **57.** 1642. **58.** 80 feet. **59.** 745. **60.** 4790 pounds. **61.** 2847 bu. **62.** $10215. **63.** 1492. **64.** 60698 ft. **65.** 1797. **66.** 1314 ct. **67.** 399 ct. **68.** $34961. **69.** 1926. **70.** 1185 tons. **71.** 584870. **72.** 2000 miles. **73.** 594. **74.** 2690 pounds. **75.** $907. **76.** 1300 acres. **77.** $422. **78.** $9404. **79.** 540.

Article 26.—**1.** 1734. **2.** 46913. **3.** 29293. **4.** 80808. **5.** 2982314. **6.** 22222212. **7.** 33333323. **8.** 34202862. **9.** 26411091. **10.** 171089. **11.** 55000085. **12.** 199998989. **13.** 367889276. **14.** 900090828. **15.** 10921812. **16.** 87242906. **17.** 8999082. **18.** 3067534217. **19.** 89640055. **20.** 800028087. **21.** 80727. **22.** 2939607. **23.** 2286722. **24.** 15928384. **25.** 228170591. **26.** 10052418. **27.** 289226824. **28.** 1010094950.

29. 864197532. **30.** 3760326. **31.** 58990502765. **32.** 25630264. **33.** 194398963. **34.** 7855426. **35.** 191833945. **36.** 28775. **37.** 4567813. **38.** 4994505. **39.** 6276511. **40.** 87845. **41.** 31199027. **42.** 1160889. **43.** 7914100. **44.** 439999099616. **45.** 32731990913. **46.** $3032. **47.** $2469. **48.** $747. **49.** 273 acres. **50.** 67 years. **51.** 1789. **52.** $1445. **53.** $26716. **54.** $37028. **55.** 2361 feet. **56.** 2964. **57.** $1557. **58.** $8750. **59.** 179. **60.** 51 years. **61.** $9242. **62.** 668. **63.** 816. **64.** 9811. **65.** 37196748. **66.** 1738. **67.** 675. **68.** 582. **69.** 1625. **70.** 1830. **71.** 5839. **72.** 897. **73.** 1405. **74.** $523. **75.** 447 acres. **76.** 1003. **77.** 9566. **78.** 49018. **79.** $1687. **80.** 4200 pounds. **81.** $20218. **82.** $21950. **83.** $2414. **84.** $3200. **85.** $20879. **86.** $16590.

Article 31.—1. 1630. **2.** 4404. **3.** 3213. **4.** 3088. **5.** 3582. **6.** 2712. **7.** 45424. **8.** 68376. **9.** 38390. **10.** 80874. **11.** 40922. **12.** 55736. **13.** 2350257. **14.** 4239396. **15.** 4617896. **16.** 2868922. **17.** 2346330. **18.** 3661820. **19.** 6251157. **20.** 5647474. **21.** 6391920. **22.** 4082406. **23.** 2373460. **24.** 5570264. **25.** 3741367872. **26.** 2016536123. **27.** 6020532702. **28.** 7716935028. **29.** 9336976580. **30.** 6766294344. **31.** 4120819551. **32.** 5367983103. **33.** 7838070273. **34.** 6601. **35.** 10846. **36.** 9384. **37.** 15810. **38.** 9650. **39.** 12272. **40.** 33285. **41.** 21132. **42.** 35446. **43.** 262668. **44.** 182031. **45.** 278855. **46.** 181482. **47.** 528126. **48.** 352674. **49.** 543567. **50.** 224284. **51.** 76242. **52.** 31602. **53.** 291984. **54.** 243004. **55.** 445842. **56.** 766476. **57.** 223244. **58.** 665042. **59.** 374808. **60.** 892248. **61.** 3093120. **62.** 3589662. **63.** 3446546. **64.** 3856152. **65.** 3228646. **66.** 5769525. **67.** 18076200. **68.** 3378012. **69.** 1943212675. **70.** 3399899130. **71.** 3544904538. **72.** 41343239335. **73.** 7853233038. **74.** 27708855662. **75.** 9279625278. **76.** $6975. **77.** $6975. **78.** 16464 yd. **79.** 1215136 ct. **80.** 247101 lb. **81.** 241920 ems. **82.** 655960 lb. **83.** $98945. **84.** 214727 links. **85.** 120955 lb. **86.** 5695 men. **87.** $46494. **88.** 112683264 gal. **89.** 95091975 mi. **90.** 92512 lb. **91.** $404499. **92.** 45824 trees. **93.** 2108295 yd. **94.** 133152 lb. **95.** 7218882 vols. **96.** 205592 men.

Article 32.—**1.** 2985192. **2.** 8035104. **3.** 26710607. **4.** 194553198. **5.** 64065096. **6.** 18757728. **7.** 170321895. **8.** 604085568. **9.** 230351550. **10.** 26907755. **11.** 19039104. **12.** 72785952. **13.** 30948864. **14.** 52287552. **15.** 24088504. **16.** 73180665. **17.** 33273456. **18.** 70882476. **19.** 43096405. **20.** 52202416.

Article 33.—**1.** 28734000. **2.** 4986500. **3.** 6200945000. **4.** 3845030000. **5.** 46835700. **6.** 40050008000. **7.** 4007089300000. **8.** 37088900000. **9.** 268938450000. **10.** 3477926700. **11.** 4859602300000. **12.** 76540063000.

Article 34.—**1.** 26550. **2.** 3454360. **3.** 438570000. **4.** 1578960000. **5.** 3745950000. **6.** 38467552000. **7.** 3581783200000. **8.** 256576320000. **9.** 254356320. **10.** 23387136000. **11.** 56762721600000. **12.** 127264680000. **13.** 26980167900000. **14.** 4141190060. **15.** 551374704000. **16.** 70740913000. **17.** 13815594000000. **18.** 32213776000000. **19.** 131065010400. **20.** 128610595000.

Article 41.—**1.** 15226312. **2.** 8643753. **3.** 1428570380. **4.** 161401387. **5.** 49114887. **6.** 246913077. **7.** 164608718. **8.** 12345679. **9.** 37037037. **10.** 7008946. **11.** 10580037. **12.** 19146923. **13.** 90455625. **14.** 97393690. **15.** 1410934745. **16.** 69360054. **17.** 2000558288. **18.** 505279134. **19.** 86420132. **20.** 94909300. **21.** 4365777. **22.** 146090535. **23.** 98229774. **24.** 15432016. **25.** 70072815. **26.** 793651200. **27.** 68685608. **28.** 102863457. **29.** 333667334. **30.** 58007569. **31.** 934598. **32.** 920072. **33.** 8896037. **34.** 3208901. **35.** 7583366. **36.** 11201960. **37.** 7855064. **38.** 2600209. **39.** 5900470. **40.** $742. **41.** 1274. **42.** 415. **43.** 1204205. **44.** $162. **45.** 570 hr. **46.** 504. **47.** 575. **48.** 72. **49.** 349 lb. **50.** 429 miles. **51.** 128 weeks. **52.** 694. **53.** $2402. **54.** 2499. **55.** 273. **56.** 1296. **57.** $1028480. **58.** 15702. **59.** 2668.

Article 42.—**1.** 2738. **2.** 4386. **3.** 4623. **4.** 5387. **5.** 9876. **6.** 3875. **7.** 4639. **8.** 9375. **9.** 3896. **10.** 7199. **11.** 50731. **12.** 79308. **13.** 40065. **14.** 40508. **15.** 89490. **16.** 30972. **17.** 92312. **18.** 69234. **19.** 37401. **20.** 38495. **21.** 70193. **22.** 2038904. **23.** 50783. **24.** $30700\frac{11}{611}$. **25.** 68040. **26.** 38905. **27.** $133136\frac{32}{338}$. **28.** 19909. **29.** 40893. **30.** 60907. **31.** 38729. **32.** 70625. **33.** 4075008. **34.** $121440187\frac{7882}{8251}$. **35.** $67872653\frac{2232}{3456}$. **36.** $75690587\frac{1171}{4567}$. **37.** $80448947\frac{1934}{5678}$. **38.** 395. **39.** 156. **40.** 501. **41.** $305. **42.** 65. **43.** 285 days. **44.** 49 miles. **45.** 154 years. **46.** 78 miles. **47.** 3003. **48.** 1674 bu. **49.** 9208 lb. **50.** 7934. **51.** 1925. **52.** 107 min. **53.** 189 yd.

Article 43.—**1.** $188\frac{12}{24}$. **2.** 12649. **3.** $11641\frac{6}{32}$. **4.** $60813\frac{10}{45}$. **5.** $98508\frac{8}{48}$. **6.** 20864. **7.** $496796\frac{9}{27}$. **8.** $133643\frac{11}{28}$. **9.** 1514097. **10.** 1894074. **11.** $264550\frac{11}{42}$. **12.** $56811\frac{42}{63}$.

Article 44.—**1.** $47389\frac{256}{1000}$. **2.** $3678540\frac{1}{100}$. **3.** $2700000\frac{8746}{10000}$. **4.** $12345678\frac{92}{100}$. **5.** $3704605\frac{504}{1000}$. **6.** $98979\frac{69594}{100000}$. **7.** $1300270\frac{5}{100}$. **8.** $123843\frac{658}{1000}$. **9.** $44872\frac{362592}{1000000}$. **10.** $500070\frac{40}{10000}$. **11.** $3726483952\frac{7}{10}$. **12.** 430000. **13.** $12345654\frac{321}{1000}$. **14.** $754000\frac{400}{10000000000}$. **15.** $4763859\frac{2143}{10000}$.

Article 45.—**1.** $11823\frac{36}{40}$. **2.** $889842\frac{133}{140}$. **3.** $7098\frac{5324}{8000}$. **4.** $1809855\frac{882}{1900}$. **5.** $560300\frac{58}{470}$. **6.** $182344\frac{2062}{4050}$. **7.** $365137\frac{7713}{8800}$. **8.** $101604\frac{2967}{3400}$. **9.** $7153\frac{101384}{107000}$. **10.** 1282840750. **11.** $1415\frac{19500}{706700}$. **12.** $4092783\frac{49000}{97000}$. **13.** $18614\frac{1067467}{3050600}$. **14.** $10990\frac{19899}{90990}$.

Article 49.—**1.** $3296. **2.** 146640 ct. **3.** $13950. **4.** 359 A. **5.** 108419. **6.** 35 cows. **7.** 145 mules. **8.** 3088. **9.** 336735 ct. **10.** $1672. **11.** $308. **12.** $35. **13.** 2184. **14.** 51 men. **15.** 15 pounds. **16.** $7600. **17.** $16988. **18.** $10360. **19.** 69. **20.** 169. **21.** 3820 ct. **22.** 72. **23.** $10388. **24.** 448. **25.** $3736. **26.** $6240. **27.** $17001. **28.** 33462 lb. **29.** 948. **30.** $1855. **31.** 230. **32.** 244477. **33.** 97 horses. **34.** 385.

35. 82 hogs. **36.** 276676. **37.** $16. **38.** 800 times. **39.** $70. **40.** 1229 yd. **41.** 107677 yd. **42.** 2106320 lb. **43.** $1068. **44.** 15625 yd. **45.** $4140. **46.** 268850 lb. **47.** 12250 bu. **48.** 362. **49.** 262 A. **50.** 350 A. **51.** $2214. **52.** 35100 ct. **53.** 216.

Article 53.—**1.** $13.93. **2.** $87.493. **3.** $29.08. **4.** $157.50. **5.** $9.099. **6.** $12.002. **7.** $500.10. **8.** $200.003. **9.** $99.90. **10.** $90.99.

Article 55.—**1.** 9300 ct. **2.** $8. **3.** 460 m. **4.** 18 ct. 7 m. **5.** 760 ct. **6.** 45000 m. **7.** $3.009. **8.** 8917 ct. **9.** 70000 ct. **10.** 10000000 m. **11.** 4044 m. **12.** 46702 ct. **13.** 46700 ct. **14.** 83009 m. **15.** $123.

Article 56.—**1.** $227.75. **2.** $206. **3.** $1544. **4.** $2028.66. **5.** $63.95. **6.** $2646.95. **7.** $3857.85.

Article 57.—**1.** $33.34. **2.** $50.33. **3.** $23.91. **4.** $224.20. **5.** $89.10. **6.** $62.37. **7.** $309.91. **8.** $15138.60. **9.** $6317.82. **10.** $520.32. **11.** $370.40. **12.** $170.87.

Article 58.—**1.** $199.032. **2.** $354.06. **3.** $3675. **4.** $520.52. **5.** $547.20. **6.** $10803.20. **7.** $22224. **8.** $24.804. **9.** $121.176. **10.** $261090. **11.** $38082.80. **12.** $330.75. **13.** $10693.20. **14.** $3005.60. **15.** $393.228. **16.** $742.26. **17.** $114.72. **18.** $115.72. **19.** $877.50. **20.** $900. **21.** $3388.56. **22.** $27. **23.** $128.25. **24.** $99. **25.** $1263.50. **26.** $640. **27.** $13525.92. **28.** $783. **29.** $563.28. **30.** $384. **31.** $1275. **32.** $398.40. **33.** $3738.24. **34.** $6494.40. **35.** $13125. **36.** $7140.

Article 59.—**1.** 150. **2.** 525. **3.** 625. **4.** 740. **5.** 438. **6.** 735. **7.** 4760. **8.** 7090. **9.** 182 yards. **10.** 160 sheep. **11.** 6460 needles. **12.** 796 acres. **13.** 200. **14.** 152. **15.** 2500. **16.** $24.87. **17.** $13.572. **18.** $40.795. **19.** $48.448.

20. $15.56. **21.** $5.72. **22.** $3.056. **23.** $7.009. **24.** $113.89. **25.** $2.80. **26.** $48.04. **27.** 22 ct. 5 m. **28.** 62 ct. 5 m. **29.** $.055. **30.** $.075. **31.** $10104.20. **32.** $1.15. **33.** 3 ct. 5 m. **34.** $9. **35.** 48 pounds.

Article 60.—**1.** $4000. **2.** $100.95. **3.** 18 ct. **4.** 45 bu. **5.** $24.50. **6.** $62.58. **7.** $96.32. **8.** $81.40. **9.** $5.948. **10.** $37.98. **11.** $1072.95. **12.** $71.50. **13.** $2673.40. **14.** $500.50. **15.** $9.25. **16.** 400. **17.** 216. **18.** 80000. **19.** 36000. **20.** 166. **21.** $1071.72. **22.** $462.25. **23.** 349 days. **24.** $203. **25.** 2 ct. **26.** 79400 lb. **27.** $654.02. **28.** $59. **29.** 48 gallons. **30.** 70 miles. **31.** 3758. **32.** $2.35. **33.** $288.40. **34.** $67.54. **35.** $16.14. **36.** $99.73.

Article 63.—**1.** 309 pt. **2.** 581 pt. **3.** 1201 pt. **4.** 2310 pt. **5.** 2864 qt. **6.** 74 bu. 3 pk. 2 qt. 1 pt. **7.** 180 bu. 6 qt. **8.** 6399 pt. **9.** 37313 pt. **10.** 1929 bu. **11.** 78928 pt. **12.** 1639424 pt. **13.** 400 bu. 1 pk. **14.** 1543 pk. 1 qt. **15.** 224000000 qt.

Article 64.—**1.** 310 pt. **2.** 32 gal. 1 gi. **3.** 701072 pt. **4.** 2996 gi. **5.** 2983 gal. 1 qt. 1 pt. **6.** 276544 gi. **7.** 3194 gi. **8.** 466 qt. 1 pt. **9.** 2365 gi. **10.** 143 gal. **11.** 115500 cubic in. **12.** 226 gal.

Article 65.—**1.** 6000 lb. **2.** 11300 lb. **3.** 18150 lb. **4.** 15999 lb. **5.** 26013 lb. **6.** 155200 oz. **7.** 96325 oz. **8.** 6 T. 9 cwt. 45 lb. **9.** 49 T. 4 cwt. **10.** 438 T. 5 cwt. 43 lb. **11.** 1239744000 oz. **12.** 5 T. 5 lb. **13.** 143771 lb. **14.** 355 T. 17 cwt. 71 lb. **15.** 1250 T. **16.** 6 T. **17.** 281 T. 5 cwt. **18.** 34 T. 11 cwt. 20 lb. **19.** 499 T. 19 cwt. 99 lb. 15 oz. **20.** 9 T. 19 cwt. 92 lb.

Article 66.—**1.** 1797 in. **2.** 1915 in. **3.** 13320 rd. **4.** 2796 in. **5.** 1584960 rd. **6.** 157 yd. 2 ft. 2 in. **7.** 119 mi. 177 rd. **8.** 17939 in. **9.** 1168 mi. 85 rd. **10.** 1100 yd. 1 in. **11.** 12672320 rd. **12.** 123 mi. 241 rd.

Article 67.—1. 1220 sq.rd. **2.** 355200 sq.rd. **3.** 1948659 sq.rd. **4.** 24598 sq. in. **5.** 3993690 sq. rd. **6.** 128403 sq. in. **7.** 5120000000000 sq. rd. **8.** 771604 sq. yd. 8 sq. ft. 64 sq. in.

Articles 68 and 69.—1. 30 sq. yd. **2.** 66 sq. yd. **3.** 142 sq. yd. 2 sq. ft. **4.** 40 sq. yd. **5.** 80 sq. yd. **6.** 27 A. **7.** 38 A. **8.** 62 A. 80 sq. rd. **9.** $85.80. **10.** $12. **11.** $674.50. **12.** $38.40. **13.** 120 rd. **14.** 20 mi. **15.** 780 bu. **16.** 9 yd. **17.** 9 yd.

Article 70.—1. 74 cu. yd. 18 cu. ft. **2.** 140268 cu. in. **3.** 16 cu. yd. **4.** 77 C. **5.** 2625943 cu. in. **6.** 240 cu. yd. **7.** 30 C. **8.** 5120 cu. yd. **9.** $6600. **10.** $375. **11.** 10368. **12.** $570.

Article 71.—1. 268200 sec. **2.** 110880 min. **3.** 2084583 sec. **4.** 5475600 sec. **5.** 3715243 sec. 6. 1 wk. 2 da. **7.** 31 da. 17 hr. 18 min. **8.** 7560000000 sec. **9.** 7 wk. 1 da. **10.** 525600 min. **11.** 132480 min. **12.** 2419200 sec. **13.** 158112000 sec. **14.** 26280 hr. **15.** 63244800 times. **16.** 200000 min.

Article 73.—1. 103104 gr. **2.** 103698 gr. **3.** 143999 gr. **4.** 15 lb. 1 oz. 19 pwt. 4 gr. **5.** 211 lb. 1 oz. **6.** 7506000 pwt. **7.** 2 lb. 7 oz. 5 pwt. **8.** 24964 gr. **9.** 57840 gr. **10.** 21814 gr. **11.** 2603 ℈. **12.** 84007 gr. **13.** 7 ℔ 11 ℥ 1 ʒ 17 gr. **14.** 36 ℔ 2 ℥ 6 ʒ. **15.** 42 ℔ 10 ℥ 3 ʒ. **16.** 896 f. ℥. **17.** 24000 ♏. **18.** 72707 f. ʒ. **19.** 648 lines. **20.** 15 hands. **21.** 51 mi. **22.** 4 yd. **23.** 5 ft. 8 in. **24.** 80 spans. **25.** 117 hands. **26.** 40 fathoms. **27.** 4 fathoms 1 foot. **28.** 100 rd. **29.** $135457''$. **30.** $68419''$. **31.** $10^\circ 31' 4''$. **32.** $1620000''$. **33.** 360. **34.** 2160. **35.** 8640. **36.** 25 dozens. **37.** 50 gross. **38.** $72. **39.** $70.56. **40.** $192. **41.** $17.28. **42.** $10.40. **43.** $30.24. **44.** $2.52. **45.** $90.72. **46.** $17.28. **47.** 5760 sheets. **48.** 3840 leaves. **49.** 34560 pages. **50.** 125 reams.

Article 74.—1. 1788 in. **2.** 40392 gr. **3.** 134 sq. yd. 6 sq. ft. **4.** $3^\circ 28' 20''$. **5.** 10 cu. yd. 21 cu. ft. 1152 cu. in. **6.** 17740 gr. **7.** 1 wk. 2 da. 23 hr. 59 min. 50 sec. **8.** 52 bu. 1 pt. **9.** 2016

dozens. **10.** 15300 lb. **11.** 103 yd. 2 ft. 2 in. **12.** 3317760
cu. in. **13.** 709 gal. 3 qt. **14.** 5184 barrels. **15.** 750 gross.
16. 110592 qt. **17.** 165 lb. 7 oz. 10 pwt. **18.** 448224 oz.
19. 23552 f. ʒ. **20.** 33 wk. 12 hr. **21.** 949 gal. 3 qt. 1 pt.
22. 4 sq. mi. 162 A. 150 sq. rd. **23.** 76800 rd. **24.** 631 pt.
25. 11491220 sec. **26.** 99510 rd. **27.** 1 T. 11 cwt. **28.** 1 wk.
4 da. 13 hr. 46 min. 40 sec. **29.** 81 C. **30.** 30816000 gr.
31. 385 bu. 3 pk. 1 qt. **32.** 6832800 min. **33.** 599616 cu. in.
34. 78039 lb. **35.** 49928 gr. **36.** 59940 sq. in. **37.** 1234
gal. 2 qt. **38.** 277 yd. 2 ft. 4 in. **39.** 20 bu. 2 qt. **40.** 5740 gr.
41. 512005 sq. rd. **42.** 768 cu. yd. **43.** 199680 leaves.
44. 13° 13′. **45.** 125000 gal. **46.** 7 ℥ 2 ʒ 1 ℈. **47.** 99 bu. 3 pk.
7 qt. 1 pt. **48.** 11520 sheets. **49.** 612 sq. yd. 4 sq. ft. 135 sq. in.
50. 31 T. 5 cwt. **51.** 2855 in. **52.** 4204096 cu. in. **53.** 6 sq. mi.
560 A. **54.** 8816 pt. **55.** 3510055 sec. **56.** 4290 rd.
57. 320000 lb. **58.** 961600 oz. **59.** 4 cu. yd. 18 cu. ft.
60. 865 gal. **61.** 864 scores. **62.** 14 T. 5 cwt. 49 lb. 5 oz.
63. 156 bu. 1 pk. **64.** 50423″. **65.** 1180 gal. **66.** 771 sq. yd.
5 sq. ft. 64 sq. in. **67.** 187 yd. **68.** 11 f. ℥. **69.** 36161 pt.
70. 5 wk. 5 da. **71.** 300 reams. **72.** 9 T. **73.** 62020 sq. rd.
74. 16320 rd. **75.** 18 C. 70 cu. ft. **76.** $25.20. **77.** $24.96.
78. 2 cwt. 50 lb. **79.** 120 gal. **80.** $36.27. **81.** 120. **82.** 368
dozen. **83.** $75. **84.** $16. **85.** $136.80. **86.** 1496. **87.** 800.
88. 1 min. 45 sec. **89.** 768. **90.** 1° 20′. **91.** $61.25.
92. 5400 lb. **93.** 7 lb. 6 oz. **94.** 2250 C. **95.** 56 doz. **96.** 60.
97. 640. **98.** $3.92. **99.** 4096 bu. **100.** 200 sq. yd. **101.** 5600.
102. $760. **103.** 400 doz. **104.** 2 da. 32 min. **105.** 4 hr.
106. 6 bu. 1 pk. **107.** 125 reams. **108.** 2000 gal. **109.** $9360.
110. $54.72. **111.** $354. **112.** $18. **113.** $.035. **114.** $121.50.
115. 6 da. 16 hr. **116.** $112.50. **117.** 160 T. **118.** $144.
119. 3 da. 4 hr. **120.** $162. **121.** 133 cu. ft. 1176 cu. in.
122. $3.60. **123.** $11650.80. **124.** $247.50. **125.** 2592 score.
126. 3 bu. 3 pk. 6 qt. **127.** $224. **128.** 376. **129.** 282.
130. $460.80. **131.** $8640. **132.** 75 doz. **133.** 331 gal.
134. $66. **135.** 16 da. **136.** 320 wk. **137.** 147 barrels.
138. 1040 bags. **139.** 81 da. **140.** $171.18. **141.** $.075.
142. $76.80. **143.** 45 gal. **144.** 13824. 145. $2.40.
146. 72 sheets.

Article 75.—1. 60 bu. **2.** 900 bu. **3.** 192 gal. 2 qt. **4.** 31 T. 16 cwt. 11 lb. **5.** 151 gal. 1 pt. **6.** 4 T. 10 cwt. **7.** 177 gal. 3 qt. **8.** 79 yd. **9.** 57 yd. 1 ft. 3 in. **10.** 500 A. 38 sq. rd. **11.** 127 sq. yd. 3 sq. ft. 43 sq. in. **12.** 34 sq. mi. 330 A. **13.** 152 cu. yd. 6 cu. ft. **14.** 377 C. 7 cu. ft. 1130 cu. in. **15.** 57 da. 9 hr. 26 min. **16.** 5 wk. 6 hr. 32 min. **17.** 42 lb. 11 oz. **18.** 3 ℥ 5 ʒ. **19.** 2 ℔ 8 ℥. **20.** 23 score and 3. **21.** 119° 50′. **22.** 61° 1′ 1″. **23.** 35 Cong. 15 f. ℥. **24.** 1 O. 4 f. ℥. **25.** 361 gal. 3 qt. **26.** 253 C. 88 cu. ft. **27.** 258 dozen. **28.** 4 T. 18 cwt. **29.** 102 A. **30.** 149 da. 14 hr. **31.** 100 mi. 160 rd. **32.** 24 da. 23 hr. 36 min. 2 sec.

Article 76.—1. 19 bu. 3 pk. 5 qt. **2.** 19 bu. 1 pk. 6 qt. **3.** 50 gal. 1 pt. 2 gi. **4.** 149 gal. 1 qt. 1 pt. **5.** 1 T. 15 cwt. 18 lb. **6.** 9 cwt. 89 lb. 6 oz. **7.** 23 mi. 250 rd. **8.** 7 yd. 11 in. **9.** 62 yd. 2 ft. 10 in. **10.** 4 sq. mi. 370 A. **11.** 17 sq. yd. 5 sq. ft. 99 sq. in. **12.** 199 sq. mi. 639 A. 110 sq. rd. **13.** 27 cu. yd. 17 cu. ft. 1628 cu. in. **14.** 62 C. 127 cu. ft. 1706 cu. in. **15.** 2 hr. 46 min. 2 sec. **16.** 4 wk. 1 da. 23 hr. 57 min. 56 sec. **17.** 5 lb. 7 oz. 7 pwt. **18.** 2 ℔ 9 ℥ 4 ʒ 2 ℈. **19.** 4° 48′ 40″. **20.** 6 reams 16 quires. **21.** 1 gross 8 dozen. **22.** 6 f. ℥ 2 f. ʒ. **23.** 14 bu. 6 qt. **24.** 176 bu. 2 pk. **25.** 1 wk. 1 da. 7 hr. **26.** 316 gal. 3 qt. **27.** 83 A. 40 sq. rd. **28.** 3 cwt. 58 lb. **29.** 18 C. 113 cu. ft. **30.** 2 T. 18 cwt. 10 lb. **31.** 8° 23′ 40″. **32.** 4 ℥ 3 ʒ 10 gr. **33.** 276 T. 19 cwt. 70 lb. **34.** 96 hr. 18 min. **35.** 21 C. 32 cu. ft. **36.** 13 bu. 3 pk. **37.** 13 da. 11 hr. 3 min.

Article 77.—1. 1 yr. 7 mo. 18 da. **2.** 84 yr. 2 mo. 19 da. **3.** 67 yr. 9 mo. 22 da. **4.** 155 yr. 6 mo. 13 da. **5.** 1 yr. 10 mo. 14 da. **6.** 6 yr. 8 mo. 24 da. **7.** 46 yr. 4 mo. 6 da. **8.** 85 yr. 11 mo. 23 da.

Article 78.—1. 119 da. **2.** 64 da. **3.** 146 da. **4.** 277 da. **5.** 203 da. **6.** 195 da. **7.** 361 da. **8.** 162 da.

Article 79.—1. 29 bu. 1 pk. 4 qt. **2.** 63 gal. 3 qt. **3.** 1 T. 12 cwt. 75 lb. **4.** 64 yd. 1 ft. 5 in. **5.** 23 sq. yd. **6.** 2 cu. yd. 20 cu. ft. 88 cu. in. **7.** 6 lb. 8 oz. 18 pwt. **8.** 2 ℔ 5 ℥. **9.** 227

gal. 1 qt. **10.** 78° 12′. **11.** 20 reams 10 quires. **12.** 276 mi. 230 rd. **13.** 55 da. 7 hr. 35 min. 24 sec. **14.** 43 T. 15 cwt. 34 lb. **15.** 138 bu. 4 qt. **16.** 1073 yd. 1 ft. **17.** 37 bu. 2 pk. **18.** 24 da. 10 hr. 20 min. **19.** 1 hr. 54 min. 40 sec. **20.** 274 T. 15 cwt. 40 lb. **21.** 489 sq. yd. 120 sq. in. **22.** 41 bu.

Article 80.—1. 3 bu. 2 pk. 3 qt. **2.** 3 cwt. 72 lb. 9 oz. **3.** 3 yd. 2 ft. 4 in. **4.** 7 sq. ft. 88 sq. in. **5.** 3 hr. 30 min. 40 sec. **6.** 3 pwt. 14 gr. **7.** 1 ℥ 2 ℈ 10 gr. **8.** 7 gal. 2 qt. 1 gi. **9.** 7 yd. 8 in. **10.** 1 sq. yd. 2 sq. ft. 24 sq. in. **11.** 2 da. 7 hr. 20 min. **12.** 1 cu. yd. 864 cu. in. **13.** 23 bu. 3 pk. 1 qt. **14.** 5 gal. 1 qt. 1 pt. 3 gi. **15.** 98 lb. 5 oz. **16.** 5 cu. yd. 15 cu. ft. **17.** 16 da. 7 hr. 34 min. **18.** 32′ 26″. **19.** 249 bu. 1 pk. 4 qt. **20.** 7 mi. 206 rd. **21.** 3 T. 9 cwt. 40 lb. **22.** 1 bu. 2 pk. 7 qt.

Articles 81 and 82.—1. 2 hr. 40 min. **2.** 2 hr. 13 min. 20 sec. **3.** 2 hr. 25 min. 8 sec. **4.** 4 hr. 39 min. 24 sec. **5.** 6 hr. 40 min. 40 sec. **6.** 3 hr. 16 min. 54 sec. **7.** 4 hr. 24 min. 3 sec. **8.** 4 hr. 41 min. 9 sec. **9.** 6 hr. 36 min. 36 sec. **10.** 7 hr. 27 min. 26 sec. **11.** 3 hr. 55 min. 53 sec. **12.** 6 hr. 31 min. 32 sec. **13.** 169° 18′ 15″. **14.** 104° 49′ 15″. **15.** 152° 32′ 30″. **16.** 109° 21′ 45″. **17.** 228° 37′ 15″. **18.** 71° 17′ 30″. **19.** 82° 21′ 15″. **20.** 11° 56′ 45″. **21.** 1 hr. 56 min. slow. **22.** 3 hr. 8 min. fast. **23.** Shortened 3 min. **24.** 5 hr. 32 min. **25.** 10 hr. 36 min. A.M. **26.** 2 hr. 32 min. A.M. **27.** 6 hr. 20 min. P.M. **28.** 10 hr. 16 min. A.M. **29.** 6 P.M. previous day. **30.** 5 hr. 39 min.

Article 87.—1. 3, 17. **2.** 2, 2, 13. **3** 2, 31. **4.** 3, 3, 7. **5.** 2, 2, 2, 3, 3. **6.** 3, 5, 5. **7.** 2, 2, 19. **8.** 2, 2, 2, 3, 5 **9.** 2, 2, 3, 11. **10.** 2, 2, 2, 3, 7. **11.** 2, 2, 7, 7. **12.** 2, 3, 3, 11. **13.** 2, 2, 3, 17. **14.** 3, 3, 23. **15.** 2, 2, 3, 3, 7. **16.** 3, 11, 17. **17.** 2, 3, 3, 7, 7. **18.** 2, 2, 3, 3, 23. **19.** 2, 11, 11, 11. **20.** 3, 3, 7, 7, 7. **21.** 2, 2, 3, 3, 11, 11.

Article 88.—1. 2, 2, 5. **2.** 2, 3, 5. **3.** 2, 2, 2, 5. **4.** 3, 3, 5. **5.** 2, 3, 7. **6.** 2, 2, 3, 3, 3. **7.** 2, 3, 3, 3. **8.** 2, 11. **9.** 3, 7. **10.** 5, 7. **11.** 3, 11. **12.** 2, 2, 3. **13.** 13. **14.** 2, 2, 3. **15.** 2, 2, 2. **16.** 3, 5. **17.** 2, 2, 2, 3. **18.** 13. **19.** 2, 7. **20.** 11. **21.** 7. **22.** 2, 3.

Article 89.—**1.** 12. **2.** 10. **3.** 9. **4.** 7. **5.** 4. **6.** 78. **7.** 49. **8.** 11. **9.** 9. **10.** 82. **11.** 49. **12.** 21. **13.** 144. **14.** 144. **15.** 37. **16.** 27. **17.** 14. **18.** 20. **19.** 36. **20.** 27. **21.** 7. **22.** 17. **23.** 9. **24.** 15. **25.** 3. **26.** 9. **27.** 2.

Article 90.—**1.** 240. **2.** 720. **3.** 240. **4.** 400. **5.** 3024. **6.** 840. **7.** 1980. **8.** 4620. **9.** 7920. **10.** 720. **11.** 720. **12.** 360. **13.** 3024. **14.** 14762. **15.** 4199. **16.** 4225. **17.** 5145. **18.** 2250. **19.** 600. **20.** 1848. **21.** 25025. **22.** 2288. **23.** 144. **24.** 2880. **25.** 702. **26.** 2304. **27.** 3960. **28.** 16200. **29.** 30870. **30.** 8610.

Article 91.—**1.** 9 times. **2.** 3. **3.** 24 times. **4.** 6 times. **5.** 15. **6.** 54. **7.** 24. **8.** 32. **9.** 24. **10.** 16. **11.** 36. **12.** 102. **13.** 360. **14.** 120. **15.** 18 (hundred).

Article 103.—**1.** $\frac{98}{7}$. **2.** $\frac{253}{11}$. **3.** $\frac{161}{23}$. **4.** $\frac{1134}{18}$. **5.** $\frac{810}{9}$. **6.** $\frac{992}{32}$. **7.** $\frac{168}{56}$. **8.** $\frac{208}{8}$. **9.** $\frac{2835}{9}$. **10.** $\frac{2400}{12}$. **11.** $\frac{666}{18}$. **12.** $\frac{1360}{40}$. **13.** $\frac{280}{20}$. **14.** $\frac{351}{13}$. **15.** $\frac{496}{16}$. **16.** $\frac{1474}{22}$. **17.** $\frac{1710}{90}$. **18.** $\frac{2349}{29}$.

Article 104.—**1.** $\frac{127}{8}$. **2.** $\frac{138}{7}$. **3.** $\frac{892}{9}$. **4.** $\frac{731}{10}$. **5.** $\frac{548}{15}$. **6.** $\frac{767}{18}$. **7.** $\frac{1234}{7}$. **8.** $\frac{362}{19}$. **9.** $\frac{521}{18}$. **10.** $\frac{995}{22}$. **11.** $\frac{5337}{73}$. **12.** $\frac{2903}{100}$. **13.** $\frac{3000}{11}$. **14.** $\frac{10696}{27}$. **15.** $\frac{7871}{14}$. **16.** $\frac{10001}{100}$. **17.** $\frac{10923}{16}$. **18.** $\frac{5303}{41}$. **19.** $\frac{3223}{111}$. **20.** $\frac{400}{19}$. **21.** $\frac{7300}{99}$.

Article 105.—**1.** $76\frac{1}{6}$. **2.** 46. **3.** 177. **4.** $123\frac{9}{10}$. **5.** $362\frac{4}{13}$. **6.** $174\frac{7}{15}$. **7.** $243\frac{1}{19}$. **8.** $145\frac{3}{17}$. **9.** $163\frac{4}{23}$. **10.** $33\frac{13}{22}$. **11.** $403\frac{5}{14}$. **12.** $152\frac{21}{26}$. **13.** 230. **14.** $141\frac{25}{33}$. **15.** 39. **16.** $98\frac{76}{100}$. **17.** 81. **18.** $82\frac{4}{15}$. **19.** 218. **20.** $536\frac{17}{23}$. **21.** $48\frac{22}{97}$.

Article 106.—**1.** $\frac{12}{33}$. **2.** $\frac{25}{60}$ **3.** $\frac{15}{40}$. **4.** $\frac{28}{35}$. **5.** $\frac{85}{100}$. **6.** $\frac{112}{126}$. **7.** $\frac{80}{105}$. **8.** $\frac{144}{156}$. **9.** $\frac{153}{171}$. **10.** $\frac{238}{280}$. **11.** $\frac{210}{345}$. **12.** $\frac{204}{336}$. **13.** $\frac{240}{464}$. **14.** $\frac{221}{416}$. **15.** $\frac{972}{1368}$. **16.** $\frac{7128}{7744}$. **17.** $\frac{4161}{4560}$. **18.** $\frac{221}{3604}$. **19.** $\frac{203}{1911}$. **20.** $\frac{6086}{6698}$.

Article 107.—**1.** $\frac{6}{7}$. **2.** $\frac{2}{3}$. **3.** $\frac{27}{47}$. **4.** $\frac{81}{143}$. **5.** $\frac{11}{27}$. **6.** $\frac{37}{90}$. **7.** $\frac{11}{12}$. **8.** $\frac{16}{21}$. **9.** $\frac{25}{47}$. **10.** $\frac{2}{7}$. **11.** $\frac{41}{43}$. **12.** $\frac{37}{50}$. **13.** $\frac{96}{121}$. **14.** $\frac{35}{44}$. **15.** $\frac{9}{17}$. **16.** $\frac{4}{5}$. **17.** $\frac{7}{11}$. **18.** $\frac{2}{3}$. **19.** $\frac{13}{27}$. **20.** $\frac{25}{64}$. **21.** $\frac{4001}{5001}$.

Article 108.—**1.** $\frac{40}{60}, \frac{15}{60}, \frac{36}{60}$. **2.** $\frac{72}{90}, \frac{75}{90}, \frac{80}{90}$. **3.** $\frac{21}{56}, \frac{42}{56}, \frac{24}{56}$. **4.** $\frac{40}{90}, \frac{63}{90}, \frac{48}{90}$. **5.** $\frac{24}{60}, \frac{18}{60}, \frac{16}{60}, \frac{27}{60}$. **6.** $\frac{42}{48}, \frac{28}{48}, \frac{21}{48}, \frac{14}{48}$. **7.** $\frac{108}{120}, \frac{70}{120}, \frac{54}{120}, \frac{35}{120}$. **8.** $\frac{32}{120}, \frac{25}{120}, \frac{28}{120}, \frac{27}{120}$. **9.** $\frac{156}{240}, \frac{78}{240}, \frac{52}{240}, \frac{39}{240}$. **10.** $\frac{1287}{2002}, \frac{819}{2002}, \frac{693}{2002}$. **11.** $\frac{56}{72}, \frac{60}{72}, \frac{54}{72}, \frac{27}{72}, \frac{30}{72}$. **12.** $\frac{12}{100}, \frac{35}{100}, \frac{90}{100}, \frac{22}{100}$. **13.** $\frac{27}{36}, \frac{6}{36}, \frac{28}{36}, \frac{33}{36}, \frac{12}{36}$. **14.** $\frac{528}{1056}, \frac{88}{1056}, \frac{48}{1056}, \frac{33}{1056}$. **15.** $\frac{36}{120}, \frac{66}{120}, \frac{50}{120}, \frac{105}{120}$. **16.** $\frac{12}{144}, \frac{64}{144}, \frac{45}{144}, \frac{104}{144}$. **17.** $\frac{24}{90}, \frac{25}{90}, \frac{63}{90}, \frac{15}{90}$. **18.** $\frac{192}{720}, \frac{200}{720}, \frac{504}{720}, \frac{45}{720}$. **19.** $\frac{378}{1008}, \frac{280}{1008}, \frac{324}{1008}, \frac{147}{1008}$. **20.** $\frac{22}{30}, \frac{21}{30}, \frac{20}{30}, \frac{25}{30}$. **21.** $\frac{1540}{6930}, \frac{2079}{6930}, \frac{1980}{6930}, \frac{1890}{6930}$. **22.** $\frac{90}{144}, \frac{112}{144}, \frac{63}{144}, \frac{56}{144}$. **23.** $\frac{24}{132}, \frac{8}{132}, \frac{18}{132}, \frac{9}{132}$. **24.** $\frac{20}{12}, \frac{21}{12}, \frac{22}{12}, \frac{19}{12}$. **25.** $\frac{168}{60}, \frac{28}{60}, \frac{198}{60}, \frac{33}{60}$. **26.** $\frac{132}{144}, \frac{135}{144}, \frac{136}{144}, \frac{138}{144}$. **27.** $\frac{360}{630}, \frac{315}{630}, \frac{280}{630}, \frac{252}{630}$. **28.** $\frac{117}{144}, \frac{288}{144}, \frac{78}{144}, \frac{52}{144}, \frac{39}{144}$. **29.** $\frac{1071}{1260}, \frac{1080}{1260}, \frac{810}{1260}, \frac{1190}{1260}, \frac{1155}{1260}$. **30.** $\frac{32}{72}, \frac{27}{72}, \frac{420}{72}, \frac{126}{72}, \frac{642}{72}$.

Article 110.—**1.** $2\frac{2}{3}$. **2.** $2\frac{2}{3}$. **3.** $2\frac{5}{12}$. **4.** $2\frac{1}{2}$. **5.** $1\frac{1}{24}$. **6.** $\frac{4}{7}$. **7.** $2\frac{13}{20}$. **8.** $1\frac{29}{72}$. **9.** $\frac{11}{12}$. **10.** $1\frac{15}{16}$. **11.** $2\frac{7}{24}$. **12.** $2\frac{1}{2}$. **13.** $1\frac{17}{80}$. **14.** $2\frac{2}{45}$.

Article 111.—**1.** $1\frac{9}{16}$. **2.** $2\frac{5}{56}$. **3.** $2\frac{5}{8}$. **4.** $2\frac{8}{15}$. **5.** $6\frac{13}{56}$. **6.** $1\frac{1121}{1716}$. **7.** $1.\frac{107}{216}$. **8.** $2\frac{391}{420}$. **9.** $2\frac{101}{120}$. **10.** $23\frac{19}{24}$. **11.** $29\frac{71}{120}$. **12.** $98\frac{7}{12}$. **13.** $154\frac{5}{8}$. **14.** $555\frac{7}{8}$. **15.** $1498\frac{19}{24}$. **16.** $2\frac{4}{5}$. **17.** $2\frac{1}{40}$. **18.** $5\frac{23}{24}$. **19.** $14\frac{1}{24}$. **20.** $12\frac{35}{36}$. **21.** $13\frac{5}{12}$. **22.** $2\frac{19}{60}$. **23.** $7\frac{19}{24}$. **24.** $36\frac{1}{8}$. **25.** 55. **26.** $7\frac{1}{18}$. **27.** $2\frac{25}{56}$. **28.** $948\frac{11}{504}$. **29.** $174\frac{71}{120}$. **30.** $35\frac{43}{60}$.

Article 113.—**1.** $13\frac{5}{8}$. **2.** $24\frac{3}{10}$. **3.** $8\frac{4}{9}$. **4.** $9\frac{2}{5}$. **5.** $72\frac{1}{2}$. **6.** $11\frac{3}{5}$. **7.** $8\frac{3}{4}$. **8.** $159\frac{1}{3}$. **9.** $9\frac{11}{12}$. **10.** $19\frac{18}{25}$. **11.** $11\frac{2}{3}$. **12.** $199\frac{3}{4}$. **13.** $142\frac{19}{24}$. **14.** $74\frac{8}{9}$. **15.** $287\frac{1}{2}$. **16.** $26\frac{1}{5}$. **17.** $352\frac{2}{5}$. **18.** $368\frac{31}{49}$. **19.** $11\frac{22}{25}$. **20.** $327\frac{89}{100}$. **21.** $186\frac{18}{23}$. **22.** $53\frac{15}{16}$. **23.** $876\frac{1}{2}$. **24.** $279\frac{31}{60}$.

Article 114.—**1.** $\frac{1}{24}$. **2.** $\frac{13}{77}$. **3.** $\frac{1}{60}$. **4.** $\frac{29}{144}$. **5.** $\frac{23}{60}$. **6.** $\frac{29}{60}$. **7.** $\frac{13}{36}$. **8.** $\frac{15}{56}$. **9.** $\frac{13}{80}$. **10.** $\frac{7}{132}$. **11.** $3\frac{5}{12}$. **12.** $3\frac{17}{24}$. **13.** $1\frac{43}{252}$. **14.** $7\frac{3}{16}$. **15.** $1\frac{4}{21}$. **16.** $8\frac{191}{342}$. **17.** $5\frac{173}{220}$. **18.** $652\frac{8}{21}$. **19.** $578\frac{27}{28}$. **20.** $4\frac{211}{240}$. **21.** $21\frac{569}{600}$. **22.** $102\frac{39}{40}$. **23.** $8989\frac{7}{66}$.

Article 115.—1. $\frac{63}{80}$. **2.** $\frac{2}{9}$. **3.** $\frac{3}{10}$. **4.** $\frac{7}{18}$. **5.** $\frac{51}{250}$. **6.** $2\frac{1}{4}$. **7.** $\frac{1}{9}$. **8.** $\frac{5}{8}$. **9.** $\frac{10}{63}$. **10.** $1\frac{5}{7}$. **11.** $14\frac{6}{11}$. **12.** $8\frac{4}{7}$. **13.** $145\frac{3}{5}$. **14.** $34\frac{2}{7}$. **15.** 154. **16.** 84. **17.** $320\frac{2}{5}$. **18.** 675. **19.** $3473\frac{1}{3}$. **20.** $189\frac{1}{16}$. **21.** $2441406\frac{1}{4}$. **22.** $32\frac{14}{15}$. **23.** $306\frac{2}{3}$. **24.** 500. **25.** 1960. **26.** $26\frac{2}{3}$. **27.** $9\frac{6}{25}$. **28.** 840. **29.** $31\frac{1}{33}$. **30.** 32130. **31.** 5200. **32.** $48\frac{8}{9}$.

Article 116.—1. $63\frac{7}{11}$. **2.** $156\frac{3}{5}$. **3.** $77\frac{1}{2}$. **4.** $21\frac{7}{9}$. **5.** $\frac{72}{91}$. **6.** $18\frac{19}{30}$. **7.** $17\frac{1}{19}$. **8.** $37\frac{1}{3}$. **9.** $1\frac{67}{120}$. **10.** $662\frac{1}{2}$. **11.** $100\frac{4}{5}$. **12.** $56\frac{8}{19}$.

Article 117.—1. $\frac{27}{38}$. **2.** $\frac{17}{28}$. **3.** $1\frac{1}{9}$. **4.** $8\frac{1}{3}$. **5.** $\frac{85}{168}$. **6.** $1\frac{14}{195}$. **7.** $\frac{1}{45}$. **8.** $10\frac{26}{45}$. **9.** $10\frac{4}{15}$. **10.** $\frac{1}{675}$. **11.** $6\frac{3}{7}$. **12.** 7. **13.** $4\frac{7}{12}$. **14.** $10\frac{1}{5}$. **15.** $1\frac{7}{17}$. **16.** $2\frac{59}{128}$. **17.** $\frac{5}{78}$. **18.** $23\frac{4}{7}$. **19.** $\frac{3}{40}$. **20.** $5\frac{7}{9}$. **21.** $\frac{931}{2250}$. **22.** $2\frac{1}{2}$. **23.** $1\frac{1}{3}$. **24.** $84\frac{7}{12}$. **25.** $\frac{27}{35}$. **26.** $24\frac{14}{15}$. **27.** $5\frac{35}{57}$. **28.** $\frac{105}{116}$.

Article 118.—1. $31\frac{1}{4}$ ct. **2.** $56\frac{1}{4}$ ct. **3.** $64\frac{7}{12}$ ct. **4.** $85. **5.** $\$11\frac{1}{5}$. **6.** $\$6\frac{9}{16}$. **7.** $41280. **8.** $\$10\frac{4}{5}$. **9.** $\$4.84\frac{3}{8}$. **10.** 45 ct. **11.** $1. **12.** $177.30. **13.** $2\frac{5}{6}$. **14.** $7\frac{15}{28}$. **15.** $31\frac{17}{25}$. **16.** $89\frac{1}{10}$ mi. **17.** $\$136\frac{2}{3}$. **18.** 19 A. **19.** $9\frac{11}{16}$ C. **20.** $16. **21.** $125. **22.** $\$12\frac{13}{16}$. **23.** $\$1.37\frac{1}{2}$. **24.** $2\frac{32}{45}$ A.

Article 119.—1. $1\frac{1}{6}$. **2.** $\frac{6}{7}$. **3.** $1\frac{1}{2}$. **4.** $6\frac{2}{3}$. **5.** $21\frac{1}{3}$. **6.** $\frac{3}{160}$. **7.** $1\frac{1}{84}$. **8.** $5\frac{13}{36}$. **9.** $\frac{2}{5}$. **10.** $3\frac{1}{13}$. **11.** $17\frac{1}{2}$. **12.** $\frac{4}{15}$. **13.** $4\frac{2}{5}$. **14.** $4\frac{2}{7}$. **15.** $48\frac{6}{13}$. **16.** $\frac{2}{125}$. **17.** 1700. **18.** $3\frac{9}{11}$. **19.** $1\frac{47}{120}$. **20.** $5\frac{5}{7}$. **21.** $\frac{50}{63}$. **22.** 375. **23.** $9\frac{1}{5}$. **24.** $95\frac{3}{25}$. **25.** $\frac{18}{65}$. **26.** $\frac{11}{500}$. **27.** $21\frac{7}{16}$. **28.** $\frac{3}{5}$. **29.** $1127\frac{1}{4}$. **30.** $2\frac{2402}{2967}$. **31.** $1\frac{11}{24}$ ct. **32.** $\$34\frac{11}{14}$. **33.** $57\frac{11}{20}$ A. **34.** $\frac{1}{12}$ yd. **35.** $17\frac{7}{9}$ ct. **36.** $17\frac{19}{43}$ lb. **37.** $\frac{4}{15}$ lb. **38.** 45. **39.** $\frac{1}{24}$ oz. **40.** $\$3\frac{3}{16}$. **41.** $9\frac{3}{8}$ da. **42.** $\$\frac{16}{95}$. **43.** $12\frac{6}{7}$ yd. **44.** $8\frac{16}{25}$ lb. **45.** $7\frac{9}{25}$ da.

Article 120.—1. $\frac{3}{8}$. **2.** $\frac{4}{15}$. **3.** $\frac{1}{49}$. **4.** $\frac{13}{15}$. **5.** $\frac{7}{10}$. **6.** $\frac{1}{12}$. **7.** $\frac{9}{14}$. **8.** $\frac{72}{77}$. **9.** $\frac{1}{24}$. **10.** $\frac{9}{196}$. **11.** $\frac{3}{20}$. **12.** $\frac{15}{77}$. **13.** $\frac{7}{10}$. **14.** $\frac{7}{9}$. **15.** $\frac{1}{30}$. **16.** $\frac{35}{72}$.

Article 121.—**1.** $\frac{63}{80}$. **2.** $\frac{20}{21}$. **3.** $\frac{32}{45}$. **4.** $\frac{21}{880}$. **5.** $\frac{11}{53}$. **6.** $\frac{65}{132}$. **7.** $3\frac{1}{5}$. **8.** $\frac{21}{464}$. **9.** $\frac{369}{1240}$. **10.** $\frac{5}{49}$. **11.** $\frac{35}{48}$. **12.** $\frac{2}{3}$. **13.** $\frac{40}{129}$. **14.** $\frac{4}{9}$. **15.** $\frac{4}{9}$.

Article 122.—**1.** $2\frac{13}{16}$. **2.** $3\frac{1}{5}$. **3.** $4\frac{31}{56}$ lb. **4.** $\$13\frac{3}{4}$. **5.** $1\frac{3}{5}$. **6.** $\$61\frac{3}{5}$. **7.** $3\frac{3}{14}$ yd. **8.** $33\frac{2}{3}$ lb. **9.** $5\frac{1}{3}$ times. **10.** 8. **11.** $13\frac{8}{9}$ A. **12.** $\frac{27}{98}$. **13.** 40. **14.** $1\frac{61}{64}$. **15.** $\frac{1}{100}$. **16.** $\$16\frac{4}{5}$. **17.** $13\frac{1}{3}$ yd.

Article 123.—**1.** 132 yd. **2.** 4840 sq. yd. **3.** 40 yr. 80 da. **4.** $\$3.82\frac{1}{2}$. **5.** 22869 sq. ft. **6.** $\$180\frac{2}{5}$. **7.** 952 sq. rd. **8.** \$53.20. **9.** \$123.75. **10.** $\$33.47\frac{1}{2}$. **11.** 112392 hr. **12.** $\$15.31\frac{1}{4}$. **13.** \$21.25. **14.** $35\frac{11}{15}$ ct. **15.** $29\frac{1}{7}$ ct. **16.** $\$1.89\frac{5}{8}$. **17.** $32\frac{5}{8}$ ct. **18.** 10 mi. 12 rd. 2 ft. **19.** 18150 sq. yd. **20.** 2 mi. 4 rd. **21.** 18817920 sq. in. **22.** 12 rd. **23.** 9600. **24.** 77 yr. $35\frac{3}{4}$ da.

Articles 124 and 125.—**1.** $\frac{3}{4}$ qt. **2.** $\frac{28}{45}$ pt. **3.** $\frac{4}{5}$ oz. **4.** $\frac{121}{125}$ sq. yd. **5.** $\frac{2}{5}$ cu. ft. **6.** $\frac{3}{4}$ da. **7.** $\frac{17}{25}$ oz. **8.** $\frac{18}{25}$ pwt. **9.** $\frac{11}{20}$ ℈. **10.** $\frac{64}{65}$ sq. rd. **11.** $\frac{2187}{15625}$ cu. in. **12.** $\frac{24}{25}$ sec. **13.** $\frac{1}{125}$ pt. **14.** $\frac{132}{175}$ min. **15.** $\frac{384}{875}$ gi. **16.** 2 qt. 3 gi. **17.** 12 cwt. 72 lb. $11\frac{7}{11}$ oz. **18.** 302 rd. 1 yd. 8 in. **19.** 153 sq. rd. 10 sq. yd. 108 sq. in. **20.** 202 da. 22 hr. **21.** 9 oz. 6 pwt. 16 gr. **22.** 3 qt. 1 pt. $3\frac{7}{15}$ gi. **23.** 7 ʒ 1 ℈ 10 gr. **24.** 9 cwt. 37 lb. 8 oz. **25.** 2 yd. **26.** 1′ 48″. **27.** 5 A. 46 sq. rd. 8 sq. yd. 4 sq. ft. 72 sq. in. **28.** 3 rd. 1 yd. $3\frac{3}{5}$ in. **29.** 39 cu. ft. $874\frac{2}{3}$ cu. in. **30.** 3 f. ℥ 1 f. ʒ 36 ♏. **31.** 10 hr. 57 min. $46\frac{2}{3}$ sec.

Article 126.—**1.** $\frac{1}{1800}$ da. **2.** $\frac{1}{2560}$ C. **3.** $\frac{1}{1152}$ sq. yd. **4.** $\frac{1}{2250}$ cwt. **5.** $\frac{2}{19}$ gal. **6.** $\frac{1}{10}$ bu. **7.** $\frac{1}{1600}$ oz. **8.** $\frac{1}{3072}$ cu. yd. **9.** $\frac{1}{88}$ lb. **10.** $\frac{1}{240}$ mi. **11.** $\frac{3}{10240000}$ sq. mi. **12.** $\frac{1}{90}$ yr. **13.** $\frac{1}{2880}$ T. **14.** $\frac{1}{216}$ chain. **15.** $\frac{9}{112}$ gal. **16.** $\frac{1}{512}$ bu.

Article 127.—**1.** $\frac{4}{15}$. **2.** $\frac{34}{65}$. **3.** $\frac{1}{72}$. **4.** $\frac{5}{26}$. **5.** $\frac{1}{9}$. **6.** $\frac{807}{2420}$. **7.** $\frac{11}{40}$. **8.** $\frac{5}{61}$. **9.** $\frac{50}{171}$. **10.** $\frac{3}{10}$. **11.** $\frac{161}{320}$. **12.** $\frac{7}{24}$. **13.** $\frac{1}{360}$.

Article 128.—**1.** 1 sq. ft. 72 sq. in. **2.** 124 cu. ft. **3.** 44′ 12″. **4.** 4 oz. 12 pwt. **5.** 6 cwt. 70 lb. **6.** 1 Cong. 3 O. 5 f. ℥ 2 f. ʒ 40 ♏. **7.** 191 rd. 2 yd. 1 ft. 4 in. **8.** 3 rd. 2 yd. 2 ft. 5 in. **9.** 5 da. 17 hr. 16 min. **10.** 3 pk. 7 qt. **11.** 2 qt. 1 pt. **12.** 12 cwt. 9 lb. 4 oz. **13.** 87 rd. 3 yd. 2 ft. 6 in. **14.** 2 ʒ 1 ℈. **15.** 70 cu. ft.

Article 129.—**1.** $\frac{19}{30}$. **2.** 145 A. 72 sq. rd. 22 sq. yd. **3.** $5\frac{1}{4}$. **4.** $13\frac{1}{3}$. **5.** $\frac{56}{126}$. **6.** $\frac{9}{13}$. **7.** $\frac{18}{20}$. **8.** $7\frac{1}{5}$. **9.** 21. **10.** $\frac{17}{35}$. **11.** $\frac{49}{77}$. **12.** $\frac{1}{125}$. **13.** $\frac{8}{31}$ lb. **14.** \$$5\frac{5}{14}$. **15.** \$131.25. **16.** \$$2\frac{7}{8}$. **17.** $\frac{4}{75}$. **18.** $26\frac{2}{3}$ T. **19.** \$$62\frac{13}{20}$. **20.** $23\frac{6}{11}$. **21.** $\frac{3}{7}$. **22.** \$55. **23.** $\frac{9}{25}$. **24.** 2 cwt. 57 lb. 11 oz. **25.** $544\frac{4}{5}$. **26.** 270. **27.** 264. **28.** $\frac{60}{72}$, $\frac{64}{72}$, $\frac{42}{72}$, $\frac{45}{72}$. **29.** 18. **30.** \$678. **31.** \$11.75. **32.** 60. **33.** \$70. **34.** \$3368. **35.** \$$4\frac{1}{40}$. **36.** \$396.80. **37.** $1638\frac{21}{22}$ A. **38.** \$$1415\frac{11}{26}$. **39.** $\frac{9}{50}$. **40.** 6 A. 125 sq. rd.

Article 130.—**1.** \$112.50. **2.** \$49. **3.** \$77. **4.** \$420.625. **5.** \$180. **6.** \$85.89. **7.** \$605.25. **8.** \$1280.50. **9.** \$31.25. **10.** \$1351.50. **11.** \$298.50. **12.** \$222. **13.** \$370.50. **14.** \$631. **15.** \$14.375. **16.** \$42.40. **17.** \$47.43. **18.** \$$1.68\frac{3}{4}$. **19.** \$1.50. **20.** \$6.468. **21.** \$13.50. **22.** \$13.41. **23.** \$11.85. **24.** \$14.90. **25.** \$30.54. **26.** \$25.30. **27.** 21 bu. **28.** $42\frac{1}{2}$ yd. **29.** \$6.25. **30.** \$1.25. **31.** \$$12.33\frac{1}{3}$. **32.** \$$1.33\frac{1}{3}$. **33.** $83\frac{1}{3}$ A. **34.** \$$58.66\frac{2}{3}$. **35.** \$8.05. **36.** \$137.64.

Article 141.—**1.** $\frac{7}{8}$. **2.** $\frac{16}{25}$. **3.** $\frac{64}{125}$. **4.** $\frac{5}{8}$. **5.** $\frac{1}{40}$. **6.** $\frac{32}{125}$. **7.** $\frac{1}{400}$. **8.** $\frac{139}{625}$. **9.** $\frac{39}{40}$. **10.** $\frac{21}{2500}$. **11.** $\frac{3}{16}$. **12.** $\frac{15}{32}$. **13.** $4\frac{9}{200}$. **14.** $26\frac{9}{50}$. **15.** $\frac{1}{80}$. **16.** $19\frac{5}{8}$. **17.** $300\frac{1}{4}$. **18.** $46\frac{7}{8}$. **19.** $13\frac{23}{25}$. **20.** $20\frac{1}{50}$. **21.** $\frac{11}{16}$. **22.** $14\frac{3}{160}$. **23.** $9\frac{1}{125}$. **24.** $\frac{11}{32}$.

Article 142.—**1.** .375. **2.** .45. **3.** .3125. **4.** .44. **5.** .26. **6.** .1875. **7.** .40625. **8.** .53125. **9.** 1.3125. **10.** .01875. **11.** .00125. **12.** .068. **13.** .018. **14.** .85625. **15.** .0171875. **16.** .953125. **17.** 1.78. **18.** .56179+. **19.** .2394+. **20.** .4. **21.** .75. **22.** .9423+. **23.** .135. **24.** .0418+.

Article 143.— **1.** 153.13. **2.** 146.23. **3.** 600. **4.** .458843. **5.** 662.2829. **6.** 694.532. **7.** 989.1009. **8.** 3551.979. **9.** 192.06. **10.** 2767.9932. **11.** 1872.448. **12.** 5517.789. **13.** 599.4. **14.** 1472.827755.

Article 144.— **1.** 27.488. **2.** 9.17. **3.** 35.8761. **4.** 253.125. **5.** 256.7989. **6.** 225.612. **7.** 8.4476. **8.** 88.888. **9.** 16.92924. **10.** 18.825. **11.** 49.911. **12.** 124.1376. **13.** .576. **14.** 88.850034. **15.** 50895.3573.

Article 147.— **1.** .57227. **2.** 222.5. **3.** 740.25. **4.** .01575. **5.** 2377.05. **6.** .0006. **7.** .093. **8.** .00135. **9.** .9702. **10.** 3696.3. **11.** .0021. **12.** 2250. **13.** .031777. **14.** .02121696. **15.** 4207.5. **16.** 169.119. **17.** 294.06. **18.** .0797449. **19.** 730675.2. **20.** 729. **21.** 80000. **22.** 4503744. **23.** 310. **24.** 94.87.

Article 150.— **1.** 1.67. **2.** 7.53. **3.** 2.115. **4.** 2.5. **5.** .024. **6.** 14.95. **7.** .00345. **8.** 12.5. **9.** 400.3. **10.** 4000. **11.** .21. **12.** 41000. **13.** .96875. **14.** .000025. **15.** 4.5. **16.** .0625. **17.** 9.25. **18.** .75. **19.** 10000. **20.** .32. **21.** .06636+. **22.** .301003+. **23.** .0000066+. **24.** 98.21428+.

Article 151.— **1.** .8 pt. **2.** .2184 pt. **3.** .86 lb. **4.** .99 in. **5.** .768 sq. rd. **6.** .11664 cu. in. **7.** .972 sec. **8.** .48 cu. ft. **9.** .7452 sq. in.

Article 152.— **1.** 1 pk. 6 qt. **2.** 1 qt. 1 pt. 2 gi. **3.** 3 cwt. 12 lb. 8 oz. **4.** 50 rd. **5.** 250 A. **6.** 89 cu. ft. 1036.8 cu. in. **7.** 138 da. 19 hr. 4 min. 48 sec. **8.** 16° 55′ 12″.

Article 153.— **1.** .0055 bu. **2.** .015 gal. **3.** .0005 sq. yd. **4.** .0000125 cu. yd. **5.** .01475 bu. **6.** .0003375 da. **7.** .000256 cwt. **8.** .04875 gal. **9.** .0000015 da. **10.** .000234375 bu. **11.** .000000625 C. **12.** .00002 yr. **13.** .0000125 mi. **14.** .00024 T. **15.** .000000027+ A.

Article 154.—1. 1 hr. 12 min. **2.** $16.24. **3.** 5 A. **4.** $2.185 **5.** 118 lb. 2 oz. **6.** 42 rd. **7.** 36 C. 32 cu. ft. **8.** 128 rd. 2 yd. 1 ft. .6 in. **9.** 14 cwt. 95 lb. **10.** 32 gal. 1 qt. 1 pt. **11.** $9990. **12.** 7 qt. 1 pt. **13.** $61.32. **14.** 233 mi. 132.8 rd. **15.** 38 da. 5 hr. 48 min. **16.** .375. **17.** 1 pk. 7 qt. .4 pt. **18.** 42 sq. rd. **19.** 1 cwt. 33 lb. 12 oz. **20.** $109.20. **21.** 20 yd. 1 ft. 10.5 in. **22.** 158 lb. 8 oz. **23.** $121.80. **24.** $65.73. **25.** 81 ct. **26.** 281 da. 5 hr. 49 min. 12 sec. **27.** 9 hr. 13 min. 7.5 sec. **28.** $6. **29.** 3 mi. 40 rd. **30.** $612.50.

Article 156.—1. 394500 dm. **2.** .09364 Km. **3.** 1.23456 Mm. **4.** 98765 Dm. **5.** .000034 Mm. **6.** 74600 cm. **7.** .837 Mm. **8.** 3700 m. **9.** 46000000 dm. **10.** 5.8 Hm. **11.** 374500000 cm. **12.** .6725 Km. **13.** 8.9364 Dm. **14.** 4.56 Hm.

Article 157.—1. 37.468 Ha. **2.** 49320 ca. **3.** 3.8743 a. **4.** 3.8743 a. **5.** 4387.5 m^2. **6.** .0000457 Ha. **7.** .89734 Ha. **8.** 583900 m^2. **9.** .3843 Ha. **10.** 397000 ca.

Article 158.—1. 48 l. **2.** 39500 cl. **3.** .4937 Hl. **4.** 583900 cl. **5.** 4.57 l. **6.** 678.9 cl. **7.** 346.92 Dl. **8.** 4.2789 l. **9.** 3.2584 Hl. **10.** .047 Dl. **11.** 3800000 dl. **12.** 2.97 Dl. **13.** .04683 Hl. **14.** 3870000 dl. **15.** 49000 l. **16.** .37282 m^3. **17.** .678 m^3. **18.** 303 dl.

Article 159.—1. .065 M. T. **2.** 4893100 mg. **3.** 465.3 Dg. **4.** .6543 Q. **5.** 87000 Kg. **6.** .000937 g. **7.** 123456 dg. **8.** 8.734 Dg. **9.** 88736000 cg. **10.** .000000086 Q. **11.** .0000765 M.T. **12.** .3945 Hg. **13.** 3894000 gr. **14.** 87300000000 mg. **15.** 89.9 Mg. **16.** 4890 dg. **17.** .4 Mg. **18.** 12 Kg. **19.** 9.876541 Q. **20.** 34560 g. **21.** 4800.48 Hg. **22.** 90830000 mg.

Article 160.—1. 43 yd. 2 ft. 2.8 in. **2.** 123 A. 88 sq. rd. **3.** 8 cwt. 26 lb. 11.6 oz. **4.** 126 rd. 4 yd. 6 in. + **5.** 14 T. 6 cwt. 59.8 lb. **6.** 25 C. 110.8 cu. ft. **7.** 2 lb. 4 oz. 2 pwt. 15 gr.

8. 654 cu. yd. **9.** 747.5 sq. yd. **10.** 148 sq. rd. 8 sq. yd. **11.** 127 bu. 2 pk. 6 qt. **12.** 2.54 + m. **13.** 160.9347 + Km. **14.** 83.612 + m^2. **15.** 40.4694 + Ha. **16.** 76.4526 m^3. nearly. **17.** 12.14 + a. **18.** 16.3295 M. T. nearly. **19.** 160 Hl. **20.** 249.834 + l. **21.** 500 g. **22.** 278.7068 m^2. nearly. **23.** 20 Hl. **24.** 1 Kg.

Article 161.—**1.** $41.8874. **2.** $295.275. **3.** $68.975. **4.** $2266.89 +. **5.** 38.4 lb. **6.** $27000. **7.** $46.80. **8.** $85. **9.** $1400. **10.** $3800. **11.** $10800. **12.** $75. **13.** $14. **14.** 8 hr. 20 min.

Article 164.—**1.** 259. **2.** 156. **3.** 207. **4.** 99.2. **5.** 65. **6.** 3.3. **7.** 7.25. **8.** .21. **9.** 199. **10.** 420. **11.** 42. **12.** .5188 +. **13.** 6400. **14.** $\frac{1}{100}$. **15.** 396 bu. **16.** 5 da. 22 hr. 48 min. **17.** 48 ct. **18.** 355 A. **19.** 1 T. 11 cwt. 80 lb. **20.** 3 gal. 3 qt. 1 pt. **21.** 3 bu. 2 pk. **22.** 58 gal. **23.** $\frac{1}{400}$. **24.** $\frac{1}{15}$. **25.** $2\frac{7}{8}$. **26.** 144.0285.

Article 165.—**1.** 12. **2.** 75. **3.** 17. **4.** 75. **5.** 75. **6.** 16. **7.** 44. **8.** 200. **9.** 1000. **10.** 75. **11.** 125. **12.** .2. **13.** $22\frac{1}{2}$. **14.** $12\frac{1}{2}$. **15.** .02. **16.** $36\frac{1}{2}$. **17.** 40. **18.** 150. **19.** 150. **20.** 60.

Article 166.—**1.** 70. **2.** 225. **3.** 63000. **4.** 175. **5.** 320. **6.** $5\frac{1}{7}$. **7.** 390. **8.** 75. **9.** $2666\frac{2}{3}$. **10.** 17.5. **11.** 242. **12.** 15 bu. 2 pk. 4 qt. **13.** 3 da. 11 hr. 20 min. **14.** 18 gal. 3 qt. **15.** 82 T. **16.** 23 A. 20 sq. rd.

Article 167.—**1.** 1300. **2.** 400. **3.** 555. **4.** 1295. **5.** 150. **6.** 37.5. **7.** $\frac{3}{4}$. **8.** 20. **9.** $6\frac{2}{3}$. **10.** 42000. **11.** $55\frac{5}{9}$. **12.** 30.4.

Article 169.—**1.** $1900. **2.** 95. **3.** 16. **4.** 128. **5.** $1600. **6.** 456. **7.** 150 ft. **8.** 48 A. **9.** 600 A. **10.** 160 A. **11.** 400 A. **12.** 1728 mi. **13.** 5 ft. 6 in. **14.** 42 lb. Troy. **15.** 1 oz. 8 pwt.

16 gr. **16.** 2580 gr. **17.** 1260 oz. **18.** 550 bu. **19.** $13\frac{1}{2}$ wk. **20.** 620. **21.** 74 %. **22.** 46000 doz. **23.** 365. **24.** 15 %. **25.** $\frac{1}{2}$ %. **26.** 126 A. **27.** 105.84 A. **28.** 294 A. **29.** 1395 bu. **30.** 175 A. **31.** 637 T. 10 cwt.

Article 172.—**1.** \$98.50. **2.** \$2717. **3.** $1\frac{2}{3}$ %. **4.** $2\frac{2}{5}$ %. **5.** \$58.50. **6.** \$1068. **7.** \$210.20. **8.** \$1275. **9.** \$20. **10.** \$47045. **11.** \$45. **12.** \$218.875. **13.** $1\frac{1}{2}$ %. **14.** \$15. **15.** \$462612.50.

Article 173.—**1.** \$1254. **2.** \$2880. **3.** \$850. **4.** \$2750. **5.** \$2750. **6.** \$326. **7.** \$300.

Article 174.—**1.** \$42. **2.** \$3.75. **3.** \$370. **4.** \$15. **5.** \$294. **6.** $6\frac{4}{5}$ %. **7.** 6 %. **8.** 20 %. **9.** 25 %. **10.** $70\frac{2}{3}$ %. **11.** $77\frac{7}{9}$ %. **12.** 220 %. **13.** 20 %. **14.** 25 %. **15.** $33\frac{1}{3}$ %. **16.** \$1.25. **17.** $6\frac{2}{3}$ %. **18.** 20 %. **19.** $16\frac{2}{3}$ %. **20.** $3\frac{7}{11}$ %. **21.** \$1340. **22.** 10 ct. a yd. **23.** \$7843.14 nearly. **24.** \$8163.27. **25.** \$8160. **26.** \$7840. **27.** $166\frac{2}{3}$ %. **28.** \$3171.875. **29.** 25 %. **30.** $66\frac{2}{3}$ %.

Article 175.—**1.** $7\frac{11}{27}$ %. **2.** \$817.50. **3.** \$60. **4.** 28 %. **5.** \$8791.20. **6.** \$250. **7.** 12 %. **8.** 40 %. **9.** \$4620. **10.** 25 %. **11.** $5\frac{5}{19}$ %. **12.** 5 %. **13.** $37\frac{1}{2}$ %. **14.** $33\frac{1}{3}$ %. **15.** 25 %.

Article 177.—**1.** $\frac{1}{5}$ %. **2.** $\frac{3}{10}$ %. **3.** \$117. **4.** $\frac{1}{10}$ %. **5.** \$12.25. **6.** 250. **7.** \$1378. **8.** \$66.25.

Article 178.—**1.** \$1950. **2.** \$172.50. **3.** 2240. **4.** 30 %. **5.** \$261. **6.** $7\frac{1}{2}$ %. **7.** \$1680. **8.** 350.

Article 179.—**1.** \$3555. **2.** \$35770. **3.** \$6210. **4.** 52. **5.** 532. **6.** $\frac{1}{4}$ %. **7.** \$112.50. **8.** $98\frac{2}{51}$ ct. **9.** $41\frac{1}{4}$ %. **10.** \$1431. **11.** \$1439.94. **12.** 216. **13.** \$1590.

Article 180.—**1.** \$468. **2.** 10 %. **3.** \$444. **4.** 70. **5.** \$294. **6.** \$300. **7.** \$100. **8.** \$91.80. **9.** 80 %. **10.** 60 %. **11.** 120 %. **12.** $4\frac{11}{16}$ %. **13.** 24 %. **14.** \$3.

Article 183.—**1.** \$45. **2.** \$45. **3.** \$7.20. **4.** \$240. **5.** \$273. **6.** 55 ct. **7.** \$608.40. **8.** \$80. **9.** \$9185.72. **10.** \$526.40. **11.** \$963.50. **12.** \$1088.91. **13.** \$70.56. **14.** \$39.60. **15.** \$270.03. **16.** \$1428.16. **17.** \$438.25. **18.** \$816.52. **19.** \$500. **20.** \$1073.40. **21.** \$180. **22.** \$12. **23.** \$18000. **24.** \$18.08. **25.** \$3.60. **26.** \$1.10. **27.** \$80.76. **28.** \$20.09. **29.** \$31.76. **30.** \$13.34. **31.** \$198.75. **32.** \$976.50. **33.** \$487. **34.** \$600.855. **35.** \$4179.15. **36.** \$380.87. **37.** \$3. **38.** \$1.65. **39.** \$1.16. **40.** 20 ct. **41.** \$1.72. **42.** \$4.41. **43.** \$4747.90. **44.** \$6.02. **45.** \$480.80. **46.** \$16265.60. **47.** \$388.275. **48.** \$475.67. **49.** \$87. **50.** \$39.75. **51.** \$73.20. **52.** \$119.20. **53.** \$83.50. **54.** \$223.425. **55.** \$150.70. **56.** \$455.41. **57.** \$512. **58.** \$879. **59.** \$846.25. **60.** \$1404.16. **61.** \$556.76. **62.** \$97.19. **63.** \$1696.27. **64.** \$5622.65. **65.** \$130.76. **66.** \$76.85. **67.** \$19.20. **68.** \$57.76. **69.** \$383.47. **70.** \$278.42. **71.** \$109.13. **72.** \$8258.90. **73.** \$696.72. **74.** \$549.28. **75.** \$630.45. **76.** \$430.42. **77.** \$507.74. **78.** \$787.35.

Article 184.—**1.** \$.062. **2.** \$.097. **3.** \$.294$\frac{1}{3}$. **4.** \$439$\frac{2}{3}$. **5.** \$.250$\frac{1}{3}$. **6.** \$.609$\frac{1}{3}$. **7.** \$.480$\frac{1}{3}$. **8.** \$.239$\frac{2}{3}$. **9.** \$.0225. **10.** \$.07. **11.** \$.061$\frac{1}{3}$. **12.** \$.07. **13.** \$.016. **14.** \$.023$\frac{1}{4}$. **15.** \$.042$\frac{7}{36}$. **16.** \$.020$\frac{1}{6}$. **17.** \$.02$\frac{11}{72}$. **18.** \$.002$\frac{5}{6}$. **19.** \$.14. **20.** \$.078$\frac{1}{6}$. **21.** \$.080$\frac{8}{9}$. **22.** \$.38. **23.** \$.420$\frac{5}{6}$. **24.** \$13. **25.** \$88.50. **26.** \$77.04. **27.** \$78.12. **28.** \$245. **29.** \$191.59. **30.** \$16.87. **31.** \$55.80. **32.** \$14.75. **33.** \$15.48. **34.** \$80.48. **35.** \$4844.44. **36.** \$6.38. **37.** \$.31. **38.** \$1460.70. **39.** \$756.16. **40.** \$1018.36. **41.** \$105.71. **42.** \$6712.60. **43.** \$3. **44.** \$439.80. **45.** \$86.32. **46.** \$1365. **47.** \$63.58. **48.** \$631.94. **49.** \$809.65. **50.** \$110.08.

Article 185.—**1.** 3 yr. **2.** 2 yr. 6 mo. **3.** 2 yr. 2 mo. **4.** 25 yr. **5.** 12 yr. 6 mo. **6.** 2 yr. 6 mo. **7.** 20 yr. **8.** 5 yr 8 mo. **9.** 2 mo. 20 da. **10.** 1 yr. 7 mo. 6 da. **11.** 11 yr. 1 mo.

10 da. **12.** 3 yr. 1 mo. 15 da. **13.** 3 yr. 4 mo. **14.** 12 yr. 6 mo. **15.** 3 mo. 6 da. **16.** 6 yr. 3 mo. **17.** 31 yr. 3 mo. **18.** 1 yr. 11 mo. 21 da. **19.** 1 yr. 10 mo. 6 da. **20.** 3 mo.

Article 186.—**1.** 6 %. **2.** 8 %. **3.** 6 %. **4.** 5 %. **5.** $8\frac{1}{3}$ %. **6.** 5 %. **7.** 8 %. **8.** 5 %. **9.** 8 %. **10.** 30 %. **11.** 72 %. **12.** $6\frac{2}{3}$ %. **13.** $3\frac{1}{2}$ %. **14.** 4 %. **15.** $4\frac{1}{2}$ %. **16.** 120 %. **17.** $4\frac{31}{36}$ %. **18.** $2\frac{1}{2}$ %. **19.** 3 %. **20.** $4\frac{1}{2}$ %.

Article 187.—**1.** $260. **2.** $725. **3.** $200. **4.** $24500. **5.** $17600. **6.** $90. **7.** $720. **8.** $4500. **9.** $1964.40. **10.** $424.80. **11.** $612. **12.** $360.

Article 188.—**1.** $600. **2.** $800. **3.** $180. **4.** $120. **5.** $135. **6.** $45. **7.** $410. **8.** $150. **9.** $197.50. **10.** $175. **11.** $242.50. **12.** $880.

Article 190.—**1.** $441. **2.** $693. **3.** $491.30. **4.** $629.86. **5.** $138.66. **6.** $137.92. **7.** $67.42. **8.** $563.26. **9.** $339.72. **10.** $17.20. **11.** $31.38. **12.** $1040.60. **13.** $4.86. **14.** $5.51.

Article 191.—**1.** $595.40. **2.** $596.75. **3.** $252. **4.** $1052.64. **5.** $2004. **6.** $312.75. **7.** $1834.87. **8.** $242.80.

Article 192.—**1.** $455.76. **2.** $464.40. **3.** $605. **4.** $605. **5.** $677.97. **6.** $465.93. **7.** $915.06. **8.** $623.42.

Article 193.—**1.** $218.10. **2.** $14.70. **3.** $110.50. **4.** $2.32. **5.** $3.30.

Article 196.—**1.** Sept. 6–9; $4.20, $395.80. **2.** June 16–19; $9.30, $440.70. **3.** July 17–20; $9.30, $390.70. **4.** Sept. 14–17; $6.04, $513.96. **5.** Sept. 16–19; $8.37, $531.63. **6.** April 25–28; $1.26, $78.74. **7.** April 15–18; $1.86, $178.14. **8.** Oct. 19–22;

$6.12, $473.88. **9.** Jan. 13–16; $4.92. $315.08. **10.** April 26–29; $18.54, $791.46. **11.** Aug. 28–31; 53 ct., $88.87. **12.** Feb. 18–21; 50 ct., $13.43. **13.** Dec. 5–8; $5.89, $394.10. **14.** Mar. 17–20; $20.30, $1102.03. **15.** Nov. 18–21, 1880; 92 da., $6.13, $393.87. **16.** Oct. 24–27, 1870; 83 da., $13.83, $486.17. **17.** April 19–22, 1880; 66 da., $3.30, $446.70. **18.** Jan. 12–15, 1876; 55 da., $5.50, $714.50. **19.** Aug. 19–22, 1877; 57 da., $2.28, $357.72. **20.** Aug. 17–20, 1877; 55 da., $2.20, $357.80. **21.** July 11–14, 1875; 41 da., $8.03, $775.26. **22.** April 16–19, 1884; 66 da., $6.74, $401.46. **23.** April 13–16, 1846; 44 da., $8.12, $730.48. **24.** Nov. 9–12, 1884; 121 da., $25.71, $611.79. **25.** July 16–19, 1883; 180 da., $18.75, $450. **26.** Sept. 14–17, 1888; 63 da., $71.08, $5006.42. **27.** May 1–4, 1880; 110 da., $14.71, $466.78.

Article 197.—**1.** $500. **2.** $600. **3.** $750. **4.** $804.02. **5.** $1016. **6.** $60. **7.** $120. **8.** $2000.

Article 199.—**1.** $375; $75. **2.** $625; $275. **3.** $500; $185. **4.** $720; $90. **5.** $300; $59. **6.** $420; $28.70. **7.** $420; $202.30. **8.** $280; $93.10. **9.** $420; $196.21. **10.** $583.70; $304.30. **11.** $186. **12.** $77. **13.** $22.80. **14.** $100.10. **15.** $21.21. **16.** $436.90. **17.** $276.43. **18.** $31.53. **19.** $4.48. **20.** 56 ct. **21.** $240. **22.** $60. **23.** $431. **24.** $1621.60. **25.** $1738.18.

Article 201.—**1.** $4709.40. **2.** $726.35. **3.** $4952.47. **4.** $1356.60. **5.** $375.71. **6.** $2359.67. **7.** $994.50. **8.** $989.50. **9.** $2379.40. **10.** $1482. **11.** $800. **12.** $800. **13.** $1892.21. **14.** $1002.51.

Article 202.—**1.** $3853.85. **2.** $1384.70. **3.** £1093 10 s. **4.** 4224.75 fr. **5.** $980. **6.** $1152. **7.** $916.79. **8.** 4145.08 m.

Article 204.—**1.** $33.60. **2.** $84. **3.** $92. **4.** $61.50. **5.** $8800. **6.** $\frac{4}{5}$. **7.** $\frac{4}{5}$ %.

Article 205.—**1.** \$193.08. **2.** \$25.50. **3.** Son, \$18.60. **4.** \$2854.712.

Article 208.—**1.** $2\frac{1}{2}$ mills on \$1. **2.** 23 mills on \$1. **3.** \$2640000. **4.** 6.08 mills on \$1.

Article 209.—**1.** 2.56 mills on \$1. **2.** \$22.20. **3.** \$15.86. **4.** \$16.63. **5.** \$5.85. **6.** \$7.17. **7.** \$7.67. **8.** \$4.03. **9.** 25.324 mills. **10.** \$22.13. **11.** \$4927.04. **12.** \$35927.67. **13.** \$2.13. **14.** \$21.48. **15.** \$214.85. **16.** \$2148.69.

Article 211.—**1.** \$33.60. **2.** \$54.60. **3.** 12 ct. **4.** 48 ct. **5.** 24 ct. **6.** 30 ct. **7.** 15 ct. **8.** 15 ct. **9.** \$3.84. **10.** \$32.40. **11.** \$10. **12.** \$584. **13.** 750. **14.** 750.

Article 212.—**1.** \$103. **2.** \$19.20. **3.** \$375. **4.** \$25.20. **5.** \$26.90. **6.** \$1869.65. **7.** \$207. **8.** \$153.72. **9.** \$651.22. **10.** \$1834.64. **11.** \$14583.80. **12.** \$1536.50. **13.** \$803. **14.** \$606.60.

Article 214.—**1.** 20. **2.** 10. **3.** 24. **4.** $5\frac{15}{17}$. **5.** $6\frac{2}{5}$. **6.** $\frac{2}{19}$. **7.** $2\frac{1}{2}$. **8.** $1\frac{3}{5}$. **9.** $\frac{2}{7}$. **10.** 28. **11.** $4\frac{1}{2}$. ·**12.** $3\frac{3}{4}$. **13.** $6\frac{14}{81}$. **14.** $\frac{2}{45}$. **15.** $\frac{4}{81}$. **16.** $\frac{1}{175}$. **17.** 60. **18.** $2\frac{94}{99}$. **19.** 80. **20.** 75. **21.** $27\frac{1}{3}$. **22.** $\frac{3}{400}$. **23.** 56. **24.** $196\frac{12}{13}$.

Article 215.—**1.** 700. **2.** 28000. **3.** $332\frac{1}{2}$. **4.** $\frac{16}{63}$. **5.** $52\frac{1}{2}$. **6.** 17.48. **7.** 27.95. **8.** 76 A. 128 sq. rd. **9.** 4 yd. 10 in. **10.** 5 wk. 3 da. 12 hr.

Article 216.—**1.** 19.6. **2.** 42.5 **3.** $\frac{2}{3}$. **4.** $\frac{3}{4}$. **5.** 2 pk. 5 qt. 1 pt. **6.** 275 gal. **7.** 29 min. 20 sec. **8.** 165 liters.

Article 217.—**1.** $4\frac{1}{2}$. **2.** 21. **3.** $\frac{5}{9}$. **4.** $1\frac{1}{2}$. **5.** 20. **6.** 168. **7.** 22. **8.** 9.

Article 219.—**1.** 5:4. **2.** 7:3. **3.** 7:3. **4.** 111:11. **5.** 11:5. **6.** 4:3. **7.** 4:13. **8.** 7:11. **9.** 4:3. **10.** 216:7. **11.** 16:1. **12.** 1:6.

Article 220.—**1.** 105:64. **2.** 201:28. **3.** 135:52. **4.** 280:207. **5.** 20:27. **6.** 16:15. **7.** 8:3. **8.** 6:5.

Article 223.—**1.** 68. **2.** 21. **3.** 8. **4.** 96. **5.** $13\frac{3}{4}$. **6.** $82\frac{1}{8}$. **7.** $64\frac{8}{9}$. **8.** $64\frac{8}{9}$. **9.** $\frac{72}{73}$. **10.** 86.4. **11.** 28. **12.** 4. **13.** $10\frac{1}{5}$. **14.** 3 cwt. 44 lb.

Article 224.—**1.** $1025. **2.** $93. **3.** $6250. **4.** $45.50. **5.** 105. **6.** $4387.50. **7.** $129.60. **8.** $98. **9.** $3.23. **10.** $184. **11.** $65.80. **12.** 138 hr. **13.** 36 wk. **14.** $113\frac{7}{11}$ bu. **15.** 80 hr. **16.** $25\frac{3}{5}$ mi. **17.** $2\frac{2}{3}$ qt. **18.** 54 sec. **19.** 7 T. 10 cwt. **20.** 32. **21.** 280 bu. **22.** 1260 bu. 1 pk. **23.** 2 lb. 3 oz. **24.** 6600. **25.** $50\frac{1}{2}$ mi. **26.** 48 C. **27.** 106 A. 40 sq. rd. **28.** 55 yd. **29.** 105. **30.** 140. **31.** 56 ct. **32.** 84 ct. **33.** $536. **34.** $40. **35.** 45 da. **36.** $1.45. **37.** $675.78. **38.** $30.60. **39.** 572. **40.** $43.20. **41.** $126.50. **42.** 140 cu. ft. **43.** $232\frac{1}{2}$ lb. **44.** $16. **45.** 592. **46.** 1140. **47.** $7980. **48.** $20\frac{1}{5}$ ct. **49.** 192. **50.** 882. **51.** 648. **52.** $587.25. **53.** $\frac{9}{14}$ in. **54.** 3 min. 48 sec. **55.** 137 hr. 15 min. **56.** 18. **57.** $16.68. **58.** 11 T. **59.** $389.43.

Article 225.—**1.** $118.80. **2.** 18. **3.** 12 da. **4.** $2400. **5.** 24 lots. **6.** 18 rd. **7.** $10\frac{4}{5}$ rd. **8.** $57.76. **9.** 22 cows. **10.** 151 bu. 1 pk. **11.** 1100 mi. **12.** 5120 books. **13.** 16 rabbits. **14.** 10 cats. **15.** $7175. **16.** 2 lb. 10 oz. **17.** $450. **18.** 2:1. **19.** $134.75. **20.** 60 men. **21.** $89.76. **22.** $28.97. **23.** 160. **24.** 6 men. **25.** 13 hr. 7 min. 30 sec. **26.** $952.50. **27.** $168.75.

Article 226.—**1.** 1st., $937.50; 2d., $562.50. **2.** A. $1062.50; B. $937.50. **3.** A. $63; B. $56; C. $91. **4.** 1692 and 2256. **5.** 2256 and 1692. **6.** 987, 1316 and 1645. **7.** 1680, 1260 and 1008. **8.** 9.48 and 10.08. **9.** 3.92 and .005. **10.** A. $32.40; B. $43.20. **11.** $600, $540, $300. **12.** First society, $27.50; second, $16.50. **13.** A. $10.13; B. $9.49; C. $12.66; D. $6.96; E. $10.76.

Article 227.—1. 42 ct. **2.** 26 ct. **3.** $141.

Article 228.—**1.** General Average $1\frac{1}{5}$ %. **2.** A. 75 bl.; B. 60 bl.; C. 25 bl. **3.** $25. **4.** $1842.75.

Article 229.—**1.** A. $240; B. $540. **2.** A. $80.05; B. $72.05. **3.** A. $990; B. $1320. **4.** A. $240; B. $216; C. $120. **5.** A. $184; B. $230. **6.** A. $69.30; B. $148.50. **7.** A. $2100; B. $2205. **8.** $212.50.

Article 230.—**1.** 3 mo. 6 da. **2.** 5 mo. **3.** 8 mo. **4.** 4 mo. **5.** 10 da. **6.** 90 da. **7.** 29 da. **8.** 8 da. **9.** May 15. **10.** 10 mo. **11.** Aug. 14. **12.** May 3. **13.** Sept. 2. **14.** April 5. **15.** April 1. **16.** Nov. 20.

Article 232.—**1.** 11 ct. per lb. **2.** $6.80 per oz. **3.** 26 ct. per lb. **4.** $1.80 per gal. **5.** $1.80 per gal. **6.** 9 min. $23\frac{11}{13}$ sec. **7.** 29.87 in. **8.** 5 ft. 7 in. **9.** 12 mi. 205 rd. per hr. **10.** 12 meetings. **11.** 16 members. **12.** 321 sq. ft.

Article 234.—**1.** 6561. **2.** 32768. **3.** 390625. **4.** 286.29151. **5.** 4802.49. **6.** 166.375. **7.** $1785\frac{1}{16}$. **8.** 4173.281. **9.** $9823\frac{1}{81}$. **10.** $3\frac{3337}{4096}$. **11.** 95481. **12.** 2919.2409. **13.** $3672\frac{9}{25}$. **14.** $\frac{100}{441}$. **15.** $2\frac{79}{441}$. **16.** $228\frac{28}{81}$. **17.** $915\frac{1}{16}$. **18.** $36\frac{481}{1600}$. **19.** $1938\frac{1}{1936}$. **20.** 46656. **21.** 1953125. **22.** 1157625. **23.** $2370\frac{10}{27}$. **24.** 6967.871. **25.** 41781923. **26.** $\frac{4913}{42875}$. **27.** 1124.864. **28.** $1076\frac{57}{64}$. **29.** 68574961. **30.** 1477.6336. **31.** $12155\frac{1}{16}$. **32.** $1234567\frac{73}{81}$. **33.** 4978.7136. **34.** 614656. **35.** $\frac{28561}{38416}$. **36.** $55277\frac{19}{81}$. **37.** $138\frac{438}{2401}$. **38.** 16850581551. **39.** $16455646\frac{47}{1024}$. **40.** 12762815625. **41.** 10648. **42.** 272.25. **43.** $90266\frac{70}{81}$. **44.** 6967.871. **45.** 14641. **46.** $11\frac{25}{64}$.

Article 238.—**1.** 12. **2.** 38. **3.** 88. **4.** 25. **5.** 75. **6.** 125. **7.** 175. **8.** 225. **9.** 425. **10.** 1.1. **11.** 3.9. **12.** 103. **13.** 97. **14.** 24. **15.** 74. **16.** $9\frac{4}{5}$. **17.** $14\frac{2}{3}$. **18.** $35\frac{1}{7}$. **19.** $7\frac{1}{14}$. **20.** $\frac{55}{63}$. **21.** 3.53553+. **22.** 31.62277+. **23.** 2.28035+. **24.** 4.01248+. **25.** 16.0312+. **26.** 5.06951+. **27.** 3.47706+.

Article 239.—**1.** 35. **2.** 48. **3.** 64. **4.** 105. **5.** 72. **6.** 135. **7.** 150. **8.** 375. **9.** 11.2.

Article 240.—**1.** 75. **2.** 9 ft. **3.** 28 ft. **4.** 65 ft. **5.** 85 ft. **6.** 48 ft. **7.** 53 ft. **8.** 96 ft. **9.** 84.8528+ ft. **10.** 5 in. **11.** 219 mi. **12.** 122 ft. **13.** 56.5685+ ft. **14.** 92.1954+ mi. **15.** 255 mi.

Article 241.—**1.** 240 rd. **2.** 17 rd. **3.** 60 rd. **4.** 40 rd. **5.** 3613 rd. **6.** 60 rd.

Article 244.—**1.** 24. **2.** 43. **3.** 63. **4.** 74. **5.** 68. **6.** 39 **7.** 205. **8.** 513. **9.** 907. **10.** 85.3. **11.** 6.56. **12.** .313. **13.** 1.4422+. **14.** 6.6943+. **15.** .213. **16.** .0129. **17.** $\frac{4}{81}$. **18.** .7368+. **19.** .34199+. **20.** .15874+. **21.** $8\frac{2}{5}$. **22.** .85498+.

Article 245.—**1.** 1 ft. 11 in. **2.** 14 ft. **3.** 125. **4.** 91125. **5.** $5\frac{1}{2}$ in. **6.** 1 ft. 3.119+ in.

Article 247.—**1.** 45 sq. yd. **2.** 60 A. **3.** 250 sq. ft. **4.** 165 A. **5.** 10 A. **6.** 32 A. **7.** 80 sq. yd. **8.** 40.5 m^2. **9.** 146 sq. yd. 6 sq. ft. **10.** 22 A. **11.** 1440. **12.** 90 A. **13.** 40 yd. **14.** 13 ft. 6 in. **15.** 12 yd.

Article 248.—**1.** 270 sq.ft. **2.** 10 A. 128 sq. rd. **3.** 10800 sq.ft.

Article 249.—**1.** 400 sq. ft. **2.** 880 sq. yd. **3.** 4 sq. yd. **4.** 2400 sq. ft. **5.** 2400 sq. ft. **6.** 6 A. 140 sq. rd. **7.** 1734 sq. yd. **8.** 1170 sq. yd. **9.** 8 A. 64 sq. rd.

Article 250.—**1.** 37 A. 80 sq. rd. **2.** 2450 sq. ft. **3.** 48 sq. rd. **4.** $36000.

Article 251.—**1.** 62.832 ft. **2.** 6.366 + ft. **3.** 163.3632 ft. **4.** 282.744 ft. **5.** 1 ft. 5.825 + in. **6.** 54.1125 + rd. **7.** 1 mi. 214.072 rd. **8.** 70 ft. 8.232 in.

Article 252.—1. 1963.5 sq. ft. **2.** 340 sq. ft. 127.5 sq. in. **3.** 9.62115 sq. in. **4.** 1256.64 sq. yd. **5.** 33.85+ ft.. **6.** 26.58 + ft. **7.** 5026.56 sq. ft. **8.** 141.372 sq. rd.

Article 254.—1. 432 sq. ft. **2.** 40 sq. ft. **3.** 64 sq. ft. **4.** 41 sq. ft. 104.31 sq. in. **5.** 1 sq. ft. 19.3632 sq. in. **6.** 92 sq. ft. 143.07 sq. in.

Article 255.—1. 40 cu. in. **2.** 200 cu. in. **3.** 25 cu. ft. **4.** 10 in. **5.** 1 cu. ft. 726.375 cu. in. **6.** 2 ft. 1 in.

Article 256.—1. 12 sq. ft. **2.** 1 sq. ft. 6.7968 sq. in. **3.** 10 sq. ft. 130.8 sq. in. **4.** 17 sq. ft. 65.28 sq. in.

Article 257.—1. 36 cu. ft. **2.** 768 cu. in. **3.** 83.776 cu. ft. **4.** 139 cu. ft. 1082.88 cu. in. **5.** 366.69 + cu. in.

Article 258.—1. 1520.5344 sq. in. **2.** 201.0624 sq. ft. **3.** 19089068.46 sq. mi. **4.** 317 sq. ft. 54 + sq. in.

Article 259.—1. 285 cu. ft. 328 + cu. in. **2.** 19 cu. ft. 678.4 cu. in. **3.** 5884962406.4 cu. mi. **4.** 450 T. 5 cwt. 92 lb.

Article 260.—1. $15.64. **2.** $4.16. **3.** $13.35. **4.** $24.61. **5.** $212.22. **6.** $369.45.

Article 261.—1. 15 ft. **2.** 56 ft. **3.** 125 ft. **4.** 400 ft. **5.** 896 ft. **6.** 39 ft.

Article 262.—1. 32000. **2.** 72. **3.** $420. **4.** $637.24. **5.** 44800. **6.** $324.

Article 263.—1. 585 bu. **2.** $1446\frac{3}{7}$ bu. **3.** 187 bu. 2 pk. **4.** 401 bu. nearly. **5.** 646.272 bu. **6.** 512 gal. **7.** 165 bu. **8.** 3166.7 + gal. **9.** 5184 bl. **10.** $113.98.

Article 265.—**1.** 960. **2.** 580. **3.** $480. **4.** 782. **5.** 700 ft. **6.** .003604.

Article 266.—**1.** 7. **2.** 126. **3.** 37. **4.** 60 ct. **5.** 54.

Article 267.—**1.** 840. **2.** $6750. **3.** 530. **4.** 330. **5.** 4815. **6.** 4185. **7.** 13635. **8.** 660.

Article 269.—**1.** 135. **2.** 375. **3.** .375. **4.** $\frac{1}{648}$. **5.** 87480.

Article 270.—**1.** 6138. **2.** 765. **3.** $8\frac{728}{729}$. **4.** 3. **5.** 9. **6.** $\frac{4}{27}$.

Miscellaneous Examples.

1. $\frac{8}{13}$. **2.** $\frac{11}{45}$. **3.** $\frac{5}{32}$. **4.** $96.88. **5.** $14.85. **6.** 42 da. **7.** $32. **8.** $61.20. **9.** $471.44. **10.** 3514.24 fr. **11.** $176.40. **12.** $63½. **13.** $154.14. **14.** 25 sq. ft. 19.1232 sq. in. **15.** $250. **16.** 5 bu. **17.** $40.84. **18.** $369.53. **19.** $64.58. **20.** $462. **21.** 15.31 + yd. **22.** $348.40. **23.** $64.68. **24.** $1100. **25.** A. $234, B. $312. **26.** $6250. **27.** $\frac{16}{60}$, $\frac{45}{60}$, $\frac{40}{60}$. **28.** $70. **29.** 1266. **30.** $51.45. **31.** 432 gal. **32.** 6 A. 28.4 sq. rd. **33.** 33⅓ %. **34.** $36. **35.** 54 %. **36.** 1 A. 123 sq. rd. 12 sq. yd. 5 sq. ft. 107 sq. in. **37.** 2305. **38.** 502.656 ft. **39.** 77. **40.** 7½ bu. **41.** 174240 min. **42.** 44 sq. yd. **43.** $47.63. **44.** $134.09. **45.** $4.83. **46.** $100.80. **47.** 10 cwt. 50 lb. **48.** $487.50. **49.** 25 %. **50.** 110.23 lb. **51.** $78.74. **52.** 5 bu. 3 pk. 6 qt. **53.** $202.50. **54.** 5 ft. **55.** 838.1 fr. **56.** $\frac{14}{75}$. **57.** $14000. **58.** 9 hr. **59.** $166.60. **60.** $78.75. **61.** 3600. **62.** 420 bu. **63.** July 13. **64.** 392.7 sq. in. **65.** $\frac{425}{450}$, $\frac{420}{450}$, $\frac{324}{450}$, $\frac{315}{450}$. **66.** 16 doz. **67.** $668. **68.** Gain 1¼ %. **69.** $158.40. **70.** 36.576 + m. **71.** 567. **72.** 12. **73.** $734.68. **74.** 3½ %. **75.** 1478.4 Kg. **76.** $12 a yd. **77.** $2367.63. **78.** $2.50. **79.** $613.33. **80.** A. $2200, B. $1672. **81.** $121.38. **82.** $\frac{14}{37}$. **83.** $1702.12. **84.** 1152 times. **85.** $51.19. **86.** $320. **87.** 325. **88.** 3 gal. **89.** 1256.64 sq. yd. **90.** 408⅔. **91.** 125 C. **92.** 106. **93.** 904.7808 cu. in. **94.** $3.33. **95.** $\frac{1}{144}$. **96.** 16 A. 40 sq. rd.

97. \$66. **98.** $10\frac{5}{22}$ %. **99.** \$27.16. **100.** \$87. **101.** \$22.50. **102.** $\frac{81}{160}$. **103.** \$435.60. **104.** \$205.16. **105.** \$320. **106.** \$18.77. **107.** \$849.42. **108.** 3 pk. **109.** 17 sq. ft. 65.28 sq. in. **110.** 189.268 + l. **111.** 31 yr. 3 mo. **112.** 615.7536 sq. in. **113.** \$564.10. **114.** 24.72 + rd. **115.** $7\frac{1}{2}$ %. **116.** 74000. **117.** 390600. **118.** 1440 A. **119.** \$20.20. **120.** \$2625. **121.** \$38.54. **122.** 2 yr. 9 mo. 20 da. **123.** $\frac{9}{25}$. **124.** 10 mi. 230 rd. **125.** 48000. **126.** \$148.50. **127.** $\frac{24}{25}$. **128.** $21\frac{29}{40}$. **129.** \$6672. **130.** \$60. **131.** \$44.50. **132.** $\frac{5}{8}$ %. **133.** 44602.3424 cu. in. **134.** \$180.25. **135.** 720. **136.** 6 mi. 128 rd. **137.** \$1620. **138.** 176 bu. **139.** 108. **140.** £1=\$$4.86\frac{1}{4}$. **141.** 800. **142.** 20. **143.** 4 wk. 6 da. 17 hr. 20 min. **144.** A. \$33825; B. \$20500. **145.** June 26, 1815. **146.** 1 mi. 80 rd. **147.** 2 ft. 8 in. **148.** 1 T. 7 cwt. 55 lb. **149.** $42\frac{1}{4}$. **150.** 350 A. **151.** \$540. **152.** 2 yr. 4 mo. 25 da. **153.** \$342.63. **154.** 125 da. **155.** Nov. 4. **156.** \$4. **157.** 35. **158.** 22680 fr. **159.** \$945.25. **160.** \$59.73. **161.** 5575.2928 cu. in. **162.** 12.45 P. M. **163.** 64 %. **164.** \$307.18. **165.** 20178. **166.** 2 pk. 3 qt. **167** \$1170. **168.** \$3048.63. **169.** \$315. **170.** \$480. **171.** 6.25 Km. **172.** $\frac{3}{5}$. **173.** May 1, 1886. **174.** 8 mi. 240 rd. **175.** \$590.40. **176.** 21200 lb. **177.** $7\frac{31}{60}$. **178.** 9 %. **179.** 45. **180.** 82.024 +. **181.** 21 lb. **182.** 11 rd. **183.** 6 hr. 58 min. A. M. **184.** \$43.80. **185.** 2 m. **186.** A. \$700; B. \$650. **187.** \$1103.60. **188.** \$589.50. **189.** Aug. 26. **190.** \$2506.31. **191.** \$496.87. **192.** \$19.95. **193.** 4 hr. 10 min. **194.** \$750. **195.** \$4.50. **196.** 476. **197.** June 17. **198.** .06857 +. **199.** 2 hr. **200.** \$453.60. **201.** \$3891.73. **202.** 16 m. **203.** \$108. **204.** \$918. **205.** 137° 30′ W. Long. **206.** 8 %. **207.** July 20. **208.** 3200. **209.** 3262 gal. 3 qt. **210.** \$285. **211.** $\frac{13}{18}$. **212.** 56.5685 + rd. **213.** A. \$825; B. \$660. **214.** 60 ft. **215.** \$113.60. **216.** 8 %. **217.** 2123.7216 sq. in. **218.** $\frac{11}{17}$. **219.** 405 cu. ft. **220.** $1\frac{3}{10}$ % discount. **221.** Feb. 28, 1873. **222.** \$800. **223.** \$60. **224.** 20000. **225.** 6 %. **226.** \$4900.50. **227.** \$671.55. **228.** 42 sq. ft. 78.12 sq. in. **229.** A. \$275; B. \$198. **230.** 1413.72 sq. yd. **231.** $\frac{21}{320}$. **232.** 36 ct. **233.** 120. **234.** $4\frac{1}{2}$ %. **235.** \$2.50. **236.** \$60.75. **237.** \$6600. **238.** 175. **239.** 6.32455 +. **240.** 52.3259 +. **241.** 1000. **242.** 9 ft. 4 in.

243. \$1093.75. **244.** 285. **245.** $4\frac{1}{2}$ %. **246.** \$891.65. **247.** .708928+. **248.** 90 ct. **249.** £1 = \$4.86. **250.** 2 ft. **251.** A. \$750; B. \$600. **252.** April 18, 1893. **253.** 26400 bu. **254.** Gain 4 hr. 42 min. **255.** \$2700. **256.** 2 cwt. 34 lb. **257.** \$793.53. **258.** 256. **259.** 1600 A. **260.** \$400. **261.** \$12699.36. **262.** 7 mo. **263.** .000079507. **264.** $\frac{2}{5}$. **265.** \$666.27. **266.** 1044.48 bl. **267.** 50 in. **268.** 76. **269.** March 3, 1884. **270.** 4680 sq. ft. **271.** .48. **272.** \$107.20. **273.** 180 cu. ft. **274.** $16\frac{55}{72}$. **275.** \$5280. **276.** 4 %. **277.** 30 A. 100 sq. rd. **278.** $8\frac{1}{3}$ %. **279.** 1 A. 108 sq. rd. 18 sq. yd. **280.** 40. **281.** \$931.91. **282.** $11\frac{1}{9}$. **283.** $13\frac{1}{3}$ A. **284.** $\frac{32}{36}$, $\frac{48}{36}$, $\frac{24}{36}$, $\frac{21}{36}$. **285.** 49.0875 cu. ft. **286.** 44 %. **287.** 16777216. **288.** \$9100. **289.** 22 bu. 2 pk. **290.** \$4550. **291.** 9. **292.** Nov. 30, 1884. **293.** £1026 13 s. $10\frac{1}{2}$ d. **294.** \$249.34. **295.** $3\frac{11}{15}$ da. **296.** \$2414.27. **297.** 11 in. **298.** A. \$27000; B. \$12000. **299.** $1\frac{23}{52}$ %. **300.** 7 mo. **301.** 2146 sq. ft. **302.** \$240. **303.** 28. **304.** March 23, 1892. **305.** 32.863 + ft. **306.** $\frac{15}{34}$. **307.** 22164361129. **308.** 11421 + gal. **309.** June 14. **310.** 6 feet. **311.** 90. **312.** \$1022.34. **313.** April 22, 1880. **314.** $17\frac{1}{2}$ A. **315.** 2 yr. 9 mo. **316.** 13 da. **317.** 24 ct. **318.** \$45. **319.** 10 ft. 8 in. **320.** \$398.25. **321.** Lost 4 %. **322.** \$4570. **323.** $\frac{103}{120}$. **324.** 20 %. **325.** 36 ct. **326.** \$12960. **327.** 203.717 + A. **328.** 8 hr. 43 min. P. M. of the previous day. **329.** $5\frac{1}{2}$ in. **330.** 54. **331.** \$165. **332.** \$80.99. **333.** 565. **334.** $292\frac{1}{2}$ sq. in. **335.** 58.67 ft. nearly. **336.** $2\frac{3}{5}$ %. **337.** 25 m. **338.** 40 %. **339.** 2072.54 marks. **340.** Oct. 21,1875. **341.** $21\frac{11}{18}$. **342.** \$325.20. **343.** 5.25 fr. **344.** $7\frac{1}{2}$ %. **345.** 8 %. **346.** 44 %. **347.** 3 oz. 2 pwt. 6 gr. **348.** \$873.03. **349.** $12\frac{1}{2}$ %. **350.** 94 bu. 2 pk. **351.** $\frac{784}{840}$, $\frac{924}{840}$, $\frac{735}{840}$, $\frac{540}{840}$. **352.** 9.0719 + M. T. **353.** $44\frac{4}{9}$ ct. **354.** \$340. **355.** 1 fr. = 19 ct. 7 m. **356.** \$2577.25. **357.** \$10. **358.** 50 ft. **359.** \$14.16. **360.** 4879681. **361.** $5\frac{5}{19}$ %. **362.** .52083 +. **363.** 2463.0144 sq. in. **364.** A. \$75; B. \$45; C. \$30. **365.** \$45. **366.** 2nd term 3. **367.** 85 ft. **368.** Oct. 28. **369.** \$9.45. **370.** 40 ft. **371.** 22.05 a. **372.** \$20000. **373.** Dec. 2, 1869. **374.** \$34.20. **375.** \$5877. **376.** 8 dm. **377.** \$864. **378.** \$846.45. **379.** 1.963 + cu. ft. **380.** May 13, 1891. **381.** $\frac{216}{15625}$. **382.** \$1022.36. **383.** 1256.64 sq. yd. **384.** 38. **385.** E. Long. 14° 10′. **386.** Nov. 1, 1883. **387.** 9 %.

388. \$509.95. **389.** 120 sq. rd. **390.** 17 Mg. **391.** 7 ft.
392. Sept. 20, 1884. **393.** $26\frac{11}{64}$ %. **394.** \$10250. **395.** $37\frac{25}{27}$.
396. 8250 fr. **397.** \$7200. **398.** 20%. **399.** \$700.
400. 523600 cu. mi. **401.** \$158.40. **402.** 8 da. **403.** 16 da.

Who is Joseph Ray?

Joseph Ray lived as a contemporary of Abraham Lincoln. Youth in that generation finished their schoolbooks and then read the Bible, sang from the hymnbooks of Lowell Mason, and read Roman and Greek classics in the original languages. It was not unusual for a blacksmith to carry a Greek New Testament under his cap for reading during his lunch break. The literacy rate, even on the frontier, was higher than today's rate.

Ray was Professor of Mathematics for twenty-five years at a preparatory school in Ohio. He had no use for indolence and sham. He was always delighted to join his students in sports. He knew how to use balls, marbles, and tops as concrete illustrations to help young children make the transfer from solid objects to abstract figures.

From the Presidency of Abraham Lincoln to that of Teddy Roosevelt, few Americans went to school or were taught at home without considerable exposure to either Ray's Arithmetics or McGuffey's Readers—usually both. Ray and McGuffey challenged students to excellent accomplishment. Their influence on our country has certainly eclipsed Mann's and rivaled Dewey's, yet education histories, edited by humanists, seldon mention these men.

Ray's classic Arithmetics are now brought to a new generation which is in search of excellence.

Ray's Arithmetic Series

Primary Arithmetic. Reading, writing and understanding of numbers to 100; adding and subtracting with sums to 20; multiplication and division to 10's; and signs and vocabulary needed for this level of arithmetic.

Intellectual Arithmetic. Reading, writing and understanding of higher whole numbers, fractions, and mixed numbers; addition, subtraction, multiplication and division of higher numbers; computation of simple fractions; beginning ratio and percentage; and signs and vocabulary needed for all these operations.

Practical Arithmetic. Roman numerals; carrying in addition and borrowing in subtraction; measurement and compound numbers; factors; decimals and percentage; ratio and proportion; powers and roots; beginning geometry; advanced vocabulary.

Higher Arithmetic. Philosophical understandings; principles and properties of numbers; advanced study of common and decimal fractions, measurements, ratio, proportion, percentage, powers, and roots; series; business math; geometry.

Test Examples. A supply of problems for making tests to accompany study in the *Practical Arithmetic* and the *Higher Arithmetic.*

Key to Ray's Primary, Intellectual and Practical Arithmetics. Answers to problems in the three lower books.

Key to Ray's Higher Arithmetic. Answers to problems in the *Higher Arithmetic.*

Parent-Teacher Guide. Gives unit by unit helps for teaching; suggests grade levels for each book; provides progress chart samples for each grade and tests for each unit.

McGuffey's Reading Series

Primer. Begins with the alphabet, moves to simple one-syllable words such as *cat* and *fox*, then on to more difficult one-syllable words such as *horse* and *spring*.

Pictorial Primer. Begins with the alphabet. First lessons have simple three- and four-word sentences with no paragraphing.

First Reader. Follows the Primers at second or third grade. Words usually have the main alphabetic sounds, and few have silent letters. Helps to build fluency in using the phonics principles learned at primer levels.

Second Reader. Begins with fairly easy one- and two-syllable words and progresses to more difficult words. Reading selections on a variety of topics. Can be used to about fifth grade.

Third Reader. For students who have mastered basic reading skills and are fluent in easy reading. This Reader develops more advanced vocabulary and thinking skills. Can be used for two or three years, beginning at about sixth grade.

Fourth Reader. Develops advanced comprehension, requiring students to understand a variety of viewpoints and think about abstract ideas. Readings on themes such as life values, truth, religion, and freedom. Can be used at high school level.

Progressive Speller. Can be used at all grade levels. Begins with phonics rules. Covers spelling difficulty from one-syllable words to very complex words.

Parent-Teacher Guide. Explains how to teach reading and has specific ideas for using the lessons in this series of Readers. Also gives guidelines for helping children grow in all the language arts—spelling, writing, speaking, penmanship, grammar.

Materials for Teaching Phonics and Spelling

Phonics Made Plain by Michael S. Brunner. Flashcards for teaching sounds of the letters and letter combinations which make up the code for reading and writing. Wall chart for classroom reference and teaching of sounds. Instruction for use.

The ABC's and All Their Tricks by Margaret M. Bishop. A comprehensive book of phonics knowledge for teachers. Useful for study, reference, solving students' spelling problems, and answering any phonics question you can think of. Tells how to teach children of all ages who have difficulty with phonics.

A Measuring Scale for Ability in Spelling by Leonard P. Ayres. The classic book from 1915, describes the research which identified one thousand most commonly used words and arranged them into difficulty groups to use for testing children's spelling level and for teaching spelling. Includes complete directions for testing.

Mrs. Silver's Phonics Workbook and ***Mrs. Silver's Phonics Workbook Teacher's Edition*** by Claudine Silver. A lesson on each single letter and on some digraphs such as *ck*, *sh*, and *th*. Ideas enough to spend several days on each lesson and learn it well. Each sound is correlated with a Bible verse and with science, art, and other school subjects. Can be used at kindergarten or first grade level. With the McGuffey series, it should be used before the Primers. Both the student workbook and the teacher's edition are required for this program.

Phonics in Song by Leon V. Metcalf. Book of catchy tunes for teaching each letter of the alphabet and the digraphs *ch*, *sh*, *th*, and *wh*. A sing-along CD is also available.